DANGER
ABOVE

ALSO BY ROBERT ZAUSNER

Two Boys

Bad Brake

Dying to Have a Baby

DANGER ABOVE

A TRAGIC DEATH,
AN EPIC COURTROOM BATTLE

ROBERT ZAUSNER

Camino Books, Inc.
Philadelphia

Manufactured in the United States of America

1 2 3 4 5   19 18 17 16

Library of Congress Cataloging-in-Publication Data

Zausner, Robert, 1953- author.
Danger above: a tragic death, an epic courtroom battle / Robert Zausner.
Philadelphia: Camino Books, Inc., 2016
LCCN 2016004781 (print) / LCCN 2016005567 / ISBN 9781680980059
    (hardcover: alk. paper) / ISBN 9781680980066 (ebook)
LCSH Goretzka, Carrie, 1970-2009—Trials, litigation, etc. / West Penn
    Power Company—Trials, litigation, etc. / Trials—Pennsylvania—Allegheny County. /
    Wrongful death—Pennsylvania. / Electric utilities—Law and legislation—Pennsylvania. /
    Accident victims—Legal status, laws, etc.—Pennsylvania / LCGFT: Trial and arbitral
    proceedings.
LCC KF229.G67 Z38 2016 (print) / LCC KF229.G67 (ebook) / DDC
    346.74803/23—dc23

ISBN 978-1-68098-005-9
ISBN 978-1-68098-006-6 (ebook)

Jacket design: Whitney Cookman
Interior design: Jerilyn Bockorick

This book is available at a special discount on bulk purchases for promotional, business, and
educational use:

Publisher
Camino Books, Inc.
P.O. Box 59026
Philadelphia, PA 19102

www.caminobooks.com

FOR SAM AND SUE

Contents

Prologue

Reporters for major publications rarely cover civil trials. There are several reasons. For one, they can be time-consuming, often laden with technical and expert testimony. They also are mostly about money—one side trying to get it, the other trying to protect it—and not about the greater good. Reporters find themselves shut out of some of the most important aspects of the proceedings, without access to courtroom sidebars or negotiations among adversaries about settling cases before they go to juries for deliberations. And lastly, there are those pesky settlements. Very often, a reporter can spend weeks covering a case only to find that the matter is ultimately taken from a jury's hands because an agreement has been reached between the parties, with the end result being confidential. Quite suddenly, what seemed like a good story becomes no story at all, but only a waste of time.

As a reporter for *The Philadelphia Inquirer*, I was admittedly skeptical about devoting an entire year to writing a book for two civil trial lawyers. But Tom Kline and Shanin Specter assured me that their cases were more than just interesting legal stories. I took some time to study their files and what I found impressed me. It turned out that many of the cases went well beyond a matter of monetary awards. Quite a number of them had important social and governmental policy implications. I decided to take a one-year leave of absence from *The Inquirer* to write their book. I never went back to the newspaper. *Danger Above* is my fourth book about a major Kline & Specter case.

By being an insider, I am privy to much that would not be seen by a regular reporter or observer. I am there when a case is being investigated and I have unique access not only to deposition testimony, but also to the clients and attorneys who are central to the story. I have an inside track when it comes to settlement talks and to the personal tribulations experienced by those directly involved in an unfolding case. It is true that I am only a witness to one side of the behind-the-scenes action, but with *Danger Above*, I have written what I believe is an objective account—based largely on the actual legal documents and trial transcripts—of the case of *Goretzka v. West Penn Power*. And just like a sports reporter covering a long-awaited game, it was beyond my ability to change the final and, in this case, memorable outcome.

DANGER
ABOVE

Chapter 1

Shanin Specter had seen some terrible things. Never as they happened, always afterward.

Families appeared at the lawyer's door months, even years after a tragedy. He tried to bring some measure of...something—compensation, justice, closure—to a grieving mother or father, husband or wife, son or daughter. He had been doing this for nearly 30 years now, and he had come up short every time. Every single time. No compensation could equal the loss of a loved one, no legal result could make the sadness dim any faster, no jury verdict or settlement could erase the memories. But what he did was all that could be done.

Specter had seen broken and twisted bodies, children left paralyzed and palsied by a mishap at birth, by a careless doctor or an inattentive nurse. He had seen so many cases of missed cancer diagnoses lead to prolonged, painful deaths. He had seen simple mistakes lead to tragedy—a young man left in a vegetative state because of a misplaced endotracheal tube, a girl left paralyzed because of an inadequate and defective automobile seat belt, a teenage boy who was crippled and eventually died when a BB fired from a defective rifle lodged in his brain.

Specter had seen all kinds of calamity, some gruesome, all heartbreaking. But this, his latest case, was the worst.

Chapter 2

People were aware of electricity thousands of years ago. Egyptian texts dating back to 2750 B.C. refer to fish that produced an electrical charge. (Electric eels use chemicals in their bodies that can manufacture as many as 650 volts, or about five times the shocking power of a household outlet.) The ancient Egyptians believed the charges had curative properties, and they used catfish and sea rays to shock people out of maladies such as headaches or gout. In this effort they also first learned that this mysterious power could travel through conducting agents, and into humans.

Chapter 3

For previous summer vacations, the Goretzkas—Mike, Carrie and their little girls, Chloe and Carlie—had rented a beach house at the shore in Rehoboth, Delaware, and invited the entire family to make the trip down from suburban Pittsburgh. Many of them came, packing the house with relatives, plenty of food and lots of fun.

But this once, Mike wanted to get away with just his wife and kids. It was actually his brother Chuck's idea. "Michael, you can't keep taking everybody. You've got to go somewhere yourselves," he'd said more than once.

So this year, 2009, Mike had booked a trip to Disney World for the first week of June. But then he changed the plans. Mike had found out that week was marked "Gay Days Orlando," a time in which more than 150,000 gay celebrants made the trip to the Florida city. Mike was no homophobe, but he felt that might not be the perfect atmosphere for his daughters, aged four and two. So he changed the trip to the end of May.

The family had a wonderful time, going on the rides and seeing the sights, eating junk food and staying at the Wilderness Lodge, a theme hotel on the Disney World grounds. "For the first time, you look at each other at the end of the day and you're alone. It was a great feeling. It really bonded us four," Mike remembered.

They were home by the first week of June. "Going earlier was my choice. We could have gone that first week in June. We could have been at Disney that week," Mike said years later. "It haunted me for a long time."

Chapter 4

JoAnn Goretzka and her two young grandchildren were watching cartoons at around four in the afternoon while their mother, Carrie, was cooking and talking on the kitchen phone. Then the power went off.

The adults looked out the dining room window into the backyard and saw flames coming from pine trees off in the distance. Carrie dialed the power company, but the land line had gone dead. So she went to get her cell phone from her car in the garage.

A few minutes went by, then a few more. JoAnn told the kids to stay inside, to sit on the carpeted steps of the split-level home while she went to check on their mother. She walked down to the front door, opened it and took a step onto the front porch. She saw Carrie and her breath caught in her throat. Her daughter-in-law was lying on her back on the strip of grass next to the driveway. She was on fire, flames coming from her abdomen, smoke rising from her entire body. Carrie was entangled in a fallen power line. She was moaning. JoAnn didn't hesitate. She ran to Carrie. But as soon as she got to the grass and reached out, she was blown back by the force of the energized ground, her fingertips severely burned when she touched the lawn. Stunned, JoAnn did the only thing left that she could do. She screamed for help.

"Carrie! Carrie! Somebody has to help her! Somebody has to help her!'

All the while, Carrie lay feeble in the grass. Being shocked by a surging 7,200-volt line. Burning.

A neighbor, Don Thoma, chief of the local volunteer fire company, was home when he spotted smoke coming from between the two houses next to his. When he walked outside, he heard JoAnn's screams. He hurried to the Goretzka property and saw Carrie lying on the ground with the power line across her body. He edged closer but stopped in his tracks when he felt a tingle of electricity shoot up his leg. He stepped away.

Timothy Harper, another neighbor and also a volunteer fireman, arrived about the same time. He saw fire coming from Carrie's hip and smoke rising from her whole body. Thoma told Harper to run and get a fire extinguisher. Meanwhile, others had arrived at the property, but Harper shouted at them to stay back.

All the while, Carrie burned, moaning helplessly, unable to move.

Other neighbors came outside. So did Carrie's young daughters. Hearing their grandmother's screams, they sat crumpled on the porch, panicked looks on their faces as they watched their mother's anguish.

"Mommy! Mommy! Mommy is on fire! Mommy is on fire!'

Carrie remained immobile. Could she see them watching her?

Harper shouted at other neighbors who had arrived to stay back, that the wire was still "hot."

Mike Goretzka's next-door neighbor, Ron Molnar, who had been watching TV, stepped onto his porch in bare feet. He spotted Carrie and couldn't believe his eyes. "She looked like a mannequin," he would recall. "When I seen what I seen, it was like a movie. I was in shock. I just stood there."

Mike Thornburgh had been alarmed by a "huge ball of fire" that he saw rising between several houses as he was delivering mail around the corner. He heard the frantic shouts: "Help me! Help me!" He recognized JoAnn Goretzka's voice from his frequent rounds in the neighborhood. He hopped into his truck and gunned it. When he arrived at the Goretzkas', Thornburgh was horrified. He began to approach Carrie but was quickly shouted away by Harper. "He probably saved my life," Thornburgh would say later. But he felt awful. "We just stood there. We couldn't do nothing."

Then he noticed JoAnn and the girls huddled in a ball on the porch. He ran to them. He picked up one child and shouted Molnar out of his stupor—"C'mon, Ron!"—to grab the other. They tried to keep the children's faces turned away from their mother. They carried them into Molnar's house. "The kids were traumatized, they didn't say anything," Molnar would recount.

Michelle Siegel was gardening in her front yard a block away when she heard a sound "like a firecracker" and moments later heard the screams. She dropped her garden tool and ran toward the commotion. Mike Thornburgh whizzed by her in his mail truck. As she got closer to Carrie, she, too, was warned to stand back.

Carrie lay motionless, the power line holding her like an angry serpent, its venom coursing through her body. Harper doused Carrie with a fire extinguisher. He did it once, then, when the flames refused to go out, he sprayed it a second time.

Bernadine Collins, Mike's neighbor on the other side of his house, went to her fence, staring in sorrow and disbelief. Other neighbors came to the scene and soon the whole neighborhood was there, watching. Helpless.

Now, Carrie was still. It was uncertain how much she was comprehending. But she was still conscious. Harper urged Carrie, "Hold still. Don't move. Help's coming."

Collins, an older lady with short, curly white hair, stood, like everyone else, watching the terrible scene, unable to do anything for her neighbor and friend. "The only thing I heard was she was making a high, soft sound. Like a cat. It was a really pitiful sound."

Emergency personnel and power company workers arrived minutes later. Finally, after about 20 minutes, the power was shut down and one man used a long, fiberglass "hot stick" to lift the power line off Carrie. MedVac helicopter pilot Mariann Holnaider would remember that when she came on the scene, Carrie was still awake, crying and in terrible pain. Her left arm was burned so badly that bone and tendons were visible.

EMT chief Walter Lipinski administered an IO, an intraosseous needle of a heavier gauge than an IV, which can penetrate into bone marrow. "I doubt anything could have stopped the pain," he said. Eventually, 40 minutes after first being shocked by the power line, the drugs finally forced Carrie into unconsciousness.

Mike Goretzka, speeding home from work in his pickup truck, pushed his way through the neighbors and emergency workers. Seeing Carrie, he immediately knew she was in very bad shape. Mike started crying. Holnaider and Lipinski tried to comfort him, but they didn't lie to him. It was serious.

There was no room for Mike Goretzka to travel with Carrie to the hospital. Before the helicopter took off, he kissed his wife good-bye.

Carrie Goretzka died three days later.

Chapter 5

By the time Shanin Specter arrived more than three years later in West Hempfield, a sleepy little community a half hour outside of Pittsburgh, all evidence of the tragedy was gone. A cat jogged across the road. A man two houses down tended to his garden on a sunny autumn afternoon. Specter stood in front of the modest house in the middle-class neighborhood in middle America. The grass was cut and trimmed, immaculately manicured. The charred earth, the burn mark in the outline of a body, was gone.

After a little while, Mike Thornburgh pulled up and stepped out of his truck when he reached the Goretzkas' mailbox, where he once left lollipops for the girls along with the day's letters and magazines. Mike the Mailman greeted Shanin Specter with a handshake and a wary gaze. They chatted softly and walked toward the side of the house. Thornburgh talked about how he was more than just a mail carrier to the Goretzka family. How he often stopped to chat or tease the kids, who were often out front on bicycles or doodling with chalk on the asphalt driveway. He went to occasional parties at the Goretzka home.

He and Specter ambled closer to the driveway and Thornburgh stopped suddenly, as though hitting an invisible wall. He spun on his heels and turned his body away from "the spot." His lower lip started to tremble. He was physically unable to walk any farther. He just couldn't. It had been more than three years and four months, but the memory of what he had witnessed that day as his truck rounded a bend in the road still caused him pain.

Specter prodded. He pulled a file from a briefcase and opened it, showing Thornburgh a diagram of the scene. Then he withdrew a photo of the ground where the incident occurred. Mike Thornburgh's face turned away sharply as if he'd been slapped. "I can't look," he said, and he began to cry.

Chapter 6

Walter Lipinski was a mountain of a man, standing six-feet-six despite a slight stoop, even taller in the black, thick-soled Frankenstein boots he clomped around in at the Irwin, Pennsylvania, Emergency Medical Services headquarters where he was the boss. Lipinski wore a thick, gray walrus moustache and a constant scowl. He looked perpetually annoyed. He had made, by his own reckoning, about a thousand emergency calls a year over the past 37 years, bearing witness to all sorts of illnesses and accidents, hardening him to the sight of blood, death, and life's unpredictable misfortunes. He didn't seem like a man who would tear up at the mere memory of one of those scenes, of something that had happened years ago. Yet his eyes now brimmed with tears.

Specter needed to speak with Lipinski, a possible witness in the upcoming trial. But in a meeting he reluctantly agreed to have with Specter, Lipinski, like Mike Thornburgh, remained haunted by bearing witness to what had happened to Carrie Goretzka. He would never forget the first thing he noticed when he had arrived at the scene. He said the words to Specter in a barely audible tone: "I smelled burning flesh."

Chapter 7

Mike Goretzka sat in the small dining room of his home, strong arms folded on the table, his eyes downcast toward a vase filled with pink roses. The room was quiet and still, the only movement from two tiny African frogs who frolicked in their square, Lucite world resting on a credenza beneath a flowered lamp.

Goretzka, 43, was going to move from this comfortable house with its large backyard and above-ground swimming pool. He had wanted to leave, to turn his back on the bad memory, but something always stopped him. Maybe the good memories would be lost as well. Or the comfort his girls still found in things familiar. "First I decided to stay because I felt it was better for the kids. And then, just depression set in," he told Specter, shaking his head as he let the sentence slip away.

Mike Goretzka was trying to move on several years after his world had crumbled around him. He wasn't having much success. He had bought property and was having a new house built a few miles away, where he would no longer have to look at the place of his wife's demise. He was working hard at his job, where he earned a very good living, $190,000 annually, as the number two in command of a 170-employee company that provided hospice and home health care to 700 patients. And he had begun to work out again, going to a gym at lunchtime to lift weights. He ran three miles every day after work. Mike Goretzka was still in pain, but he had found the will to move forward. "When it first happened," he remembered, "I'd just go to a bar every day, just disappear…but that's no good."

Goretzka, five-feet-nine with a solid build, dark brown hair and a soft, handsome face shrouded in sadness, walked to the back of his home to show Specter his children's bedrooms. The walls of Chloe's room were hand-painted in a cheerful pattern. She had a canopy bed, but Chloe didn't sleep there and hadn't since the day of the accident. Her younger sister, Carlie, had never slept in her room, not once. They both now slept in the big bed in the master bedroom with their father. This wasn't good, Mike Goretzka knew, but it was an improvement. They had at least been able to go to the part of the house where the bedrooms were. Emotional progress had been made:

"For the first six months, they slept on the floor of the living room with me, because they couldn't go back there."

Chapter 8

Shanin Specter peered across the dining room table at Chloe and Carlie Goretzka. Images of their smiling faces looked down at him from the surrounding walls and the refrigerator nearby. The children were smiling in the photographs, but not now. They rarely smiled now.

The girls had their crayons out, hands working busily. They colored cheerful pictures of rainbows and large red hearts. Specter, who their father introduced simply as "our friend," prodded gently, asking them about school at first, then about their father. The lawyer had been warned by a psychiatrist who examined both girls that they were fragile. *Tread lightly* had been his advice.

But Specter needed to speak with them. With the trial looming, he had to determine if he would or even could call either to the witness stand. He knew that what they saw on June 2, 2009 was the most terrible sight imaginable—their mother lying in the grass being electrocuted, burning to death. Only when Mike the Mailman and another neighbor scooped them off the porch and hurried them to a next-door neighbor's house did they find some small respite from the horror.

Specter wasn't sure how to broach the subject. The children, now six and eight years old, answered his questions respectfully, with short responses. He asked, they answered. They didn't volunteer anything. Maybe they, too, knew where he was heading.

At one point, Specter asked if the kids would show him their rooms. They agreed, sliding off their chairs and walking him to the side of the house. Specter remarked about what nice rooms they had. They nodded and walk back to the dining room.

Specter asked Carlie about kindergarten and Chloe about serving in her first Mass. He told them he had four girls of his own, the oldest in college, and the youngest who was turning 12 this very day. He asked them what they wished for. *Here it comes*, Specter thought. They will finally talk about what was on his mind, and certainly theirs'. But instead they told him they wanted toys, and mentioned several dolls specifically.

"Do you know what I wish for?" Specter asked them. Both girls looked up, big brown eyes staring at his now. "I wish I had more time with my father. I'm afraid he might not be around much longer, and that I'll wish I had more time with him."

Specter didn't make the remark to coax them into conversation about their mother. He was speaking from the heart. Nine days later, on October 14, 2012, his father, former U.S. Senator Arlen Specter, passed away.

Chapter 9

"She didn't have a bad word to say about anyone," Carol Rizzo said about her sister-in-law, Carrie Goretzka.

Blonde, brown-eyed, petite at barely five-feet-one, Carrie was the only child of a broken marriage. Her father, John Salandro, and mother, JoAnn, had divorced when Carrie was five years old. "We were young. We didn't get along. It didn't work out," John remembered. His wife took Carrie and moved away, and he didn't see his daughter for a long time.

"It felt like forever. I didn't know where she was," he said. After a few years, John was reunited with Carrie. She then stayed with her mother during the week and with John during the weekends, when he was home—he had a variety of apartments over the years and later a mobile home—from his job as a candy and soda machine supplier and deliveryman.

"She was a good kid. I never had any problems with her," John, a shy, bald man, would recall years later. "She would come to my house and bring her friends over. She was good in school. She played softball. She was athletic. She was quiet, but she had a lot of friends." Soft-spoken yet gregarious, Carrie made friends wherever she went. She worked hard in school and got an associate degree in paralegal studies.

Mike Goretzka was smitten the first time he met the girl with the stunning smile in high school. He knew right away that she was the one. After several years of dating and an engagement, they got married.

Carol and Carrie later became best friends as well as workmates at Omnicare, Carrie heading the billing department and Carol, a pharmaceutical technician, working in the purchasing department of the company that provided care for the elderly. Carrie also helped her father get a job at Omnicare, delivering drugs and medical devices and working in the warehouse. She and Carol shopped together and lunched together. After Carrie left Omnicare to raise her children, she would still stop by to visit Carol and her father, sometimes bringing them lunch.

Carrie did everything for her children. She doted on them. She dressed them in matching outfits almost every day, right down to the ribbons in their hair. She made them breakfast in the morning and read to them at bedtime. When Chloe was four years old and shy at preschool, Carrie spent two hours every afternoon sitting in the hallway outside class just so that Chloe would know she was there. It made Chloe feel safe.

An only child who was never close to her own mother, Carrie bonded with Mike's family, his parents and siblings. She planned parties for grand-parents and cousins. She picked out gifts. She made everyone feel special. Everyone loved Carrie.

Chapter 10

On a stormy June night in 1752, as the story goes, an eccentric Philadelphian stood outdoors flying a kite attached to a dampened string leading to a metal key. Benjamin Franklin, who had sold many of his worldly possessions to fund experiments with electricity, noted a series of sparks jumping from the key to the back of his hand. He had proved that lightning was indeed electrical in nature. Earlier studies of electricity had dealt with static charges produced by amber—electricus was Latin for "like amber"—and charges produced using magnets. In later years, Franklin was able to harness electrical charges in a Leyden jar, the precursor of the modern-day battery. Afterward, more advanced batteries were made from layers of zinc in a device invented by Alessandro Volta, from whom the term "volt" derived.

In the 1800s, a number of inventors got into the act. Michael Faraday devised the first electric motor in 1821, and a decade later he was able to create electricity using an electromagnetic field, leading in later years to the first dynamo, or electric generator. In 1835, Joseph Henry came up with the relays to enable electricity to be sent over long distances, which led to the electric telegraph of Samuel Morse.

Englishman Stephen Gray transmitted the first electrical impulses over an extended distance in the 1700s, using dampened hemp cords suspended by silk threads, but it was not until 1882 that the first practical long-distance transmission of electricity occurred, as 1,343 volts were sent surging over 35 miles from Munich to Miesbach in Germany.

Today, more than 500,000 miles of power lines, enough to circle the earth 20 times, crisscross America's city streets, rural roads and suburban cul-de-sacs, bringing electricity to virtually every home and business. People pay the lines scant attention. Birds sit in rows atop the wires, squirrels dash across them. The lines have vanished from the daily attention span. They are simply there, like the sky or the sun. Seemingly innocuous.

Chapter 11

"This is Carrie Goretzka," Shanin Specter began, a remote control in his right hand that with a simple click displayed a large photo of the Goretzka family on a large screen, a photo taken at Disney World during happier times. Carrie, blonde and very pretty, knelt in the foreground, her children in front of her, her husband, Mike, beside her.

Specter sat at the far end of a 30-foot-long, gray-and-white marble table in a conference room of his Philadelphia law firm, Kline & Specter. Also present were Kila Baldwin and Dominic Guerrini, the young lawyers who had largely prepared the Goretzka case. Discovery—the gathering of evidence, hiring of experts and interviewing of witnesses—had been completed. Now was the time to prepare for trial. The table was littered with files and exhibits as well as photos and deposition testimony. On the morning of October 23, eight days before jury selection was scheduled, Specter was rehearsing his opening statement.

"She was a homemaker, a wife and a mother. She was a beautiful person inside and out," he continued, then paused, not for dramatic effect but simply finding it difficult to say the next sentence aloud. "She was brutally killed by electrocution when a 7,200-volt power line fell on her on her property on a clear and sunny day three years ago."

He paused again.

"On Tuesday, June 2, 2009, Carrie was at home in West Hempfield with her mother-in-law, JoAnn Goretzka, and her daughters, four-year-old Chloe and two-year-old Carlie. The family had returned from a vacation in Disney World three days before. This is one of the last photos of Carrie."

Since this was his initial practice run, Specter read through his lines in perfunctory fashion, quickly and without emotion. He was reading now not for effect but to check the facts and to synchronize his words with the exhibits he would have flashed on the large screen and TV monitors that would be placed around the courtroom.

Specter was like the movie star who, after the director uses stand-ins to get the scene just right, makes his appearance for the real takes. He had met some witnesses and the Goretzka family and would be in charge at trial, but Baldwin and Guerrini had done the basic legwork, going back more than three years. They were most familiar with the facts of the case and were on the sidelines now to coach the lead actor.

"These trees were on fire," Specter noted, a red dot from his laser pointer circling a section of a photo on the TV monitor.

"Here was the view—no, change that—Here is the view from the house. Here is the kitchen window..."

"No, that's the bedroom window," corrected Baldwin.

"OK, thanks. Here is the bedroom window."

Later, "She tried to call 911 from her cell phone, and here are the cell phone records." Then Specter said to his technician, Mike Kutys, "No, we need a highlighted version. Highlight the three calls she made, instead of this."

The process went on for several hours. Baldwin and Guerrini injected comments and opinions. Kutys, an employee of a court reporting service, worked a laptop that contained all the photos and exhibits. The exercise was like a dance, each step choreographed, photos timed to appear on screen with Specter's utterance of a particular word. "And here—click [Plaintiff's Exhibit 001636] is the view of the back of the house..."

Baldwin: "You skipped a photo."

"Accchhh!"

The exhibits, lettered from A to KK, continued to flip as Specter spoke. A few were out of order; one aerial shot of the neighborhood was upside down. Another Specter found hard to discern.

"I'll look for a better photo," promised Baldwin.

There were plenty of kinks to be worked out. A lot was at stake.

Chapter 12

Long before Shanin Specter began work on his opening speech, Bill McHugh had been standing at his stove, cooking up a batch of his signature New England clam chowder. If he hadn't been, the case might never have been solved. The secret to why the energized wire had fallen on Carrie Goretzka might never have been known.

McHugh, a divorcé who lived in the tiny town of Cavittsville, Pennsylvania, had invited his son, Bill, daughter-in-law Tina and their three-year-old daughter to join him for dinner. He knew they would accept. His chowder was his son's favorite dish.

The TV happened to be on, the nightly news happened to be airing, and the story of a live electrical wire falling in West Hempfield, Pennsylvania, happened to be the top story of the day. The three stared at the television and cringed when they heard details of the story. They saw Mike Goretzka in tears.

"I wish I knew that guy's lawyer," McHugh said aloud. "I bet I know what happened."

It was idle chatter. "I wish..." The family members ate their chowder and later said good night, never giving the incident in West Hempfield another thought. Until three days later when Tina took her daughter to the Mommy and Me preschool program at a nearby Catholic school. She bumped into her friend Carol Rizzo who was taking two little girls to the same school. The girls' names were Chloe and Carlie.

They chatted. "I don't know if you heard," Carol said finally, "but that was my sister-in-law on the news the other night."

As the two continued to talk, Tina told Carol about her father-in-law, who had been a lineman for Duquesne Light for 25 years before retiring. He had his suspicions about the fallen power line on the Goretzka property. Carol raised an eyebrow, telling Tina how her family had been having trouble finding anyone at their power company, West Penn Power, who would talk to them, never mind their lawyers.

A few weeks later, Bill McHugh got a phone call from Kila Baldwin in Philadelphia. She represented Carol's brother, Mike Goretzka, and she wanted to talk.

Chapter 13

"This is Carrie Goretzka..."

Shanin Specter was again running through his opening speech to the jury. Each version had changes and corrections, but fewer every time. "Draft number 3" had seen 116 changes. Today, "Draft number 6" required only alterations. Specter was now rehearsing not so much for style or dramatic effect as for substance, to make sure he had all the elements he wanted and none of those he didn't. Baldwin and Guerrini were in the large conference room to hear this latest version and make suggestions, which Specter then debated with them, accepting some and rejecting others. Video technician Mike Kutys was also present, making sure the visual exhibits—photos of Carrie, the Google satellite shot of the Goretzkas' neighborhood, the photos of their house, the trees in back, the power line on the side—coordinated with Specter's words.

Specter wasn't practicing so much because he was nervous. He was exacting. He didn't want his opening to seem amateurish in any way. He didn't want to be fumbling with a photo slide or struggling with an exhibit when he addressed the jury. His opening had to be seamless, with the jury focusing on his message and nothing else.

He wanted to educate and convince the jurors without seeming to be playing on their emotions. He wanted to be interesting without being theatrical. He wanted to lay out his case in simple, stark terms. First, he would need to bring Carrie to life for the jury. A photo of her with her husband and her children at Disney World flashed on a large screen.

"Carrie Goretzka was a homemaker. She was a daughter, a wife and a mother. She was a beautiful person inside and out."

Chapter 14

The chartered King Air pushed through a thick fog, headed to Pittsburgh, its twin engines groaning as the winged aluminum tube lifted off into the gray mist heading west. Inside, Specter scribbled on a yellow legal pad with cramped pen marks decipherable only to him and perhaps those able to read ancient cave markings. (And, of course, his legal assistant, Diane Grimmie.) He hadn't bothered with even a token hello to his fellow passengers and was mildly annoyed that his chartered flight to Pittsburgh was late. He had scheduled 7 a.m. for "wheels up." It was 7:02. He cut to the chase.

"Can Carrie perceive the kids perceiving her?" he asked. Kila Baldwin, blonde and energetic and with a voice that could be heard in a windstorm, and Dominic Guerrini, sharp-witted yet doe-eyed and soft-spoken, leaned forward to hear their boss over the roar of the engines. The thirty-something associate attorneys pondered the question. Part of Specter's job at trial would be to demonstrate the pain Carrie Goretzka must have suffered. The horrific physical pain she felt was unquestioned, though there was sure to be debate about the length of time that she was actually cognizant. But would the pain have been worse if she had known that her ordeal, her death essentially, was being witnessed by her own children while they sat on the porch of the family home?

"I don't know," answered Baldwin, "we'll have to ask the expert."

"Do that, please."

"Next," Specter said, "I want to go over the motions." Ten pretrial motions were being offered by his team, 21 by the defense. One by one, Specter and his younger associates examined the legal roadblocks that the defense was attempting to set up to prevent the plaintiffs from making a good case. The trio plowed through the list, ending with strategies to rebut the defense motions.

Regarding one, Specter asked Guerrini to find a court order from his last trial in Pittsburgh that allowed the jury to be shown a photo of Joe Blumer pinned under his own tow truck, his corpse blue from asphyxiation. That case had won a jury verdict of $8.75 million against the Ford Motor Company, whose defective parking brake had caused Blumer's Ford

F-350 to roll over him. As gruesome as were the photos of Joe Blumer, those of Carrie were far worse.

Then Specter asked Guerrini to retrieve a copy of a court opinion dealing with punitive damages, an opinion he once read and felt might have relevance to the Goretzka trial. Guerrini responded that he hadn't been able to unearth such a case, even on Westlaw, the universal attorneys' case repository. For this, he got cross-examined.

Specter:	"So you looked for hours and couldn't find it?
Guerrini:	"Yes. It's not on Westlaw."
Specter:	"Then how did I find it?"
Guerrini:	"I don't know."
Specter:	"But I did find it."
Guerrini:	"I'm not saying it doesn't exist, but it doesn't exist on Westlaw."
Specter:	"What are the odds it exists?"

Dominic Guerrini wasn't stupid. He smiled, but he didn't answer. Specter didn't say another word either. He didn't need to. Guerrini would find the case or lose sleep trying. Specter placed his legal pad down on his lap, signaling it was time to relax for a moment. He sipped from a water bottle. Guerrini said something about the Philadelphia Eagles. Kila Baldwin used the opportunity to remark that one of the opposing lawyers had been a jerk early in the case but more recently seemed to be a nice guy.

"I don't care what he is. I have my case to prove," Specter retorted. The cabin went quiet again. "I think we lawyers think we're more important to the process than we are. The most important thing is the facts. We have good facts and good clients. Even if we were inferior lawyers, we should still win this case."

As he finished the sentence, the plane hit a pocket of turbulence and took a sudden and nasty jolt, dropping fast, then shoving violently to one side, then the other. It was more than a bit unsettling. Except for Specter.

"Whoa!" he said, and smiled for the first time since takeoff.

Chapter 15

Bill McHugh had awakened at 3 a.m., restless. It wasn't his chowder from dinner upsetting his stomach but his mind racing with vivid memories of the police photos showing the downed wire at the Goretzka property. Before going to bed, he had been looking on his PC at a disc Baldwin had sent him. He had stared at those photos over and over again. In all his years working as a lineman for a power company, McHugh had never seen a conductor wire burn down the way this one had. There had been no storm, no lightning strike. His first theory was that the wire had been installed incorrectly in the splice that held two ends of it together. Now he inspected the photos yet again. And Bill McHugh was struck with a revelation. He waited until 8 a.m. before he called Baldwin.

"I just solved the case for you," he told her.

Indeed he had.

"I looked at the photos again and saw they used the old wire over again and didn't clean it," McHugh recalled. "It was in their [West Penn's] own standards book that if you don't clean it, it will burn down. It was what I was taught ever since I started at started at Duquesne in 1978, that you have to clean it or it can burn down."

The T&D (Transmission & Distribution) *Construction Standards Manual* used by linemen and other company employees—a thick, blue, hard-cover tome also known in the industry as "the Bible"—did stress cleaning the wire, also known as the conductor. This helped to remove corrosion and make a better connection. The manual went a step further in specifying how it was to be cleaned: "Clean conductor with wire brush." And a step beyond that, ominously noting the potential repercussion of not properly cleaning a line: "Unclean conductor will set up overheating and eventual failure of the splice."

The portion of wire cleaned with a metal brush, especially old wires—like the one at the Goretzka property, which had been up for 47 years and contained not one but three splices—would have a fairly distinctive lighter color, even from afar. Up close, the wire should have shown deep and numerous scratch marks. The power lines at the Goretzka property did not, at least as far as McHugh could see. There was no visible evidence that the wires—either at the two splices remaining stretched between the poles adjacent to the house or on the piece that had fallen to the ground—had been cleaned with a wire brush.

This became the lynchpin of the plaintiff's case. Their theory—not that it was incumbent on them to prove why the wire had fallen—was that it hadn't been cleaned properly with a wire brush before being placed into the splice. Over time, this could cause overheating. Eventually, the wire would burn up and drop to the ground.

McHugh had come up with the theory. Now other experts would run with it. Kila Baldwin went out and spoke with Chris Havlik, an employee with the company that manufactured the splices; John Dagenhart, with Clapp Research, a consulting firm for electric and communication utility systems; and Campbell Laird, the Scottish-born and highly decorated metallurgist whom Specter had worked with before.

McHugh would continue to work with the team, but he would not testify. Baldwin sent him an initial payment for his work of $2,200. McHugh told her that he didn't want the money—he just wanted to help the Goretzkas, but she insisted he take it. Over McHugh's objections, she had agreed to pay him $100 per hour for his expertise. She said she had to make the payment to formally hire him as a plaintiffs' expert. McHugh cashed the check and kept $200. He put the remaining $2,000 in an envelope and drove it over to West Hempfield. He handed it to Mike Goretzka, who politely handed it right back.

"Well," McHugh told him. "I'll put it in the bank and if you ever need it, it'll be there."

Chapter 16

It wasn't until late in the 19th century and the promise of electricity's ability to create light that the power source made its greatest strides, with the likes of Thomas Edison and George Westinghouse leading the way. What motivated this transformation of invention into commercial success was the pursuit of a different commodity—money.

The biggest hurdle to popularizing the use of electricity was not creating light, but finding a way to make that practical. The first light bulb was invented not by Thomas Edison, as most people believe, but by an Englishman, Joseph Swan, in 1878. The problem was that his was a pretty lousy light bulb. Using a steel filament, Swan's bulbs burned out quickly. They were, practically speaking, useless.

Starting a year later, Edison invented a light bulb that used a cotton thread soaked in carbon in place of a steel filament. Edison's bulb didn't burn but became incandescent; it glowed. His first bulbs made light for 40 hours, a marvel at the time. Within a year, he had made bulbs that burned for more than 1,000 hours. And thus was created the first truly functional source of electric light. Something people wanted, and were willing to buy.

Chapter 17

In Woody Allen's movie *Bananas*, the ruler of San Marcos addresses his people to announce a new set of laws. After establishing Swedish as the nation's new official language, he makes an even more bizarre announcement.

"All citizens will be required to change their underwear every half hour," he tells them, adding, "Underwear will be worn on the outside, so we can check."

Shanin Specter did not require the staff at Kline & Specter to wear their underwear on the outside, though he did have some steadfast, and sometimes unusual, rules. For one, sneakers were forbidden attire, as were flip flops. Most strictly prohibited were jeans, not only in the office but also anywhere in which a staffer or lawyer was representing the firm. This meant pants or jackets or virtually anything made of denim, blue or otherwise. If Specter saw someone wearing jeans, he would cast a disapproving glance and inform the employee of his or her transgression. Once he was even heard notifying a high-ranking attorney that he had violated the dress code by wearing black denim pants into the offices of Kline & Specter. It wasn't like Specter could fire the attorney, nor did he exactly dress him down about not dressing up, but he made sure to point out the infringement.

"You're right," responded the attorney in question, Specter's partner, Tom Kline.

Specter was a stickler on other things as well. One of his bugaboos was staples. He eschewed their use in anything handed to him, any document or report or transcript. Anything. No staples, period. Nobody dared ask why, though theories abounded. One story, entirely unfounded, held that Specter had once suffered an injury—some thought it might have been severe, maybe involving an eye—due to an errant staple. Another was that he wanted to protect his supple digits from unnecessary friction. Or perhaps many years ago he had lost a particularly nasty product liability case to a staple manufacturer.

The anti-staples rule only contributed to Specter's status as a feared sovereign whose office was situated on the top floor of the skinny glass and granite 19-floor edifice at 1525 Locust Street in Center City Philadelphia. In his presence, the staff walked on eggshells. If a mere staple could rile the king, imagine a more serious blunder.

"My aversion to staples has been vastly overblown," he said when asked about the subject. "It's like when the president tells the staff at the Oval Office that it's warm, the next day the office will be an icebox. That's the way I get treated. If I say something, it gets exaggerated the other way around."

Specter particularly disliked staples on documents comprising many pages, because it was difficult to see the top few lines on a page after several were folded back on themselves. It was especially cumbersome if he was working in the small confines of an airplane seat. To read a document, he'd often have to remove its staple manually. When dealing with dozens of documents at a time, this was time-consuming and risked pricking a finger. "At some point I asked for paper clips or gem clips instead of staples, and that's turned into an obsession on other people's part. I don't think it's that big of a deal, but I know it concerns people, and it concerns me that it concerns them."

Specter was the taskmaster in the office. If discipline was called for, even a firing, he did not hesitate. Yet he knew this gave him a persona—among the staff, not the lawyers, who generally liked working with him—of someone who was hard-hearted, even unapproachable. Rather than try to smooth this image, Specter sometimes avoided conversations with the staff.

"I often don't talk to the staff of other attorneys directly, even when they walk into my office to put something into my in-box, because I know they're nervous and if I say something, they're going to get more nervous." Why were they so nervous? "Because I have probably been intemperate at some point and it gets around the office," he acknowledged.

Indeed, on some occasions, Specter's directness and candor bubbled over into a scolding. He estimated such a reprimand occurred every six to eight weeks, generally sparked by a series of slip-ups or one egregious misstep. The target could be a staffer or an attorney. It didn't matter which.

In one such episode, overheard by several people, Specter ripped into one of his lawyers for not telling him the truth during an earlier client meeting. The lawyer explained afterward that he had fibbed to Specter in front of the client because he didn't want to embarrass her.

"You didn't want to embarrass her? So instead you lie to me?" Specter recalled his end of the conversation. "I asked you a direct question. I'm your boss. You have to answer honestly!" The lawyer apologized. To which Specter responded: "Your apology is absolutely not accepted. Now get the fuck out of my office." Weeks later, both men were seen smiling and chatting amiably and the lawyer remained at the firm.

Chapter 18

To say that Kila Baldwin and Dominic Guerrini were among Specter's favorites at the firm wouldn't be much of a secret. His regard for them was why they got on the Goretzka case. He first picked Baldwin to work up the case—to interview potential witnesses, find and hire experts and take deposition testimony. Then, after telling Guerrini that the Goretzka litigation "would be a huge case," he advised his younger colleague to "get down on your hands and knees and beg Kila" to let him come aboard. He didn't physically assume that position, but he did make the request. Nicely.

Dominic Guerrini was the "teachers' pet." The son of public school music teachers and himself pretty good on the piano, he had attended Rutgers University as an undergraduate. He then chose to attend Penn Law. Lucky he did. It was there that he took a class in trial advocacy. He picked that particular class because, after performing his due diligence, he discovered it was taught by a hands-on adjunct professor, one who had current and big-time experience in the world of trial law. Guerrini earned a rare A+ in Shanin Specter's class. But more than that, Specter said, "He just had everything. Ninety percent of the students at Penn Law School are super bright, but less than 10 percent have the interpersonal skills where I can see them doing well in a courtroom."

Shortly afterward, Kline & Specter hired Guerrini as a law clerk, and he worked at the job (in a small cubicle) for more than a year. He enjoyed plaintiff work, he liked the other lawyers, and he hoped to stay at the firm. But after he graduated from law school, Specter told him he had no spot for him at the time, but he would keep him in mind. So the young lawyer took a job at Ballard Spahr, a big-name national law firm based in Philadelphia with offices in 14 cities. Guerrini was there two months when Specter called. "If we had a position available for you, how quickly could you take it?" he asked, then suggested Guerrini come see him. Which he did, anticipating an informal chat with Specter and instead arriving—in a sport coat and khakis—for a formal interview with both Specter and partner Tom Kline. Although chided about his attire, Guerrini got a job offer. When he quit Ballard Spahr after just two months—something no one did—he was gruffly told he would have to reimburse the firm the $5,000 it had paid for a course to help him pass the bar exam after law school. Guerrini gladly wrote the check (for which he was reimbursed) and packed his belongings.

Dominic Guerrini knew the law well, and he was sharp. A good person to be at Specter's elbow before and after trial. Not unlike his boss, he possessed a quiet tenacity, both in his work and his personal life. Once a chubby college kid and still fond of fine food, he had dropped 80 pounds in recent years and he had done it the hard way, maniacally sweating off the pounds at the gym and pounding the pavement along the streets of Philadelphia. If he wasn't at work, he could usually be found at the gym, where he played squash or worked out two or even three times some days.

Kila Baldwin was picked for the Goretzka case not only because she was a skilled and trusted associate, but also because Specter found her company agreeable. Once, at a meeting with all the firm's lawyers present, Specter was asked which of his associates he would choose if they had to make a long trip together. He did not hesitate, nor did he choose some vague, diplomatic response over concern he might alienate everyone else in the room. "Kila," he said. Pressed, he explained, "We've been on a lot of trips and trials out of town together and we both survived." Small praise, but true. Not everyone could easily survive a trip with the highly demanding Shanin Specter. But Baldwin possessed traits he appreciated because he shared them. She was superbly organized and focused, awake at 4:30 a.m. every day and prepared well before arriving at the office or a courtroom. When Specter clicked off questions, Baldwin finger-snapped the answers. Like Specter, she was candid to a fault, an uncommon attribute in the world of play-it-close-to-the-vest lawyers. She never pretended to know answers she didn't have. She never tried to bullshit the boss. And when asked her opinions about witnesses or experts or trial strategy, Baldwin gave decisive answers, even though she knew Specter would often disagree and tell her so, then tell her why. She was a quick learner and a good sounding board.

She was also very intelligent. She had been accepted by Harvard as an undergraduate but chose to enroll at Penn State instead because it was less expensive. Baldwin's parents—she grew up with her mother and stepfather, her birth father was an alcoholic whom her mother had divorced long before—were hardly wealthy. "They told me, 'You better have the money to pay for this,'" she recalled, "so I didn't go to Harvard." She was able to pay most of Penn State's bill for in-state tuition on her own. Baldwin, who spoke Spanish, Italian and French, followed with a dual law degree and M.B.A. from Temple University, which had given her a scholarship. Growing up as the youngest of five children living with a mother who was an assistant to the dean of a local college and a stepfather who was a writer and English professor, she learned to become self-reliant. Since early childhood, she had only seen her birth father on occasional weekends. He wound up in her home, still suffering from alcoholism and in poor health, shortly after the Goretzka case concluded. He would die a year later at the age of 60.

Kila Baldwin was the rarest of associates at Kline & Specter—someone who had left for other employment and returned. At the time she quit, Baldwin had been assigned to the Class Action Department, where she liked neither the work nor her boss. When she told Specter she was leaving, he sat with her for nearly two hours trying to talk her out of it, even offering more money. Baldwin shed some tears but remained resolute. She took a job with a large defense firm, where she found the work less rewarding. After a year, she ran into Specter in court one day and he was friendly. Later, hearing that her old boss had been fired, she called Specter to ask if he would have her back. She would always remember his two-word response: "Yeah, absolutely."

Both Baldwin and Guerrini were glad to be where they were now. The Goretzka case was interesting. It was important. And it offered the possibility to make the firm—and them by way of bonuses—a lot of money.

Chapter 19

Shanin Specter's pedigree was well known. Both his parents were famous in Philadelphia, his father well beyond the city. Since the death of longtime Pennsylvania senator Arlen Specter, his square, skylighted office on Kline & Specter's 19th floor had sat vacant, the faces of past presidents as well as Pope John Paul II, Muammar Gaddafi and many others peering from their framed abodes on the wall into the empty space below. (The photos would later be moved to his library and archival collection, the Arlen Specter Center for Public Service at Philadelphia University.) Specter had served as Philadelphia district attorney for eight years in the 1960s and '70s. In 1980, he won election to the U.S. Senate, where he served for 30 years, including chairing the powerful Judiciary Committee. Specter lost his last Senate race in 2010 when, facing a tough Republican primary against conservative Republican Pat Toomey, he switched parties but lost in the Democratic primary. (Toomey went on to win Specter's seat.) Shanin Specter played an important role in his father's Senate campaigns.

Specter's mother, Joan, had her own success story. After earning a master's degree in food and design from Drexel University, she founded three cooking schools, wrote a foodie newspaper column and hosted a Philadelphia radio show. She also baked pies, selling them locally and growing her business into a multi-state wholesale distribution company. She ran as a Republican for Philadelphia City Council in 1979, winning that race and three more terms, remaining in office through 1995.

The power couple's son, Shanin (his only sibling, Steve, a psychiatrist, lived in Los Angeles), attended Penn Charter, a private elementary and high school in Philadelphia, Haverford College and the University of Pennsylvania Law School. While at Penn, Specter convinced the administration to let him take his third year at Cambridge University, where he earned a Master of Laws degree, or LL.M. He took to the debate floor at The Cambridge Union twice, a difficult task for any law student, never mind an American, and did well. He graduated with First Honors.

Specter started work at The Beasley Firm, the top Philadelphia plaintiff practice, where he occupied an office adjacent to an attorney named Tom

Kline. The pair prospered under the legendary James Beasley, a feisty and highly successful trial lawyer who told the two, when they left in 1995 to open their own firm, that they would never equal their success at his side. For once, Beasley was wrong.

Chapter 20

Another attorney had more than a passing interest in the Goretzka trial. Maurice Nernberg had spent 45 years practicing law when he got the biggest case of his career in 2009 quite by happenstance. His small Pittsburgh law firm, Nernberg & Associates—comprising the bald, diminutive, 70-year-old Nernberg, son David and one associate—handled general business litigation, mainly small business matters such as taxes, trustee duties, payment terms, contracts and breeches thereof. One client was Family Home Hospice, where Mike Goretzka had started sweeping and scrubbing floors at 18 and had risen to senior vice president. The number-one man, owner Norm Rish, was like a father to Mike, whose own father, Carl, had passed away from cancer in 2004.

When the incident occurred with Carrie, Mike called Norm and Norm called Nernberg, who then dialed Mike Goretzka right away, while Carrie was still alive. The two men spoke and Nernberg signed Goretzka as his newest client, though he knew his small law firm couldn't handle such an arduous matter. It didn't take him long to think of where to refer the case. The firm he decided to call was, oddly enough, one to which he had lost a verdict just a few years earlier.

Nernberg had represented a client in a case similar in some aspects to the Goretzka case. A young woman, Stephanie Wilkerson, 29, was killed in the collapse of a roof that had sheltered the pavilion of a ride called the Whip at Kennywood Park, an amusement park a half hour east of Pittsburgh. In the Wilkerson incident, a weather condition known as a "macroburst," with winds greater than 100 m.p.h., had suddenly struck the park, injuring 54 people. Park officials argued in ensuing legal proceedings that it was an "act of God" that had caused Wilkerson's death.

But Tom Kline, Specter's partner, argued otherwise. He claimed that Kennywood and its contractor, the Landau Building Company, had inadequately constructed the pavilion by using building sketches supplied by the amusement park instead of detailed and certified architectural drawings. Kennywood and Landau failed to get the proper building or occupancy permits or an inspection afterward by an engineer. "They literally built this thing from cartoons," Kline told the news media.

That case was tried in a somewhat unusual fashion, with a jury deciding the amount of compensatory damages before liability, a determination reserved for a second trial along with possible punitive damages. The jury set the award at $1.2 million if, in fact, Kennywood and Landau were found responsible for Wilkerson's death. An award could go higher, possibly much higher, if a jury also found the park and the contractor exercised reckless behavior and that punitive damages were warranted. On the eve of the second trial a settlement was reached for $1.945 million. Nernberg—who had predicted that a jury would never be coaxed into setting a million-dollar award—did not come to love Tom Kline. But he was impressed by him, and his Philadelphia law firm. "I found that when Tom Kline came into the case, the offers double."

When Nernberg landed the Goretzka case, he called Kline & Specter. But he called Kline's partner, largely because he had heard from a Pittsburgh judge whom he considered a friend, Allegheny County Common Pleas judge Michael Della Vecchia, about the wonderful job Specter had done in his courtroom in an earlier case. That trial involved a large corporation, the Ford Motor Company, and tow truck driver Joe Blumer, whose death resulted from a Ford truck with a defective parking brake.

As Nernberg put it, "I've always believed that if you couldn't do the best job for the client, I'd get them the best lawyer available." He was also getting himself the best lawyer available. As the referring attorney in the case, he stood to make a great deal of money from a large jury award—one-third of the attorney's fees in the case, which would be roughly one-third of any verdict or settlement.

When Specter got the call, he immediately flew to Pittsburgh to meet with Mike Goretzka and his older brother, Chuck, in Nernberg's office, a cluttered space in a somewhat rundown part of the city. Seated in the conference room, a cramped space curiously decorated with World War I posters and one of Richard Nixon holding a pitchfork below the words "The Almanack of Poor Richard," Mike Goretzka hired Specter.

Chapter 21

Kila Baldwin thought back to when the case had started for her, the day after Carrie Goretzka was buried. The brief note from Shanin Specter outlined the fact that a Pittsburgh attorney had referred a potentially big case, the basic details of what had happened and a brief instruction: "Please get out there ASAP."

Specter had assigned the case to Baldwin as a reward for her work on the Blumer case, on which she had toiled for more than a year, much of it learning the intricacies of a motor vehicle's braking system. She didn't know at the time, of course, that this new case would take up a good chunk of her next few years. Or that she would prove much more important than merely a lawyer to the man who lived at 23 West Hempfield Drive in West Hempfield, Pennsylvania.

After almost a six-hour drive, Baldwin arrived in the peaceful, unassuming neighborhood at a small house filled with relatives and friends who were there so the widower would not be alone. Mike Goretzka's blue eyes were rimmed with red from days of sobbing and sleepless nights. He shook Kila Baldwin's hand but could not muster even a hint of a smile. He made obligatory introductions to Carol, Amy and Chuck, his sisters and brother, his mother, JoAnn, and several other folks. Then he sat heavily on a nearby armchair, put his head in one hand and cried.

"I can't believe this happened," he mumbled through his tears.

Baldwin wanted to comfort this man she had just met, but she didn't know how. So she went about her job. She talked to family members about Carrie and the incident and then walked about the neighborhood, going from door to door and interviewing people about what they had seen while the images were still fairly fresh in their minds. She took notes and wrote summaries and had them sign statements.

Kila Baldwin surveyed the scene, peering at the wooden telephone poles and the gaggle of lines strung between them from the street to the rear of the Goretzka property. She looked in amazement and a measure of admiration at the lawn at the side of the house, the spot where Carrie had been killed. There were no signs of damage. Mike and Chuck had gotten up on the morning of the funeral and ripped up the scorched ground, then replaced it with fresh sod. Mike hadn't wanted his children to see the scarred grass and replay in their minds the terrible thing they had seen.

Baldwin tried to talk to the young Goretzka children but they avoided her, clinging to their father, at one point whining in protest when he stepped into another room and closed the door. He reopened it a few seconds later to find them howling. She looked at the easel containing photos of a happy Carrie, a reminder of just how much this family had lost.

After several hours, Baldwin couldn't take it anymore. The weight of sadness made her feel depressed, then ill, physically ill. Queasiness turned to nausea to the point at which she had to run out, afraid she was going to vomit in the Goretzkas' home. She forced herself to return the next day. And Mike Goretzka forced himself to talk about the incident. He recited the facts with little emotion, like a tape recorder. How he had gone to work, how his mother told him the lights and the TV had turned off, how Carrie had left the living room to use the phone.

"He looked like he was in a state of shock, like his mind was a million miles away," Baldwin would remember, but he was determined to help in any way he could. He made himself relay facts about Carrie, his own life, how they had met. Every now and then, he paused to sob.

In the months that followed, Kila Baldwin would offer a shoulder for Mike to lean on and to cry on. More than his lawyer, she became a therapist of sorts and, eventually, a friend. He called her in the office, at her home, on her cell phone several times a week at first. Whenever he was alone and feeling especially blue. He'd remember details he wanted to relate. Other times he just wanted to talk. And to cry.

"Carrie was my everything," he would say, his voice shaky.

"I shouldn't have gone to work that day."

"How am I going to raise two girls by myself?"

At times Mike would cry on the phone to Baldwin for nearly an hour. His candor surprised and touched her. Over the next year, she would get dozens of phone calls from him. Many ended tearfully. With each, Baldwin would try to console him, to be supportive. "I know, Mike. We're going to try to help you." Other times she would just listen and say nothing.

Chapter 22

Dominic Guerrini was a young lawyer and therefore no stranger to the inglorious grind of the discovery process in which a foundation was laid for trial. What he wasn't used to, and didn't much like, was being mocked.

"I remember getting laughed at, laughed at...I'll never forget it."

The incident, for the first time showing the intensity and potential for nastiness of the Goretzka case, occurred after Guerrini had deposed a witness in a drab conference room at the Sheraton Hotel in Greensburg, where West Penn Power is headquartered. The session had been unremarkable.

Guerrini approached Joe Starkey, West Penn Power's chief in-house counsel, who was wearing a leather Pittsburgh Steelers jacket, and asked him about the utility's responses to written questions submitted by his firm as part of discovery. One of particular interest dealt with West Penn Power's liability insurance coverage.

"Joe," said Guerrini, who at six feet and with squared shoulders towered over the smaller Starkey, "I saw from your responses there was only coverage for $35 million and I was wondering if there was any more coverage than that or if that exhausted all the coverage?"

The real answer was that there was, in fact, an excess policy for an additional $75 million, but it was not the answer Guerrini got. Instead, Starkey laughed in his face, and gave him a dismissive response.

"That's plenty of coverage for this case," he said.

Chapter 23

The discovery process was arduous and not always pleasant. But it paid dividends.

West Penn Power put up a fight on almost everything. If the plaintiffs wanted information from the company, they would have to file motions with the judge seeking to compel its cooperation. Specter's team did.

One sought something simple—the company's net worth. Avrum Levicoff, the lead defense attorney, argued that this was public information and there was no need for the company to provide it. The numbers could easily be found on the Internet. But Baldwin wanted the information to come from the company for a simple reason: so the numbers would be certified by West Penn Power and could be entered into the trial record without the need of calling a witness to do so. Michael Della Vecchia—the judge in Specter's earlier Blumer trial who was now also presiding in the Goretzka case—granted the plaintiffs' motion.

The ruling set Levicoff off on a tirade. After the motion proceedings, he followed Baldwin out of the courtroom and lambasted her outside in the hallway.

"You shouldn't be practicing in Pittsburgh; we don't do things like that out here!" he screamed at her.

Baldwin chose not to argue. "I'm sorry you disagree with the judge on this, but we're entitled to the documents," she said and walked away as quickly as she could for a woman who was eight months pregnant. Levicoff continued shouting and followed Baldwin until she managed to escape to an elevator. So scathing was the defense attorney's rebuke that two attorneys who witnessed it called later to ask if she was all right.

The motions to compel discovery paid dividends. West Penn Power finally produced documents that would prove critical during trial. There was a video produced by Hubbell, the splice manufacturer, that was shown to the linemen stressing the importance of proper conductor cleaning before installation. There was the power company's own standards manual, which also stated the importance of brushing a line before installation. And there were internal emails and documents that mentioned other "burndowns" generally and noted the power line at the Goretzka home specifically. One document mentioned Mike Goretzka's complaint about a previous fallen line on his property.

Chapter 24

While Baldwin and Guerrini were laying the foundation for the case through discovery, Specter was banging on the door of government, specifically the agency that regulates utilities in Pennsylvania, the Public Utility Commission. He was also banging the drum of public sentiment.

In a letter dated January 11, 2012, almost a year before a trial would begin, he sent the PUC a seven-page letter that began: "I write to bring to your attention a safety hazard."

The letter called for an investigation into how West Penn Power trained its linemen and inspected its power lines. It noted the incident that killed Carrie Goretzka and Specter's lawsuit against West Penn Power, a subsidiary of Allegheny Energy, which the previous year had merged with Ohio-based First Energy. The letter detailed some of what deposition testimony in the case had so far revealed, namely that the accident had been caused by an improperly cleaned power line placed into a splice connection. It pointed to the splice manufacturer's explicit instructions and the company's own standards manual calling for a wire brush to be used for cleaning, but noted that West Penn Power linemen were taught that they could use knives or pliers instead. Improperly cleaned wires could cause a buildup of oxides, which could result in overheating and a wire "burndown." Specter quoted the deposition testimony of Jason Bundren, an executive of splice maker Hubbell Electrical Products Company, to explain the importance of wire brushing a power line: "Use this as an analogy. We don't use a knife to brush our teeth."

Specter further noted that many power companies used infrared testing to check whether their splices are overheating and thus a risk for failing, but that West Penn Power did not. His letter concluded: "Allegheny Power's failure to follow proper installation instructions for the installation of automatic splices caused the death of Carrie and may cause additional lines to fall and people to die. This must be remedied."

A few days later, Specter sent a news release and a copy of the letter to the news media and drove out to Pittsburgh for a news conference. His appearance, complete with a demonstration of how the power line was not properly cleaned with a wire brush, blanketed the news, running on the ABC, CBS and Fox affiliates as well as on three radio stations, in the Associated Press, and 15 different newspaper and Internet outlets throughout Pennsylvania and even into New York and Canada. This wide media coverage, which Specter hoped would embarrass the PUC into action, was no accident. Being used to dealing with the media from his father's campaigns, he had prompted the coverage by placing a discrete call earlier to a reporter for *The Pittsburgh-Post Gazette*. He promised the paper a scoop if it agreed to two things: to hold the story until the morning of his news conference and to give it prominent play. When that day came, the story ran on the *Post-Gazette*'s front page, making it necessary news for the other media outlets.

And the Public Utility Commission, in turn, did act. It referred the case to its investigative arm, the Bureau of Investigation and Enforcement (I&E), which demanded information from West Penn Power related to Carrie's death, a demand that had so far gone unheeded. (In November 2009, five months after the incident, the power company had told the PUC staff that it was conducting an investigation and that it expected it would take six to nine months to complete.) On March 12, 2012, I&E sent another request for information, the commission's fifth.

Specter didn't let up. On March 30, less than three months after his first letter, he sent the PUC an eight-page "follow-up" containing more proof that the power company's linemen did not follow proper procedures to clean power lines. This time Specter cited the deposition testimony of some higher-ups at the utility for not doing enough to make sure the installation instructions were followed. He ended the second letter with another dire warning: "There is obviously a grave concern for the safety of those living in Allegheny Power's service area because of its practices."

Two more months passed. On May 30, I&E, finally fed up over noncompliance and prodded by Specter's news conference in Pittsburgh, wrote its own letter—a nine-page complaint against West Penn Power. In it, prosecutor Heidi L. Wushinske noted the three years of delays in providing information and wrote: "To date, the company has not complied with the commission staff's repeated requests for information." She went a step further and asked the PUC to fine West Penn Power $86,000 plus an extra $1,000 for every day it continued to ignore the agency's requests for information.

Wushinske listed various violations, claiming that "West Penn Power failed to furnish and maintain adequate, efficient, safe and reasonable service and facilities in that the company did not ensure the integrity" of its lines. The complaint recommended that the five-member PUC vote to order the company to improve line cleaning by retraining its linemen and boosting their supervision. It also sought to compel West Penn Power to inspect all of its lines, preferably using infrared technology, and replace any splices that exhibited excessive heat or signs of potential failure within one year.

But a PUC decision and the mandates imposed upon West Penn Power would have to await the outcome of the Goretzka case.

Chapter 25

Phase II of turning electricity into money was to actually bring it into peoples' homes. Enter Thomas Edison again. He started with just one house, but it was an impressive one. It belonged to John Pierpont Morgan, known as J.P. around town—New York City. There, in 1881, Edison installed a steam engine and Michael Faraday's dynamo connected to incandescent lights in the banker's home, making it the world's first electrified residence. The next year, he powered and wired Morgan's offices. Now Edison had not only two showcases for his handiwork but also, in Morgan, an investor in his future projects.

Progress came quickly in the nascent industry. Edison founded the Edison Electric Light Company in New York, and he applied for and also purchased patents involving electric lighting. Just a year after J.P. Morgan greeted dinner guests with electric light, Edison, on September 4, 1882, cranked up his Pearl Street Power Station that put out and carried enough power to light 5,000 lamps.

Meanwhile, Morgan continued to get involved in a big way. Eleven years after his house was wired with electricity, the man whose name is still carried by one of the nation's largest banks arranged the merger of two of the biggest electric companies to form General Electric. GE grew rapidly and became amazingly profitable.

Chapter 26

"This is Carrie Goretzka..."

Specter's script was now full of his own scribbled edits and instructions written in bold letters: "PAUSE," "SHOW," "USE DEMONSTRATIVES." At one point, he slashed away a page and a half of the speech. "Let's skip this part. This speech is already long," he muttered to Baldwin and Guerrini. When he reached the part about Mike and Carrie, a photo of their wedding day popped up on the screen. The young bride was beaming.

"Mike's going to be in hysterics in court at this point," commented Baldwin, whose close relationship with her client came after numerous visits and scores of phone calls, some late at night with the weeping widower. "I'm just thinking of Mike."

Specter heard her and responded: "He can leave."

By the end of this latest session, Specter made nearly 100 more changes to his script—some minor, some major. The next day, he and his crew began again from the top and made a litany of additional edits, Specter concentrating a little more now on the flow of his words, not only their meaning, but also their tone and cadence.

And again the next day—"This is Carrie Goretzka"—with Specter standing at a lectern this time. By his sixth run-through, he had become more adept with the remote controlling the photos, more sure with the red laser pointer, more in tune with the music of his own words. "I need a little more language at the beginning of this sentence. How about 'All of a sudden...' OK, let's add that there. Let's begin this sentence with 'Eventually...' It seems at the end that I've said this before. Let's cut out the earlier part and say this toward the end. It's stronger at the end."

In all, the speech went through 15 drafts before Shanin Specter would actually deliver the words in open court. After the last session in his office, finally satisfied he had honed a message that would not only capture a jury's attention but leave a lasting impression, Specter allowed himself a small smile. For the first time, he seemed content.

"How many of the jurors you think will be crying when they hear this speech?"

"All of them," said Diane Grimmie.

"I might be, and I'm not a crier," said Baldwin, looking at her boss and adding, "You might, too."

"I might," agreed Specter, who was not normally prone to displays of emotion. He looked down at his opening speech and his smile evaporated. "This is going to be hard to get through."

Chapter 27

The lead defense attorney was Avrum Levicoff of the Pittsburgh law firm of Levicoff, Silko & Deemer, which comprised three partners and nine associates, including a younger Levicoff and two Silko kids. Elizabeth Deemer would assist him on the Goretzka trial. The firm wasn't as big as Specter's, which boasted more than 30 lawyers, but it was no lightweight outfit. Neither was Levicoff.

At 60, mid-height and a tad overweight, with dark gray hair surrounding a softball-sized bald spot on the top of his head, Levicoff looked a lot older than Specter, who, at 54, was an avid athlete with a slim, almost skinny build. Levicoff wore sharp, dark suits, sometimes double-breasted, and usually with a three-point handkerchief in the breast pocket. He walked with a slight stoop. He bore a weary, pained expression but smiled easily. He had a soft voice and a matching demeanor, but he was not at all reluctant to speak up when necessary. Levicoff seemed very comfortable in the courtroom. And this certainly wasn't his first dance.

The defense attorney's knowledge of the electric utility industry was unmatched. While Specter was learning the terminology of the business on the run, Levicoff had represented West Penn Power for about five years and had a working knowledge of many pieces of equipment and gauges of conductor wire used on the job. He knew the lingo, so to speak. Avrum Levicoff was a local guy, raised in Pittsburgh's Squirrel Hill section and schooled in the city, earning magna cum laude honors from the University of Pittsburgh Law School, where he was editor of the law review. He had received a number of honors, including the American Jurisprudence Award for highest achievement in commercial law. Levicoff had two children: Eric, an orthopedic surgeon, and Edward, a lawyer in the family firm, by his first marriage, as well as 12-year-old Cara Mia from his second.

Levicoff was a trial lawyer in the true sense of the term, having taken perhaps 150 cases to a verdict. He didn't keep score, but the word was that he did quite well. And, as it happened, he was also a friend of the judge in the Goretzka trial, Michael Della Vecchia.

Chapter 28

After a request for a settlement from West Penn Power, Specter made an offer that he was fairly certain the power company would not accept. He wanted $68.1 million. When asked, and not before, he explained to the defense attorneys that the amount equaled the monetary compensation received by the power company's chief executive officer in the year of the incident. And that was the easy part. Specter—and Mike Goretzka—wanted something else: an agreement by the utility for full remediation of all its power lines. That meant inspecting each and every connection on each and every line, a herculean undertaking, no doubt, but one that Specter felt was necessary to ensure that such a tragedy never happened again. He said that anything short of such a promise—and, since Shanin Specter had a healthy skepticism about the integrity of corporate America, he also insisted on independent verification—would leave countless others potentially open to the same terrible fate as Carrie Goretzka.

A month before the trial date, a gaggle of lawyers assembled outside the courtroom of Judge Della Vecchia, whose stated goal was to try to avert a trial by reaching a settlement between the parties. The judge called them into his chambers separately. Specter walked over to Mike Goretzka before going in.

"I'm going to tell the judge we're not going to talk about money until they agree to fix the lines," he told his client. "We'll see what he says about that. We're not allowed to make them fix the lines, but we can refuse to settle if they don't."

"Why don't they just step up?" asked Goretzka.

Specter thought about the question, then replied, "I think what will be the determining factor here will be the verdict slip."

When he entered Della Vecchia's chambers, Specter stated his demand for remediation.

"I don't have any power over that," the judge answered.

"I know," said Specter, "But we're not willing to have any discussion about money until they agree to remediation."

Later Della Vecchia asked Specter if he would be willing to take a slightly lower amount. What would he say if the utility agreed to pay, for instance, $40 million to $45 million, but without a pledge to inspect the lines and make necessary repairs and upgrades? Specter did not hesitate before answering.

"I'd say no."

Della Vecchia raised an eyebrow and let Specter go back to the hallway. Then he called in the lawyers for West Penn Power. Then representatives for the utility's insurance carrier, which would be responsible for paying the bulk of any monetary settlement. Specter suspected he knew what the judge was telling them.

"He knows it's a helluva good case, a helluva good case," he told Mike Goretzka and his mother, JoAnn, out in the hallway.

Specter told the Goretzkas about another case he had litigated years earlier: Erica Lynne Pratt was a 19-year-old student at the University of Pittsburgh. On February 2, 2004, she was in the middle of a math class when she suffered a cardiac arrest. She collapsed and slumped to the ground. One student called 911. When the first campus police officer arrived in the classroom, Erica was gasping. But the officer failed to act immediately, neither assessing Erica's condition nor administering CPR for several minutes. Two students trained in CPR tried to step in to resuscitate Erica but the officer refused to allow them to help, telling them not to touch the young woman until paramedics arrived. Finally, he acted on his own, but by that time Erica had stopped breathing altogether. The result of the delay was deprivation of oxygen to her brain.

Erica Pratt suffered severe brain damage, leaving her unable to walk or feed herself and with difficulty in speaking. The case went to trial in 2007, with Specter representing the Pratt family. Evidence in the case, including testimony from a Harvard cardiologist, indicated that Erica, an otherwise healthy young woman, could have been saved from serious harm had the campus police responded appropriately. After five days of trial, the university agreed to a monetary settlement. But as part of the agreement, Specter also insisted—and Pitt agreed—to improve its emergency medical response. It pledged to hire a qualified medical director to conduct quarterly refresher courses on CPR and the use of automatic external defibrillators for the campus police and to test those officers twice yearly.

"They agreed to retrain the officers plus pay the monetary settlement. And they did it," Specter told Mike Goretzka. "They agreed to do it because they wanted to get rid of the lawsuit and because it was the right thing to do. And the situation is the same here, more so."

But West Penn Power didn't want to give up the money without a fight. Specter had seen it before, the defense going to trial to "test the waters." Its lawyers would see how jury selection went, if the panel drawn seemed sympathetic. Opening speeches would reveal how the plaintiffs' attorney sized up the case, how he made his pitch to the jury, and how the jury seemed to respond. The defense often waited for several experts to testify to see how they held up under direct and cross-examination. And plenty of times a defense attorney even waited until a jury went out to deliberate a verdict before offering a settlement.

In this case, West Penn Power, after many months of discovery, would finally make an offer, and a fairly substantial one. It came about a week before trial, and the amount indicated to Specter that the utility was ready to get serious about the case. However, it was an offer that Specter could refuse, and did. It was for $10 million.

Specter told Mike Goretzka that he believed the case, if it went to a verdict, had only a 10 percent chance of resulting in a jury award of less than $10 million. The most likely outcome—an 80 percent chance, he estimated—was that a verdict would fall somewhere between $10 million and $100 million. Specter held out a small hope, the remaining 10 percent, that the jury would return a verdict of more than $100 million.

Chapter 29

Mike Goretzka had wanted to have another child, at least one more. A boy.

"Carrie used to ask me, 'Are you disappointed we didn't have a boy?' I'd say no. But deep down inside, you want to pass on your name, your legacy. You want to play sports with them, take them hunting, to the game. Not that you can't do that with a girl, but it's different."

He and Carrie tried to have a third child. She got pregnant but miscarried. They planned to try again. Five people—parents and three children—was the perfect family, they felt. One more child would complete the package. Unless, of course, they had another daughter, in which case, Mike acknowledged with a rueful smile, "I have a feeling we would have probably tried again."

A son was unlikely now. Mike barely socialized. He wouldn't even consider dating. "Not a day goes by that I don't miss her," he said of his late wife years after her death. Instead of his family reaching the perfect five, it had been reduced to three.

Chapter 30

On the first day, Judge Della Vecchia walked into court wearing a gray cardigan instead of his black robes. It was a somewhat informal day—the lawyers in suits but no audience save Mike Goretzka, and no jury. Before the lawyers picked a jury, they would argue pretrial motions before the judge and he would rule on each. There were 31 in all, 10 now made by the plaintiffs and 21 by the defense. Each was designed to create a strategic advantage, any edge, however slight, for one side or the other, either by preventing or allowing a witness' statement or a photo to be introduced as evidence or a study to be mentioned for the jurors to hear. The motions gave an indication of the strategy that went into a case. They represented a complex tug-of-war that set the rules of engagement for the real battle to come.

Dominic Guerrini rose and asked the judge to bar an animation created by a defense expert purporting to show how Carrie had approached and touched the fallen wire as evidence that she was negligent, that her death was, at least partly, her fault. Guerrini argued the inference was not a reasonable one. Della Vecchia was not inclined to disallow the animation.

"That's their whole defense," he noted.

"That doesn't make it admissible," retorted Guerrini.

"I'm not saying they're right," the judge said about the defense's theory, "but they have the right to present it."

And so it went.

On many of the motions, Della Vecchia withheld judgment. He'd see how it went at trial before allowing leeway or admonishing one side or the other, on occasion reining them in. He was an experienced jurist. Of the large verdicts that had been awarded in his courtroom—and there had been plenty—none had ever been overturned on appeal.

Chapter 31

On a chilly mid-November morning, Specter and Baldwin briskly walked the four uphill blocks to the Allegheny County Courthouse. They exited an elevator on the seventh floor. Baldwin was, as always, a few steps behind Specter, whose smooth, quick gait left all but the best marathoners behind. As they breezed through the marble corridor, she mentioned the upcoming first phase of the trial—jury selection.

"I think we should go for women," Baldwin said. Women would be more empathetic, she felt. The victim was a woman.

"I think men," countered Specter, who often disagreed, though sometimes just to play devil's advocate. He believed that men would be more apt to feel what Mike Goretzka was feeling, and would be more able to associate with his plight.

Later, after considering the question more thoroughly, Specter disagreed with both strategies. Men or women, it didn't really matter. He had come to a simple conclusion about the jury: as long as its members were fairly intelligent and had a pulse, they couldn't help but find in the plaintiff's favor. As he would tell Baldwin: "What we want on the jury is human beings."

Specter also sought at least one juror with technical knowledge to help the rest of the jurors wend their way through the more complex testimony. And he hoped for someone, preferably more than one, who was not only smart but very smart. Specter had formed an opinion over the years, one contrary to that held by many plaintiffs' lawyers, that smart people were his strongest allies. He would even send out an "All Lawyers" memo to members of his firm saying the following:

We've spent a lot of time talking about which types of jurors are best for our clients. I've argued that the former conventional wisdom that less educated jurors were best for our clients is no longer true and we are often better off with more educated jurors. My opinion is based predominantly on three concepts: (1) less well educated people have been more susceptible to believing the insurance industry's argument that the civil justice system is out of control; (2) better educated people are better suited to understand often complex liability cases, which is especially important since we bear the burden of proof; (3) better educated people make more money and have a better appreciation that what may seem like a lot of money to some people isn't really a lot of money. There are lots of exceptions to all this, of course, and I don't use this as an exclusive method of striking prospective jurors.

Chapter 32

John Palovcak walked with a cane and an attitude. He had managed a successful car dealership in Erie for many years before poor health (chronic asthma and gout) and the cruelly long work days (from eight in the morning till ten at night by his own account) convinced him to look for a job with an employer known for offering relatively easy work and short hours—the government.

At 60, Palovcak, a graduate of Gannon College, now found himself working his 14th year as a jury clerk in Allegheny County Common Pleas Court. In this large building, where many dark-suited attorneys made in a day what Palovcak earned in a week, the jury clerk held a peculiar mix of lowly obscurity and unquestioned authority. When it was time to pick a jury, he was lord and master.

Though Palovcak walked somewhat shakily with a cane, he spoke with the firmness of a despot. In a creaky, nasally voice, he barked out orders like a general, marshalling potential jurors from one room to another, into and out of seats with rapid-fire precision. Scores, perhaps as many as 60 or 80 or even 100 (Palovcak moved them about in groups of 20) of these good, albeit often reluctant, citizens were needed to make a 12-person jury. Such a large pool was especially important when they were told at the outset that the trial could take weeks, perhaps a month or more. Many who heard that commitment sought to escape duty. It was Palovcak's job to prevent that, to make sure that those who were fit to serve did so.

Being the referee wasn't always easy. Excuses came in bunches, and Palovcak was charged with separating the good from the valid from the bogus, the true "hardships" from the embellished. "I'm real good at that," he said in between sessions in which he turned down one stated hardship after another, though also granting a few. "People say, 'I work.' I say, 'How many people don't?'" Folks with regular jobs had to serve on a jury, but those who had small businesses or were sole proprietors often got excused, as did people with planned and paid-for vacations and those with youngsters or old folks to care for—though Palovcak often asked, and often in a disbelieving tone, "Well, can't you get someone to care for them while you're in court?"

Those who claimed they lacked transportation to get to court were often asked if they couldn't get a ride or take a bus. "How'd you get here today?" Palovcak would ask. (In another case Specter would try, a juror told the judge in mid-trial that she couldn't continue to serve because she lacked the money for mass transit. Specter volunteered to pay the fare, the judge agreed, and he and the defense attorney each pulled $10 from their pockets to be given anonymously to the juror.)

Palovcak took no guff from the attorneys, either. "You can't take any," he explained. "I have to control the room."

"Sometimes one of the lawyers will say, 'I have a right to a follow-up question.' And I'll them, 'No you don't.' I'll cut them right off. Sometimes I'll have to ask a juror to leave so I can talk to them straight."

Palovcak answered questions in a clipped and fast fashion.

"Are you ever biased toward one side or the other in a case?" he was asked.

"No."

"Are you sure?"

"Asked and answered."

Probably Palovcak's proudest accomplishment in his job was that he insulated the judge from the grimy process of jury selection. Many jurors, particularly in major cases, were excused, their interviews a waste of time. Some were challenged by one side of the case or the other and were generally kept from trial. But during the course of the selection process disputes would sometimes arise that demanded a decision by the presiding judge. That is, if the jury clerk couldn't settle it first. Said Palovcak with pride, "I rarely go to the judge." And watching him work made it clear why.

At one point during jury selection in the Goretzka case, a process that took place in a room outside court, the attorneys began to squabble and things got heated. Avrum Levicoff, red-faced and raising his voice slightly, wanted to take a certain matter to a higher authority. He stood from his seat and exclaimed, "Let's go see the judge!"

Specter began to stand, too, when Palovcak swiftly intervened.

"Siddown!" he commanded, scowling at Levicoff. "You're not going anywhere."

And he didn't.

Chapter 33

Jury selection could be long and tedious. In the Goretzka trial, the proceedings bordered on the bizarre. They were conducted in a small side room with extra chairs dragged in from an adjacent courtroom to augment the odd assortment of seating already there, including a few fluffy armchairs and a love seat that Mike and JoAnn Goretzka claimed. Palovcak sat behind an old, worn desk with Specter in front and Levicoff and his jury consultant, who'd made the trip from Atlanta just for this, off to one side. An empty chair sat on the other side of the desk, reserved for potential jurors, who would be asked to step inside one by one for questioning, known as voir dire, from the French "to see to speak," though the term that has come to mean "to speak the truth."

There was one other thing about the room. It had no lights. For some unexplained reason, the electricity had shut off in a part of the building, this part. Rather than try to find a new space large enough to accommodate all the lawyers inside and 20 jurors at a clip nearby, the lawyers agreed to plow on with the available natural light that seeped in from a lone window on the far side of the room.

From the outset, it was clear that completing jury selection would take some time. While the lawyers' goal was to pick jurors who were potentially favorable to their general position, most of the prospects had a different goal in mind. And that was to go home.

Before being interviewed individually, the prospects were questioned en masse to see if any should be disqualified off the bat. They were given a brief description of the argument and asked whether they knew facts about the case, whether they knew any of the attorneys involved or had seen something in the news. The defense had insisted on asking one question that Specter didn't like: Had any of the jurors seen him on television?

Shanin Specter had been on various Pittsburgh television stations at least 15 times talking about the case: in July 2009, when he filed the suit on behalf of the Goretzkas; again the following September after the 911 tapes were released of people calling for help for Carrie; in early 2012 when he filed a complaint with the state Public Utility Commission and in May 2012 when the PUC filed a complaint against West Penn Power, blaming the company for the disaster.

The TV reports were favorable to the plaintiffs. Several noted the wire "fell on" Carrie, while others quoted Specter as saying the power line was not properly installed, and still others quoted the PUC stating that West Penn Power had not properly maintained its lines and had refused the agency's requests for information about the incident for two years. The PUC had sought to fine the company $86,000.

It made sense that Avrum Levicoff and his jury expert would want to know if prospective jurors had seen the reports. But asking those in the jury pool—and few remembered seeing anything of consequence from the TV reports—if they had seen Specter on television also had some possible unintended effects. For one, the question told the jury that the incident had been on television and was, therefore, a big deal. And it told them that Specter had been on TV, intimating that he, too, was a big deal. On the other hand, Specter worried that the TV clips suggested he was seeking publicity.

Chapter 34

The defense was sparing no expense. While Specter and Baldwin chatted almost in passing about what type of jurors they would like on the panel, West Penn Power had hired a jury consultant to help decide which 12 people they should be. Rick Fuentes, who held a master's degree and Ph.D. in applied psychology from Texas A&M University, had founded R&D Strategic Solutions in 2001 and had worked on hundreds of trials, largely with defense teams. He had written numerous articles—including "Tips for Voir Dire & Jury Selection," published in the National Bar Association magazine—and had appeared on TV programs including CNN's *Talk Back Live,* *The Phil Donahue Show* and *Court TV.* Fuentes had a surprisingly sonorous voice that did not match his soft features, though he whispered questions or advice into Levicoff's ear as the jury prospects were paraded one by one before the attorneys. "One second," Levicoff would say from time to time, halting his questioning of a potential juror to consult with Fuentes, who in turn would consult a folder presumably filled with background information on the person appearing before them. It all had an air of mystery.

Fuentes did not speak with the other defense attorneys, nor had he been introduced to Specter or his team. But he looked familiar to Specter. During a break, while the attorneys were awaiting a fresh batch of 20 prospective jurors, Specter introduced himself.

"Rick Fuentes," the jury expert responded.

"I thought I recognized you."

"Yes." Fuentes said that he, too, thought Specter looked familiar.

"We were on a case together."

"You look the same," said Fuentes in an attempt at pleasant small talk.

"No, I don't," Specter replied, always candid.

"That case settled, didn't it?" Fuentes probably knew the outcome of the older case, though jury consultants often didn't hang around after testimony began. Plus the terms of that case had been kept highly confidential. Specter was only too glad to provide an answer.

"Yes," he said, loudly enough so the insurance company lawyers in the back of the room could hear, "for a phenomenal amount of money."

Specter relayed some details of the negotiations with that defendant.

"That was a tough case for a defense attorney," he continued, on a roll now. "My client in that case was the best client ever..."

He waited a beat before delivering his gut-punch line: "until this one."

Chapter 35

Specter liked the jury that was selected of eight women and four men, fairly well educated and with jobs such as a corporate executive, account manager, engineer, pharmacist, radiology technician, quality auditor, medical secretary, computer programmer and psychological therapist. No old people sat on the jury, which was good for the plaintiffs because older people —who remembered when a Snickers bar sold for a nickel—tended to have a more conservative view of what constituted a lot of money. The jurors seemed attentive and not completely annoyed at having to be in court.

But most important, Specter got what he most wanted on the jury—a very smart person. Juror number five, George Coulston, was as close as Specter was going to get to a rocket scientist. An earnest-looking man with dark hair and glasses, Coulston, 49, held a Ph.D. in chemical engineering and applied physics from Yale University. He worked at Kennematal, the large tooling and industrial materials supplier based in Latrobe, as vice president of the company's innovation ventures group, which handled business development. Coulston would have little difficulty comprehending everything discussed at the Goretzka trial and he could, if necessary, explain it to his fellow jurors.

"Coulston is the key guy," Specter wrote in an email to Baldwin and Guerrini. He wanted his colleagues to apprise their expert witness of this and "be sure they know where number five sits."

One more thing. Specter asked Guerrini to "very quietly, please determine his political party."

Guerrini responded six minutes later. He didn't know Coulston's political affiliation, but he had found out something even more interesting.

"He gave $500 to your dad in 2008," Guerrini wrote, adding Coulston also donated $1,000 to a veteran Democratic congressman the year before.

"Holy cow," Specter responded.

Supporting Arlen Specter, a moderate Republican who would switch to the Democratic Party in 2010, was a good sign. It didn't mean that Coulston would favor Shanin Specter at the trial—or even that he knew Shanin was

Arlen Specter's son—but at least it hinted that Coulston was no conservative, pro-tort reform, kill-the-lawyers, Tea Party Republican.

A lingering question remained. Specter posed it in his final email of the day to Baldwin and Guerrini: "Does this jury have the guts to render a large award?"

Chapter 36

Trials are not a good place to learn how human beings socialize. Judges joke with the lawyers in court and sometimes when they see them out in a hallway but then can castigate them publicly: "I have one rule," Della Vecchia told Specter and Levicoff, both together and separately, "when I talk, you don't."

The lawyers themselves could be the fiercest of adversaries when at trial during the day, using the harshest of terms in shouted voices, and then go have a few drinks and a cordial dinner the same night before resuming their public animosity in court the following morning. But perhaps the oddest of interactions was reserved for the lawyers and the jurors. There was none. None at all.

The jurors in the Goretzka trial would over time become fast friends. Being confined together had that effect. While prohibited from discussing the case until the end of the trial, they were not barred from exchanging tidbits about their lives, their jobs, their families. Forced to be silent during long hours in court, they chatted eagerly during recesses, laughing loudly as they waited in the hallway for the proceedings to resume. But when Specter saw them, he averted his eyes. He wouldn't say "good morning" or "hello," not even smile or nod. More than once during the trial, he and his colleagues would hop out of an elevator if a juror stepped in. He would even leave if there was a juror in the men's room. When having lunch at one of the few eateries near the courthouse—Specter usually went to Au Bon Pain for soup on the days he ate at all—he would always cast a look around at the open tables and select one far from any jurors.

Specter wasn't being a Philly snob, as Judge Della Vecchia would explain to the jurors.

"I notice we all went out of here for lunch and we have been running into each other. None of us who are participating in this case, myself or the lawyers or the witnesses, are allowed to talk to you on the simplest of subjects. I was explaining to Mr. Specter—Mr. Levicoff knows this—that, you know, Pittsburgh/Allegheny County/Western Pennsylvania is the world's largest small town. No matter how you look at it, we all know each other.

And the lawyers will be at lunch and one of their neighbors will be a juror and the lawyers won't be allowed to talk to them, and they will get mad.

"We are not allowed to. It is not a matter of rudeness at all. It has to be no contact for fear that something could be misconstrued. I advise you that the lawyers cannot in any way, shape or form talk to you on the simplest topics, nor can I or any of the witnesses, anybody else. That's just a reminder...but it is all nice that we all know each other out in this neck of the woods."

Chapter 37

Judge Della Vecchia's generally neat and sedate courtroom had been transformed into somewhat of a circus. As the opening speeches were about to begin, the relatively small space—just three rows of bench seating for spectators—had taken on a cluttered appearance. Boxes filled with testimony and exhibits piled in the narrow space behind the last row. The plaintiffs had had 60 white cardboard boxes filled with records and documents weighing more than a ton (2,240 pounds to be exact) shipped to Pittsburgh. Two other boxes contained supplies and snacks. Stacked on top of the mountain of boxes was a case of bottled water which would be consumed and replaced several times over the course of the proceedings. The defense had a large exhibit that rested on a dolly and was covered with a tarp, though it was clear that underneath was a portion of a wooden telephone pole.

Other lawyers helping the defense or representing West Penn Power's insurance carriers took up some of the seats behind the defense table. Upcoming witnesses and friends and family of the Goretzkas occupied others. Law students filled in seats along with employees from the courthouse, some of whom had been present in the same courtroom for Specter's $8.75 million verdict in Blumer v. Ford. Some passersby stopped in just to see what all the fuss was about. People crammed into the benches until there was no more room. Some poached standing positions. Finally, Della Vecchia had to kick some people out.

"I will tell people in the gallery that we can't have people standing by the door. Not that I mean to be rude…but we can't have that. So, if you cannot find chairs, then regrettably you'll have to leave." He asked members of law firms not involved in the case to limit their members to one per firm to make room for members of the public and the news media. TV cameras were not allowed inside the courtroom, but several were posted outside the courthouse or in the hallway on certain days, particularly toward the end of the trial. One reporter, Paul Peirce, with *The Pittsburgh Tribune-Review*, would be present every day, perched in the back row from which he filed daily dispatches for the print and Internet editions.

The media presence led the judge to his next instruction, which was to admonish the jury, in his affable way and after its members had been brought into court through the throng of onlookers, to avoid discussing the case during the trial as well as paying attention to newspaper, radio or television stories about it. Della Vecchia went further, his instructions having been expanded in recent years due to technological advances.

"Do not, under any circumstances, go on any computers, laptops, iTops [sic], iPhones or any other contraption known to man to find out about this case," he ordered. And further, "Do not go on Twitter, Facebook, YouTube or any form of social media, none of which I understand."

Chapter 38

Avrum Levicoff had a tough job, defending a major utility, an entity already not beloved by the millions of people who paid their monthly electric bills, in a case in which a beautiful wife and mother of two was killed by the company's fallen power line. Not an easy job, indeed.

Levicoff's defense was risky. West Penn was going to blame Carrie, at least partially, for causing her own death. It was Carrie's fault. Noticing that the power was out and fire was burning the trees at the back of her house, she should never have left the safety of her own home and gone outside, and especially not to the side of her house where West Penn's power line was strung. The verdict slip—if the case ever went to the jury for a verdict—would even have a space for the jurors to state if, and how much of, the responsibility for the terrible incident rested with the victim. What percentage of the blame would the jury place on Carrie?

The argument raised some questions. Why did Carrie leave her house when she saw fire in the backyard trees, even though she had gone out the front? Why would she walk in the direction of the line? If the jury found she was at fault to any degree, that judgment would reduce the total amount of an award. If the jury reached a verdict awarding the Goretzkas, say, $20 million but it found Carrie was 30 percent liable, West Penn would only have to pay about $14 million.

But trying to put blame on Carrie was risky. It could inflame the jury. The panel could be made angry enough to find West Penn 100 percent at fault and award a larger monetary compensation than it otherwise might. Blaming Carrie could also tip jurors toward awarding punitive damages as well, where the award could really balloon.

Specter was glad he was not in Avrum Levicoff's shoes. "I wouldn't want to have to defend this case," he said more than once. He respected Levicoff as knowledgeable, especially well-versed in the technicalities of the electric power industry. But he did not agree with his—or was it West Penn's?—trial strategy. Specter told his colleagues that if he were heading the defense, he would handle it entirely differently.

"I would admit liability. Plain and simple. 'We were wrong. We admit it. And we're ready to pay the piper.' That's how I would handle it," he said. Specter believed the jury would find West Penn liable for its power line falling on a nice day. Why not just admit it? He would also include an apology and a plea that the jury be reasonable in its award. "Throw yourself on the mercy of the court, so to speak."

"I'd tell the jury that West Penn, although a company, is made up of people, hard-working, blue-collar people just like them," intoned Specter. "And that we work for the people of western Pennsylvania and that we provide a necessary service." He'd add that West Penn was a regional, modest-size company regulated by the government and one with a net worth of only $244 million, not many billions like major national corporations, not like Exxon Mobile's roughly $400 billion or Apple's $500 billion.

"We are taking responsibility and we are willing to compensate for what happened to Carrie Goretzka and her fine family. But please, don't push West Penn onto the financial precipice. Please be fair. That's all we ask, be fair."

Specter knew that apologies and taking responsibility went a long way with folks. He saw it in medical malpractice, where doctors who admitted errors, even egregious ones, were less likely to be sued or pay as much as those who did not. This case, he felt, would be the same. "Admit you were wrong," he maintained, "and it takes all the steam out of the case."

Near the end of the trial, Specter would ask Levicoff why he hadn't used this approach, why he didn't admit liability and hope for understanding from the jury.

"Because you had a punitive damages claim," Levicoff told him. He couldn't take the chance that an admission would lead the jury to deem a punishment necessary, and thus the likelihood of a very large award.

The jury might even find for the defense, reasoning that "things just happened" and perhaps that no party was to blame. The chances seemed slim, but one never knew with juries. This one could come to any number of conclusions, including that Carrie was partly to blame for her own demise. Or perhaps its members would feel that $10 million or $15 million was a lot of money, and enough to award the Goretzka family.

Juries were always a crap shoot.

Chapter 39

West Penn wasn't the only party the Goretzkas had sued. Specter had also filed suit against Hubbell Electrical Products Company, the maker of the splice from which the power line fell. But after the discovery process—including depositions, written questions, document production and review, and expert consultations—his team had come up with no evidence that the splice had a manufacturing flaw, no proof it might have been defective. In the meantime, West Penn Power had filed to make Hubbell part of the lawsuit. Specter didn't know what dirt, if any, West Penn Power had on its splice supplier. Specter had no grounds to continue to sue Hubbell, yet he didn't want to drop them as a defendant in case West Penn Power knew something he didn't. So he signed what was called a "tolling agreement" with Hubbell that allowed him to drop it from his suit if the company let him reserve the right to sue later on.

Specter also knew that he wanted to call a witness from Hubbell, Chris Havlik, who would blame the fallen power line on West Penn Power, specifically the alleged failure of its linemen to properly prepare the line—by vigorous cleaning with a wire brush—before installation. If Hubbell was still a defendant in the suit, that could make it seem like its witness was blaming West Penn Power simply to deflect blame for Carrie's death. A Hubbell witness might seem biased if the company had something to gain with West Penn Power taking the fall. And, truth be told, a bias of sorts did exist—Havlik was mad as hell that the utility was directing blame at Hubbell.

Only on the eve of the trial did West Penn Power let Hubbell out of the lawsuit, its insurance company lawyers happily exiting the Allegheny County Courthouse. Specter would later let Hubbell out of the tolling agreement. He didn't want the splice manufacturer to come up in this trial and take a chance that the jury might go easy on West Penn Power because it thought Specter would get a chance, as the judge put it, "to get a second bite of the apple" by suing Hubbell later on. Specter's evidence fell squarely on the power company. And that was where he wanted the jury to be focused.

Chapter 40

Man-made electricity claimed its first human life in an accident in 1879. The victim, a carpenter working on a stage in Lyons, France, came into contact with a 250-volt generator. Two years later in Buffalo, a similar thing happened when a local drunk fell onto a similar generator in front of a stunned crowd.

Eleven years after that first accidental death, electricity would be used to intentionally kill a man.

Chapter 41

Professional sports figures are often extremely superstitious—especially, it would seem, those from Philadelphia. Charles Barkley once wore the same pair of underwear (fortunately washed) for every game of a 13-game winning streak. Temple coach John Chaney threw out ties after losing games. Flyers goalie Pelle Lindbergh drank a Swedish Pripps beer not before games but between periods of games. Flyers coach Fred Shero carried rosary beads, and he wasn't even Catholic. Asked why, he replied, "It can't hurt."

Shanin Specter wasn't the superstitious type. Yet he was such a perfectionist that his habits bordered on superstition. And, he reasoned, if something worked once, it might work again. So why tempt fate? This sentiment, with a little practical strategy, was how Specter came to have a lucky lectern.

He used the same black, metal music stand—eschewing the standard wooden box lecterns found in many courtrooms—for practicing opening speeches in the office and during trials. At trial, the stand went with him. No matter the location, he wanted it in court and in place before he gave his opening speech.

Specter liked that the music stand was simple and that "the jury can see nearly all of me…I don't like those lecterns that cover your body so all that is seen is a bobbing head." The stand symbolized full disclosure, even physically. (It is notable that few of his firm's lawyers wore facial hair, many feeling that to jurors it appeared as though they had something to hide.) As for clothing, Specter wore nearly the same thing to every trial—blue suit, white shirt and red tie, with only slight variations. He did this so that his dress would become a dependable and comfortable sight, and not a distraction to a jury.

But despite his practical reason for wanting his music stand, Specter also knew that the device had been with him during some of his biggest courtroom victories. It offered him a measure of assurance. Not unlike the baseball bats that the Phillies' Richie Ashburn occasionally took to bed with him, especially when he was on a hot streak—hence his quip that he "slept with a lot of old bats."

One time, at a trial in New Jersey, Specter discovered that his music stand was not present in the courtroom with his opening speech only two hours away. Unfortunately, so was the stand, which had failed to make the trip from Philadelphia with the rest of the files, evidence, laptops and other paraphernalia. He didn't panic, not exactly. But he did fly into action, shooting orders at assistants like poisoned arrows. It was 9 a.m. and Specter wanted to be at his stand when it was his turn to speak at 11 a.m.

A staff person in Philadelphia was given the order the find the music stand, get it into a car and drive immediately to the courtroom in Morristown, almost two hours away with traffic—and there was always traffic. In case the staffer didn't arrive on time, others were sent searching for a reasonable facsimile. One associate attorney at the trial spoke with the staff of the hotel where the legal team was staying, hoping they could find a suitable alternative in one of the hotel's conference rooms. No such luck. Another lawyer searched the Internet for local schools that might be willing to loan a music stand to the cause, but she came up empty as well. Finally, one staffer found a music store that sold a stand similar to Specter's—a metal pole supporting a diagonal shelf with a solid, flat-black surface—for $50. She hopped in her car, drove to the next town and purchased the stand, getting it back to the courtroom just before Specter walked in at about 10:45.

He looked at the stand, touched it lightly with one hand and asked: "Is that my stand?"

The staffer fumbled for a second. "Uh, it's not, but it's just like it."

Specter looked at it without saying anything.

"Is it OK?" the staffer asked.

"It's fine," Specter responded, resigned if less than thrilled.

But the day was saved. At precisely 11 a.m., the assistant who had driven from the Philadelphia office did a fast walk down the hallway and into the courtroom. She had Specter's stand. Just in time for his opening speech to the jury.

The case settled three weeks into trial for $15 million.

Chapter 42

This is Carrie Goretzka.

 Carrie Goretzka was a homemaker. She was a daughter, a wife and a mother. She was a beautiful person inside and out. She was brutally killed by electrocution when a 7,200-volt power line installed and maintained by West Penn Power fell on her while she was standing on her property on a clear and sunny day three and a half years ago.

With those words, the case of *Goretzka v. West Penn Power* was under way in earnest. The opening salvo was delivered in as direct and stark a way as Specter could manage. Then he succinctly outlined his case and introduced his adversary.

We are here because you must fix responsibility for this unspeakable horror. The defendant, West Penn Power, denies responsibility. Instead, West Penn Power blames the victim, Carrie Goretzka.

Specter, who moments earlier had carried his music stand to a spot directly in front of the jury, clicked a remote control and the first photo, the one of the Goretzkas in front of the Magic Kingdom castle in Orlando, appeared on the 12-foot screen Mike Kutys had erected a day earlier (after a wrestling match in which the screen had nearly collapsed on top of him).

The family had returned from a vacation in Disney World just three days before. This is one of the last photos of Carrie taken alive.

From here, Specter detailed the chain of events that began at 4:30 p.m. on June 2, 2009, while Carrie and her mother-in-law, JoAnn, and her two little girls were watching cartoons on TV. "All of a sudden," Specter began and then told the jury how the power went out. It started to get hot inside, so Carrie went to open a rear window to let in some air. When she did, she saw trees on fire in the backyard. Specter clicked: "There's the kitchen." He explained how Carrie tried to call 911 from the house phone but it was dead. So she went to the garage to get her cell phone from her car. Knowing from experience that she couldn't get cell service inside the house, she walked toward the side of the house as she dialed. Three attempts to reach 911 failed.

Inside the house, Carlie and Chloe were getting upset. They looked at JoAnn. "Where's Mommy?" they asked. "Where's Mommy?"

Chapter 43

JoAnn ran across the driveway to try to rescue Carrie. She got as far as the grass and then she was thrown backward and down by the force of the 7,200 volts of electric power and she landed on the ground, which was itself energized by the fallen power line, and she burned her fingers. She picked herself up. She screamed at the top of her lungs, "Help me! Help me!"

Specter clicked and showed the Google Earth satellite map of the neighborhood. The Goretzka property was easily discernible by the above-ground pool he had pointed to earlier. He named those who arrived at the scene: Tim Harper, a volunteer firefighter who lived nearby; Don Thoma, another volunteer firefighter; Mike Thornburgh, the mailman; Michelle Siegel, a neighbor who had been outside gardening. None was able to get close enough to help their friend and neighbor. One used a fire extinguisher on the burning line and Carrie herself, but the power line remained charged with electricity and Carrie was shocked and burned for 20 minutes until a power company employee arrived and was able to free her of its grip using a fiberglass pole known as a "hot stick." Carrie didn't die right away, it was theorized, because the line had not come into direct contact with her heart or head and because such lines did not carry a continuous power stream but one that pulsated, turning off and on every few seconds.

Specter told how a MedEvac helicopter took Carrie to the hospital. Then for the only time in his opening, he mentioned her injuries. The mention was brief, almost in passing, and omitting the graphic descriptions of burns that were so bad they would be classified as fourth-degree, those that extend to muscle and bone. He showed no photos of Carrie at the scene or of her injuries, just the burned outline of her body on the Goretzkas' lawn.

She had a complete left arm and shoulder amputation at the hospital and several surgeries to remove pressure from her limbs before dying three days later on June 5, 2009. Carrie Goretzka was 39 years old.

Chapter 44

Specter's team was under no obligation to come up with a theory on why the power line fell. It just had to demonstrate to the jury that the tragedy was West Penn Power's fault. And who else could have been at fault? It was a beautiful, clear June day when the line fell and killed Carrie. There had been no windstorm, no hurricane, no hail. So God was out as a suspect. About 10 million Hubbell splices were on lines all over the United States and Canada, and the simple devices seemed to work perfectly. So Hubbell was out as the culprit. There had been no witness testimony about crazed birds pecking at the wires, nor were remains of electrocuted squirrels found at the scene. The possible cause was puzzling.

West Penn Power had to have made a particular mistake. According to Bill McHugh's theory, the cause was a lack of proper cleaning before installation of the wire into the splice. Specifically, the linemen had not used a wire brush. Evidence showed that the line had not been brushed, though the key part of what had fallen was largely destroyed. But the two other splices in the line where it did not burn up revealed no wire brush marks. The intact side of the fallen connection had only debatable signs of possible brushing, faint marks that were visible only under magnification. And those could have been made at some earlier date.

Specter had decided to take the theory to trial and let the experts battle it out. What wasn't open for debate—and something he found most reprehensible—was what West Penn Power had done in the wake of the Goretzka tragedy to make sure something like it never happened again. As far as Specter could tell, nothing.

Chapter 45

How and why did this power line fall on a clear and sunny day and come into contact with Carrie Goretzka?

Specter continued his opening speech with an explanation of how he theorized the line came out of a splice used to connect ends of the line—an automatic device akin to Chinese finger traps that hold the line more tightly the harder it is pulled. He told the jury that West Penn Power, with thousands of high-voltage lines strung across the community, was by law required "to use the highest degree of care practical to protect people under or near their lines."

Every day most of us walk or travel under power lines dozens of times. We don't give it a second thought. We trust, as we must, the safety and integrity of those lines.

But West Penn Power failed to use the highest degree of care, Specter asserted. He went a step further, stating that the reason the line fell—without the presence of a storm or vehicular accident or any unusual occurrence—was because it had been installed improperly. Specifically because the linemen who installed the line failed to clean the ends with a wire brush before installation as specified by the manufacturer, Hubbell, and by West Penn Power's own standards manual, which Specter noted was referred to as "the Bible." Without proper cleaning, the ends of the wire tended to oxidize, then corrode, then overheat and fail.

The line can fall. That's what failure is. When a power line, a live 7,200-volt power line, falls, it can kill.

Specter promised the jury they would hear testimony that one of the two linemen who erected that wire did not generally use a wire brush. But the problem was worse than that. He would also present a trainer who would acknowledge he didn't require use of a wire brush when he instructed linemen, and also a witness from West Penn Power's standards department who knew the cleaning technique was not being used and did nothing about it. This failure, Specter would try to convince the jury, represented reckless disregard, something he would need to prove to win punitive damages against the company.

Now, you might be wondering, well, is there somebody at West Penn Power that goes around to check on the integrity of these splices and these connections? Do they just put them up there and leave them there indefinitely? Here is the answer. Yes. That's the answer.

Now Specter presented the second of two critical pieces of information that he felt proved his case. The first was that the line came down without provocation, on a "clear and sunny day," a fact he would mention nearly 20 times during the trial. The second was that the very same line had fallen down before. That, in fact, was the reason it had been repaired using the splices in the first place. Five years before the fatal incident, the same line had fallen from the same pole and damaged Mike Goretzka's property, charring a swath of his lawn. Worse, West Penn Power never determined why the line had fallen. Workmen repaired the line using splices and put it back up, never fully investigating the cause of the failure in 2004, and never making changes to ensure it would not happen again. Worst of all, Mike Goretzka had called the company about the fallen line, stating that he feared for the safety of his family.

But most reprehensible, Specter told the jury, was perhaps something that had not occurred until right now at trial. It was West Penn Power's legal tactic, one he felt was cynical and cruel.

They are going to blame Carrie Goretzka.

Chapter 46

Electricity was still in its infancy when the "War of Currents" erupted. The generals on either side were Thomas Edison and George Westinghouse. The battle was over direct current, or DC, which Edison used, and alternating current, or AC, championed by Westinghouse. AC was the newcomer, an outgrowth of an invention in 1883 by Nikola Tesla, a Serbian-American and a onetime Edison employee. That was the same year the first lighting system used overhead power lines for service in Rochelle, New Jersey, a system known as the "Tesla coil," which transformed—hence the term transformer—electricity from low voltage to high voltage, making it possible to transport over long distances. Today, the first fully electric sports car and its company use Tesla's name.

This system allowed thinner, cheaper wires to be used to transport alternating current without losing potency. The patent rights for AC were bought by George Westinghouse, who used it in a variety of projects, including to light the 1893 World's Fair. In the same year, AC current was used to move electricity over a 22-mile line in California and later over a 20-mile line from the hydroelectric plant in Niagara Falls to the city of Buffalo.

Chapter 47

If practice made perfect, Avrum Levicoff probably wished he had practiced his opening statement—he told the jury he didn't call it a "speech"—a few more times. While Specter had meticulously choreographed every photo and exhibit with his spoken words, his opponent fumbled with his props on more than a few occasions. Instead of photos and exhibits cued and ready to go with the click of a button, Levicoff called out exhibit numbers to a technician.

> *Go to...go to number 7328 please. No, I'm sorry, 7313.*
>
> *...Let's zoom in here if we could. Is that the best we can do? All right. Back off. That's all right. Try this picture—14266. I'm sorry, 147266. There you go.*
>
> *...What I want you to notice about that, members of the jury, is that when you look at that splice...I don't know what I did with the splice. It's here somewhere.*
>
> *...You were shown a photograph... How close can you go on that? Not very good. All right. Try this one. Try 13383. There.*
>
> *...If you bring up 33393, please. This is a magnified photograph... I'm sorry, D33393. Or 33394. No. All right. Since technology fails, members of the jury, let me go back to what I used to use in my younger years—paper.*
>
> *...You are going to see what happens. No, you're not. Technology failed me again.*

Did the bungling make a difference in terms of the jury's sense of each lawyer's ability or credibility? Probably not much. But juries tended to build impressions in a cumulative manner, and even the smallest things can add up.

Levicoff tried to make light of some of his technical difficulties with self-deprecation, joking about his thinning hair, his poor hearing and his age, even though he wasn't very old. He also made up for any lost technical points with his poise in the courtroom and his relaxed manner. Early in his opening speech, he walked right up to the jury box and rested both hands on its wooden railing, speaking in a reasoned tone as close as possible to the jurors. At other times, he ambled back and forth before the jury as he spoke.

Levicoff also demonstrated an unmatched expert knowledge of the electric industry. While Specter had been brought up to speed thanks to the tutelage of Kila Baldwin and had in a few months learned the basics, he possessed nowhere near the depth of knowledge that Levicoff had for conductors (the name used for power lines or wires in the industry), automatic splices, fuses, oxidation, fault current, line chatter and vibration dynamics.

The defense lawyer seemed from time to time to seek personal sympathy from the jurors, though it certainly wasn't needed. "My opponent called me a skillful lawyer. I disavow it. But he is a skillful lawyer," Levicoff said in his opening speech about Specter, a comment meant not so much to compliment as to cast his opponent as the sly city slicker from Philly.

Levicoff took it one step further, warning the jury that this skillful advocate might "relentlessly" question his witnesses, especially company employees, and that Specter would try to make them look "stupid"— "They're hard-working people who do the best they can to do what they do as well as they can. They may not be a match for a skillful cross-examiner."

Chapter 48

The wire brush. This crude little device and its use—or lack of use—would take up more trial time than any other single item. Days of testimony would be devoted to it.

Specter was under no obligation to suggest or theorize—and certainly not to prove—why the line had fallen. That was because a power line would not ordinarily fall on a calm, clement day unless the power company had been negligent in the installation or maintenance of the line. Nevertheless, Specter claimed the cause was clear. His assertion was that the lineman had failed to brush the wire clean. Now he would go further to say that the utility had failed to adequately train its linemen on the necessity of wire brushing—even though it included the practice in its manual and supplied each truck with a special curved wire brush for that use—and that supervisors failed to check that the important preparation was done. The whole process of wire brushing, he would show, had been pooh-poohed by West Penn Power.

The company's defense was twofold. First, Specter was wrong—the wire that came down was cleaned with a wire brush, and second, even if it wasn't, it didn't matter. Wire brushing wasn't critical at all, despite what the printed materials said. So much fuss was being made over wire brushing and it didn't even matter, Levicoff held as he continued his opening statement.

> Now you heard testimony about knives being used and that sort of thing. Some of the guys probably at points do this. I can get a knife, it will do the same thing. The plaintiffs' attorney would argue it doesn't get down in the inner spaces here, but for reasons we will show you in evidence, it doesn't matter. What does matter is the outer surface. In fact, whether you brush it or don't brush it doesn't really affect the splices anyway.

Levicoff's argument was that the splices contained metal teeth that gripped down on the wire —it was actually a steel rod with seven aluminum strands wrapped around it—and so long as the teeth were holding tight, the electrical connection "will remain tight and secure." Even if oxidation was not cleaned from between the strands, a clean connection would be made. The oxidation or corrosion that Specter had targeted would not cause the line to burn up. Although during the trial Levicoff would try to show that the wire had indeed been brushed, he would continue to come back to the same theme:

It just really doesn't make much difference whether you brush or you don't brush.

He warned the jurors that over the next several weeks of trial they could expect to hear many hours of testimony on such "irrelevancies. " And, lastly, that they would hear testimony and statements seeking to play on their emotions, and that the plaintiffs' counsel would seek to sway them with a mixture of anger and sympathy. But to base a verdict on such sentiments would not be fair.

You're going to have to steel yourself against becoming so overcome with the tragedy that you take your eyes off the evidence, and that you disregard the obligation to decide the true facts.

Chapter 49

The defense was taking a big risk. It was one thing to disavow blame for a fallen power line and the death of a human being. It was another thing to blame the deceased.

Avrum Levicoff took his first steps onto this ground in his opening statement to the jury, not with delicacy but with sarcasm. He noted that Specter had already told the jury they might expect a defense tactic of blaming the victim. Levicoff added: "Now, I also heard a lot of remarks. 'West Penn Power is going to blame this. West Penn Power is going to contend that.' I almost thought maybe I didn't need to stand up and tell you what our position on many of these things actually is. But since I'm up here, I will tell you."

> *Here is our position. This is a negligence case. It's a terrible accident. It's a negligence case.*
>
> *Under our law...everyone—man, woman, corporation, utility alike—has a responsibility to exercise due care for their own safety and protection and for the safety and protection of others. Everyone.*

Levicoff told the jury that the law states that "the mere happening" of an accident does not mean negligence was involved.

> *The mere fact that a power line came down on a sunny day or any other day in and of itself proves no absence of due care anymore than the mere fact that Mrs. Goretzka walked over and came into contact with this wire is evidence of her lack of due care.*

"The mere fact that Mrs. Goretzka walked over." The sentence hung in the air. And it did create some doubt. Why, in fact, did Carrie leave the safety of her home and walk toward the power line?

Next, Levicoff sought to turn perhaps the most damning piece of plaintiff evidence on its head. It was the fact that the same power line had fallen five years earlier. The plaintiffs contended that this was a testament not only to the shoddy work of West Penn Power, but also that it never fully investigated past failures, never found out why the line had come down and damaged the homeowner's property. Levicoff's view, and it was not without some logic, was that since the same line had fallen before, Carrie should have used caution the second time around.

Unfortunately, that was the second time. It had fallen five years earlier. Mrs. Goretzka knew and understood what it meant to have a downed power line come down hot in the yard...They knew it was energized because they saw trees burning.

And there was fire not just in the rear of the property, but also in the front near where Carrie had approached, he contended, citing the testimony of a neighbor who had used a fire extinguisher on a burning tree near the front of the house.

Levicoff disputed Specter's contention that Carrie would not have seen the downed wire because it had hung for a while in the telephone lines strung beneath the power lines 18 feet high. Specter had cited the fact that Verizon Wireless had come out the next day to repair its damaged lines. But Levicoff said the plaintiffs' explanation was simply not credible. His raised voice took on a reedy tone of incredulity.

Members of the jury, the evidence will not allow you to accept that as the answer for three reasons, at least three reasons. One is that it just isn't an answer. It isn't an answer to say that someone, knowing where the line was, knowing that the line has fallen, would simply walk over to a spot directly beneath where it was without looking to see where it was.

The second reason, Levicoff contended, was that the telephone cable was bonded to a "neutral wire" just below it. The falling line would have struck the neutral wire and created a sight Carrie could not have ignored.

It's like fireworks. It draws intense electrical arcing the minute it touches. Intense, thousands of degrees, bright arcing, sparking, jumping. The minute it touches. It is unimaginable that someone would traverse [a map was shown on the screen]...that someone, even if they didn't know there was a line there, even if they didn't know the line was hot, would walk from here across to here with a phase conductor in contact for minutes with a bonded telephone cabling arrangement that would be sparking and arcing and burning...That's the degree of power. They're like many lightning bolts. It is inconceivable that if that line were tangled on that phone line as Mrs. Goretzka walked over there, she wouldn't see that.

Chapter 50

Judge Della Vecchia called Shanin Specter into his chambers and told him that West Penn Power had said it was willing to make a "substantial" move upward from its $10 million offer. But Specter would first have to prove that he was at least willing to be reasonable by lowering his demand. The only number he had mentioned so far was $68.1 million and, despite any and all entreaties, he had not moved lower by a nickel. West Penn wasn't asking for much, only that Specter lower his demand to $40 million. If he did, the utility would make a counter-offer. It didn't seem like a great concession on Specter's part, said the judge.

"No thanks," replied Specter. He had no new offer to make to West Penn Power.

The judge would continue to try to forge a settlement. At age 66 and with 11 years on the bench, Della Vecchia had built a reputation for making settlements happen. In past cases, he had helped settle some whoppers, including a lawsuit against an insurance company with 235 plaintiffs and another case involving asbestos injuries that had a total of some 90,000 claims. "That's what we're known for here, settling," he once said with a sense of pride.

He met repeatedly with Specter and Levicoff as well as representatives from West Penn Power and its insurance companies. To get some higher-ups involved in the discussions, he demanded at various points that representatives from the insurers and even West Penn Power's parent company, First Energy Corporation in Ohio, come to his chambers and join the discussion.

Yet no matter how hard the judge pushed and pried, a settlement in the Goretzka case was proving elusive. On the one hand, Della Vecchia had Specter holding firm, refusing to even mention a number as a possible counter-offer. On the other, the utility, more specifically its insurers, were also proving stubborn. "I ordered one insurance company [representative] in from New Jersey and all he said was 'No—no, no, no,'" the judge would recall after the case was over. "Early on, another one, an Irish kid, he said, and he even stood up and pointed at me as he said it: 'You'll never see an offer with a two in front of it,' meaning $20 million."

Chapter 51

I love the smell of napalm in the morning. You know, one time we had a hill bombed for 12 hours. When it was all over, I walked up…The smell, you know that gasoline smell, the whole hill smelled like…victory.

—Lieutenant Kilgore,
from the Vietnam War movie *Apocalypse Now*

Sometimes saying nothing is the best policy. Specter had refused to play ball with West Penn Power and its insurers. He would not engage in a game of offer and counter-offer when it came to settling the case. Just because West Penn Power indicated it was willing to raise its offer of $10 million didn't mean he was obliged to make a move downward. Specter would simply not respond, a tactic that could, he knew from previous cases, drive the enemy mad.

Some involved in the trial were starting to get the feeling that perhaps this was no tactic at all, that Specter was being uncooperative for a reason—he didn't really want to settle. Like Lieutenant Kilgore, Specter loved the smell of napalm in the morning, only in his case it was the musty aroma of a courtroom. Settling the case meant leaving the battlefield he loved.

Maybe Specter was dead set on the trial going to verdict, or maybe that was what he wanted the defense to believe. Whatever the truth, his intransigence paid off. Not long after his meeting with Judge Della Vecchia in which he refused to settle, West Penn Power doubled its offer to $20 million. If the new offer impressed Specter, he didn't show it. His answer remained the same.

"No thanks."

Chapter 52

Specter was duty-bound to relay the new offer to his client.

"I want to hear a verdict," Specter had said to Mike Goretzka on more than one occasion. "I want to take them down a peg. I want to prove that we're equal in the eyes of the law."

Goretzka felt the same way, only more adamantly. "I want them to explain themselves, how they destroy a family," he had said a number of times. "That's what I would like." Goretzka told Specter he had complete trust in his decision on the latest offer. "I'll let you guide me," he told Specter. In the marble and granite hallway outside the courtroom, they discussed the $20 million and together resolved to turn down the money.

"While I can't be sure, I think the jury will award more than $20 million," Specter said in a hushed voice. "You make a good living. If we lose this case, and I don't think we will, you won't want for anything."

Specter, whose firm had already invested about $750,000 in the case—on everything from food and hotels to paid experts—laughed and added, "It'll cost me a lot of money, but you'll still live the way you have. Just fine."

Specter told Goretzka that the judge wanted to speak with him directly about West Penn's offer. "He wants to make sure I'm not gaming you."

He advised Goretzka before he went to see the judge. "Here's the speech, the talking points: 'Twenty million dollars is an insult, a disgrace. It's not adequate, not for what I've gone through, not for what my kids have gone through, are going to go through. I want to hear a verdict...And I don't want any confidentiality. I want the public to know, and if we hush this up, it will be very hard for me to swallow. I'm doing this for my family and other families in the service area.'"

"I do feel that way," Goretzka added.

"You've got to look the judge in the eye and tell him, because he's not more important than you and he's not better than you."

But Goretzka had a question. "Is there any point, any number you would accept."

"Yes, in the 30 to 60 range, and even 30 million is low. And they'd have to agree to make changes, to change the training and make more inspections."

"You think this is it, their last offer, $20 million?"

"No, but we can't show weakness," Specter replied. "Tell the judge you don't need $20 million."

"I don't."

Chapter 53

It wasn't every day that someone turned down $20 million, which was why Judge Della Vecchia wanted to make sure that Mike Goretzka's lawyer wasn't gambling with his client's financial future without his being a willing participant at the craps table. When Goretzka assured the judge that he concurred with rejecting the offer, Della Vecchia asked if he would change his mind if the offer went up to $25 million.

This was a new wrinkle, but Goretzka followed the script. "No," he said, adding, "I want a jury verdict."

The judge then gave Goretzka and his attorney his take on the case. He said that the jury might be inclined to be less generous based on where they lived in Allegheny County, namely those geographic regions that tended to be more conservative, a factor the defense had evidently relied heavily upon when selecting members of the panel. And Della Vecchia knew the local demographics well. He had run for recorder of deeds for Allegheny County in 1979, winning and holding the post through 2001. A Democrat, he had also run, though unsuccessfully, for a seat on the Pennsylvania Supreme Court in 1993.

"It looks like a defense jury on paper," he said. Its members might award less than $25 million, assuming they even found for the plaintiffs.

Della Vecchia added that he felt that one juror in particular, Juror number 5, George Coulston, the VP at Kennametal—and Specter's favorite on the panel—might take the lead against the Goretzkas. Coulston was a company man and he "might not want to go against a company" like West Penn Power. He noted that both Kennametal and West Penn Power were headquartered in neighboring Westmoreland County.

"I beg to disagree with you, Your Honor," Goretzka responded. "Kennametal is a fine company and he's probably not liking what he sees."

Della Vecchia said he didn't want to see Goretzka end up with a verdict that wasn't fair. He thought he could nudge West Penn Power to a higher offer. "Would you be willing to take $30 million to $35 million?" he asked.

Goretzka took a deep breath. "Basically, judge, I'd like to see them go to jail. I'd like to see criminal charges filed."

"Well, I don't see that," responded Della Vecchia.

Specter, who had sat silently by until now, interjected, "We could seek charges with the Westmoreland County D.A."

The judge cast a smile at Specter, though he kept his eyes on Mike Goretzka. "What would you take?"

Goretzka, not normally a talkative guy, launched into a discourse of sorts.

"Well, put it this way: I trust my lawyer. If he feels there's a number we could accept. I have trust in him. I respect his decisions," he said, telling the judge that the case was about more than money for him. "You have to understand. I'm fighting for my wife."

"How would you feel if the jury came back with a verdict that was less than this offer?" Goretzka didn't hesitate. "That's a chance you take. I'd be fine with it." Would he really?

"You know what, judge?" Goretzka continued, his face stern as he stared at the judge, "Everybody goes home after this. You go home. The lawyers go home. The jurors go home. And everybody resumes their normal life. I'm left with this my entire life—two kids without a mother, a husband without a wife."

The judge didn't push any further.

Chapter 54

Mike Goretzka, who had been glum at best from the moment Shanin Specter and his colleagues had met him, had a marked improvement in his mood after leaving the judge's chambers. Goretzka didn't care about the money. He felt that it was "blood money," a payoff by the company in exchange for his wife's life. No amount would do. But the new offer showed that West Penn's resolve was weakening, that Goretzka and his family and his lawyers were winning. For the first time since the trial had begun, Mike Goretzka slept a little sounder that night.

As everyone filed back into the courtroom Tuesday morning, Goretzka caught Dominic Guerrini by the arm as he walked by. He had a question. It wasn't about the case or the trial but about *Monday Night Football* and Guerrini's favored team.

"Did the Eagles win last night?" he asked. Then Goretzka, a diehard Steelers fan, smiled broadly, perhaps his first smile in a week. He knew damned well the Eagles had lost.

Chapter 55

Harvey Hubbell II never became a household name like his contemporaries Thomas Edison and George Westinghouse, but in the world of electricity, he was no slouch. While he did not invent the light bulb or bring electricity to the far-flung masses, he was responsible for allowing folks to move a lamp or a toaster from one room to another without paying an electrician to hard-wire a connection. Harvey Hubbell II was the inventor of something so simple it is rarely given a second thought nowadays—the plug.

In 1888, Hubbell quit his job as manager of a manufacturing company and started his own company, making a number of products for which he held patents, including machines that slotted screw heads. He later turned his attention to electricity, tinkering with how to use and control this relatively new source of power. He devised the first toggle-action light switch, which replaced the two-button system, and the pull-chain electric light socket, "which many of us still have in our basements today," future company employee Chris Havlik would say at a trial in Pittsburgh more than a century later. (Hubbell also devised a mechanism to lock light bulbs into sockets, which was particularly useful in trains, where bulbs had previously crashed to the floor because of vibration or had disappeared in the hands of passengers who decided the bulbs would be of better use in their homes.)

Hubbell's greatest invention popped into his brain while he was walking past a penny arcade in New York City one day in 1904. Peering inside, he noticed a janitor struggling to move electric arcade games—one featured two boxers who threw electrically powered punches in a miniature ring—from one spot to another so he could sweep under the machines. With every move, the janitor had to detach the power supply wires from separate post terminals in the walls, carefully identifying each wire and then reattaching them in different places in the wall. Hubbell went from the arcade to his lab, where he came up with a product with permanent wires attached in the proper sequence and polarity that could be easily and safely connected and disconnected to fixed wall receptacles. His unknowing lab rat, as the story went, was the janitor, who was presented one day with Hubbell's "separable plug." The janitor was thrilled. Not long afterward, Hubbell applied for a patent for the plug and corresponding receptacles, including his "duplex receptacle." By 1920, Harvey Hubbell Inc. had sold more than 50 million of the receptacles, now called sockets.

Hubbell went on to patent 45 inventions and his company, headquartered in Shelton, Connecticut, grew to become a worldwide manufacturer of electrical and electronic products with annual revenues approaching three billion dollars. Along the way, Hubbell Inc. gobbled up more than 30 companies, including its 1997 acquisition of the Fargo Manufacturing Company, which made products for the utility industry's transmission and distribution power lines. One of them was the automatic splice, of which some 100 million were sold. The product allowed ends of a power line to be coupled, with one end of a wire pushed inside an aluminum sleeve where it would be grabbed by a set of metal "jaws" or teeth with the weight of the line creating tension to hold it in place. It was inside one of those simple yet ingenious devices that a power line burned and detached on the afternoon of June 2, 2009 in West Hempfield, Pennsylvania.

Chapter 56

Chris Havlik was the plaintiffs' first witness. Havlik was angry. West Penn Power had sued his company, Hubbell Electrical Products, and Havlik knew damned well nothing was wrong with its product. Hubbell had sold many millions of splices to utilities across the country without incident, and certainly nothing like what had occurred on the Goretzka property in 2009. He wanted to tell this to the world, or at least those who would be listening in Courtroom 710 in Allegheny County Court.

Havlik was more than eager. He started answering Specter's questions in such a rapid-fire fashion that the attorney had to tell him to put on the brakes.

"Hold on! I want you to slow down." He smiled before asking his next question.

"Are you nervous?"

"Yes."

"Have you ever testified before in court?"

"No."

Chris Havlik, 45, a nice-looking fellow with short-cropped brown hair and wearing a navy jacket over a dark blue shirt and a light-colored rep tie, calmed down a bit as Specter took him, mentally anyway, to more comfortable ground. Havlik told about Harvey Hubbell, whose company invented the electrical cable splicing system. Then how he had inspected some 250 splices over the years and how he and quality manager Chris Andrews and other members of a product performance team had examined the splice from which the power line had fallen at the Goretzkas' house. The proceeding got testy from there on between the lawyers, first with Levicoff raising an objection, then with Specter objecting to the objection.

> *Levicoff:* "Objection, Your Honor. Who did this review, Chris? Him? The team?"
>
> *Specter:* "I object to his speaking objection." Specter would not let his opponent get away with making comments before the jury.

Now it was Della Vecchia's turn to echo what Specter had said only minutes earlier. "Hold on!" The judge removed his glasses and rubbed his face. This was going to be a long trial. The courtroom was silent for a half minute before Della Vecchia overruled Levicoff's objection. "I'll let it go through," he said.

Havlik went on to give his theory of what caused the line to fall. It was the same theory that the plaintiffs' side would repeat throughout the trial. West Penn Power's linemen did not properly clean the line before installing it into the splice, which caused oxidation, which caused corrosion, which caused resistance, which caused heat, which caused the line to burn down.

This assertion was supported in a letter Chris Havlik and his team— having examined the pieces of the failed line at the request of West Penn Power in the first place—had sent to the utility. It stated: "Poor cleaning probably started the problem by causing the splice to run hot."

Just to make the point clear, Specter had Havlik step down from the witness stand and demonstrate how to properly wire-brush a piece of used, weathered power line. Havlik, just inches from the jurors in the front of two rows, did so with gusto. "In a minute or less, you can get it into the condition that it's ready to install," he said. When he was done, he walked again past the jurors so each could inspect the exhibit. One put on her glasses for a better look. "You can see with the naked eye that there are brush marks on the wire," Havlik noted.

"Is it ever OK to use a knife?" Specter asked.

"No, it will scratch only the outer surfaces," replied Havlik, again walking before the jurors and showing them wires cleaned with a brush and one scraped with a knife. "In the short term, the connection will be solid, but in the long term, it is very suspect."

Specter then showed his witness parts of the wire that were spliced but did not fail, asking, "Do you see any evidence of cleaning here?" And Havlik, again walking pieces of wire in front of the jurors, repeated, "No...I don't see any evidence."

Specter mentioned a report conducted for the defense that noted evidence of brushing when the unfailed part of the failed splice was examined, but only under magnification. "So," he wanted to know, "if there was brushing, was it sufficient?"

"No."

Chapter 57

Something peculiar happened to Chris Havlik on cross-examination by Avrum Levicoff. He had been holding up fine under fire, but then suddenly he seemed bewildered. To answer questions posed by Levicoff, Havlik on several occasions reached into a marked plastic bag for a piece of evidence only to find the wrong object. Or to discover that the evidence in the bag didn't match what he had been describing up on the video screen. He looked like an embarrassed magician who had reached into a hat for a rabbit only to pull out a mouse, or nothing at all. It wasn't good for his credibility. Levicoff had the plaintiffs' first witness on the ropes and was going for a first-round knockdown.

Specter and Kila Baldwin looked at each other. *What the hell was going on? What was wrong with their once-confident witness?* "They're sandbagging him!" Baldwin exclaimed in a loud whisper. Somehow the evidence, which in recent months had been in the possession of the defense, had gotten mixed up. Some of it was missing. Specter jumped to his feet and asked for a sidebar with the judge. Della Vecchia excused the jury for a five-minute break to discuss the issue.

After some searching, it turned out that three pieces of evidence (among hundreds) had been misplaced or were missing. Was that why Havlik was having a difficult time? Nobody knew what had happened to the evidence. Levicoff admitted to some confusion. But Specter told the judge that West Penn Power had already acknowledged—only two days earlier—that 15 other items had been missing from its custody. Specter suggested, "Your Honor, I would say that there is a correlation between the missing 15 and those three pieces missing from this bag." In other words, the same party that lost 15 pieces of evidence probably was to blame for misplacing three others. "To say the least," the judge commented, "this particular chain of evidence has been confused and mishandled, to say the very least." Kila Baldwin opined that this was no honest mistake, that the defense knew the missing objects would leave Chris Havlik tied in knots, looking foolish in front of the jury.

Specter lodged an objection with Della Vecchia. The judge, seeming angered over the missing evidence, sustained the objection and told Levicoff to go on to another line of questioning, his opportunity to score a first-round knockdown gone.

But Specter went a step further. He asked for a mistrial. He felt that Levicoff had insinuated that something fishy had gone on with the evidence and that perhaps Havlik was behind it. (That would later prove to be untrue.) "I didn't want to start the trial over," Specter would say later, "but I wanted the judge and Levicoff to know how upset I was and that this had to be cured."

The judge denied a mistrial. But after dismissing the jury for the day, he did demand that both parties—including lead counsel—get together and go over all the evidence piece by piece, evidence number by evidence number, to try to find what was missing and if they couldn't, to determine exactly what had vanished.

Chapter 58

All the lawyers gathered in the evening in a conference room at Levicoff's law firm to try to solve the mystery of the missing evidence. They reviewed each item while a videographer recorded everything, moving about to capture close-ups of pieces of metal and wires being removed from plastic bags marked with exhibit numbers. The office was closed except for a receptionist who had stayed late to let everyone in and, hopefully before too long, out. Specter was visibly cranky, missing his nightly squash game and being made late for dinner. He sat at a chair far from the action and scrolled through his Blackberry, answering the day's messages that had piled up over the afternoon.

The items of evidence were counted and catalogued in a painstaking process that took several hours and that failed to produce the missing pieces or even a clue as to their whereabouts. Eventually, the lost evidence would be discovered. The objects all along had been in the possession of one of the defense's own witnesses, metals expert Joe Turek.

Specter was burned up about the entire episode. He was angry at West Penn Power for misplacing evidence. He was angry that his witness had come across, at least toward the end of his testimony, as a bit of a buffoon. Specter pressed the issue with the judge. He wanted—demanded—that the judge somehow set things straight. That the jury be informed that Havlik wasn't "confused," as Levicoff had suggested, but that he had been handicapped by the misplacing of evidence.

Judge Della Vecchia said he would think about it as the trial progressed, and he did. With the agreement of both sides, he would read a statement twice during the trial. The one-page statement read:

Ladies and gentlemen of the jury, you may remember the testimony of Mr. Havlik. He was the gentleman from Alabama, and there was some discussion about what evidence he saw, some parts may be missing or something like that. In that regard the lawyers have asked me to read to you the following stipulations. This has been agreed upon by both lawyers.

During Mr. Havlik's testimony, Mr. Havlik stated certain evidence from the unfailed south side of the splice that failed was missing. Questions were asked by counsel with respect to whether Mr. Havlik was confused as to what evidence was missing. At the Court's direction, an investigation was undertaken by West Penn's counsel and Plaintiff's counsel to determine whether evidence was missing. This investigation concluded that the items to which Mr. Havlik referred was not made available to him in the days before he testified and was not in the box of evidence marked as Exhibit 8. However, Mr. Havlik examined this piece of evidence in 2010 and '11. Had it been present in the courtroom, Mr. Havlik would have testified that it did not show evidence of wire brushing and that it was consistent with his conclusions as to the cause of what he characterized as the burndown. With respect to whether Mr. Havlik was confused as to what evidence was missing, Mr. Havlik was not confused. He correctly identified the various items about which he spoke.

No adverse inference will be drawn by you against the Goretzkas, their attorney, or Mr. Havlik, either from the questions about allegedly missing evidence or alleged confusion of the identity of the evidence.

Chapter 59

Perhaps the most potent part of Chris Havlik's testimony had not come in anything he had said. It had come in the form of a video, the training film that for years Hubbell sent to its customers. It had been made by a business that Hubbell had taken over, the Fargo Manufacturing Company. The video—on how to use its splice properly—was issued to all utility companies that had purchased the devices.

West Penn Power's linemen were supposed to have watched the video, which made it clear that it was important to clean the conductor—the industry term for a power line—with a wire brush before installation. The video was 13 minutes and 55 seconds long.

"While the installation of these splices is straightforward, involving a minimum of simple steps, there are a few key procedures to be followed to assure permanent performance," it noted at the outset.

The video used a cutaway, or cross-section, to provide a look inside the tapered aluminum device. It showed in a diagram how a line is pushed inside the opening of an end until it stops, then the installer pulls back, causing the metal teeth in a set of circular jaws to bite into the conductor. From that point on, the harder the line is pulled, the tighter the teeth bite down.

"Now, let's look," the video continued, "at the installation process that should be followed in the field. First, it is important to properly prepare the conductor prior to installation." And the primary aspect of that, the recorded voice noted, is to "carefully clean the conductor with a wire brush."

The point was stressed: "This must be done in every installation to assure that oxides are removed. Remember, oxidation is undetectable to the naked eye. It even exists on new conductors, and can cause serious resistance problems if not removed."

The video included a laboratory demonstration that tested and measured three pieces of power line—one new wire that was brushed, one new wire that was unbrushed and one older, weathered piece that was unbrushed. The new line that went unbrushed showed almost as much resistance as the weathered piece. Conclusion: wire brushing made a difference.

To make sure there was no possible way this lesson could be missed, the video recapped its main topics with a list of important checkpoints: "Now let's review some of the things that must be avoided during installation. It included seven "nevers," the third of which was: "Never install a conductor without wire brushing, no matter how clean it looks."

Chapter 60

Specter had wondered how Walter Lipinski would hold up on the witness stand. Would this menacing-looking hulk, who appeared none too happy about being in a courtroom, relive the grim scene that unfolded in the Goretzkas' side yard or would he break down in the retelling of the tragic events? And how would the paramedic and EMS boss handle the defense's cross-examination? Would he respond to adversarial queries in a civil and calm fashion or would he get ruffled, perhaps angrily starting from the stand to crack a few skulls? As a witness, Lipinski was a bit of a wild card. In the end, a simple gesture, a hand motion, would prove the most memorable piece of his testimony.

Lipinksi lumbered into the courtroom wearing a maroon shirt and silver tie, no jacket, along with black pants and black cowboy boots that made him appear even taller than God had made him. The man was out of his element. Clearly, he would have been more comfortable pulling a bloody body out of a car wreck than wearing his silk noose in an Allegheny County courtroom. But Lipinski took his responsibilities seriously, so here he was.

He shifted his considerable weight several times in the witness stand as Specter questioned him, his answers short and clipped but quite certain, bolstered by his booming voice. Lipinski read off his report of the accident scene, ticking off the timeline in matter-of-fact fashion: 16:34 he got the call, 16:50 he arrived at the scene, 17:04 he checked Carrie's vital signs after administering drugs. And what had occurred: "sparks were coming off her body and actual flames...The line was entangled with her, her torso, chest, abdomen and left arm...She was hollering and moaning....."

While the witness answered, Specter had photos flash on a screen at the side of the courtroom, not of Carrie but of the house, the yard, the burn mark on the lawn. Mike Goretzka stared straight ahead, his eyes blinking. He finally surrendered to the flood of tears and closed his eyes, allowing his head to bob downward. Norm Rish, his boss, seated in the second row, gently patted his back. Specter held a laser and made its red dot appear on the photos, with Lipinski identifying the outline of the scorched ground. "This may be her head, this is her arms..."

The testimony became increasingly graphic. Lipinski described how Carrie appeared in awful pain while she remained conscious, burns on her face, her chest, her neck. He could see open tissue in some parts of her body, exposed bone in others. Her eyes were open and she was moaning, her head thrashing from side to side.

Lipinski told how he used a drill to insert an intraosseous (IO) line into the bone in the victim's leg so he could administer medication and painkillers. He doubted she would survive. But with drugs her vital signs improved. Finally, he helped load her into an ambulance.

Perhaps the most difficult task Lipinski performed happened when he "saw a gentleman in the back of the closed ambulance crying." Lipinski opened the back doors of the vehicle and let Mike Goretzka see his wife. He saw the pain wash over Mike Goretzka's face. He tried to console him the best he could. Lipinski, who had maintained his composure throughout his testimony, related to the jury members: "I told him that for her he had to be strong."

The direct examination over, Judge Della Vecchia called a recess. "The jurors need a break," he said.

Liz Deemer rose for the defense. Specter knew she would question details of Lipinski's account. He didn't know how his witness would react, either with his answers or his demeanor.

Deemer questioned whether the fallen line had in fact become entangled around Carrie. "Do you recall that for a fact?" she asked.

"Yes."

With that answer, she whipped out a copy of Lipinski's deposition testimony. She pointed to page nine, where he had said it "looks like" the wire had become entangled, then to the next page, where he had said the line was not fully around the victim, not 360 degrees around her body.

This aroused the first glimmer of anger from Lipinski. "I'm not talking about 360 degrees," he responded, "maybe you are."

Next, Deemer attempted to use Lipinski's testimony to back up the defense theory that Carrie had come out of her house and grabbed the power line, thus making her partly culpable for her own fate. But whether or not he knew this was the defense's goal, Lipinski wasn't having any part of it.

Asked where Carrie's left arm had been badly burned, the suspected point of initial contact, Lipinski described an area of her left forearm.

"So," said Deemer, "closer to the wrist than the forearm?"

But this was not what Lipinski had said or suggested. And he let the defense counsel know it.

"No!" he bellowed, "right in the middle." With this, he held up his own left arm and with his right hand made a karate-chop gesture directly in the middle of his own, large forearm. The spot he pointed to was far from his wrist and farther from his hand.

Chapter 61

Dr. Larry Jones had what most people would consider an awful job. He attended to burn victims, between 1,000 and 2,000 per year. A professor of surgery at Ohio State University and director of the burn center at its hospital, Jones had reviewed the photos and medical records of Carrie Goretzka for the plaintiffs. Jones, who had dark hair and sported a thick goatee flecked with gray, had 23 years previous experience at the burn center at Mercy Hospital in Pittsburgh, where Carrie was treated and died.

Under examination by Dominic Guerrini, he described in detail the various degrees of burns—first degree, a burn to the top layer of skin; second degree, in which the skin blisters; third degree, which extends through all the layers of skin; fourth degree, a burn extending into muscle; and fifth degree, a burn that went through the muscle and into bone. Jones testified that Carrie had second- to fifth-degree burns on 80 to 90 percent of her body, including her face and neck, her torso and her extremities. He went into further detail about muscle and exposed bone. As he did, Mike Goretzka sighed heavily, his hands over his eyes and his head bent down as he listened to the gruesome testimony.

Jones, looking at photos Guerrini handed to him but did not display for the jury, said that Carrie had multiple contact wounds but that it was not possible to differentiate between entry and exit wounds.

"Can anyone come to this courtroom and say what the initial point of contact was between Carrie Goretzka and that wire?" Guerrini asked.

"No."

"Why not?"

"There were no witnesses, and the patient did not survive to tell us."

Referring to Levicoff, Guerrini recalled, "The lawyer, in his opening speech, suggested that Mrs. Goretzka grabbed or touched the live power line..."

Levicoff interrupted, objecting to the characterization.

"I'll rephrase," offered Guerrini, continuing to ask whether the injuries Jones saw in the photographs were "consistent with Carrie Goretzka grabbing or touching the live power line with her left hand?"

"No."

"Why not?"

"Because the hand, even though it's burned, is intact. The area of largest tissue destruction which would represent a contact point is in the forearm."

Guerrini asked if those injuries to her forearm were "consistent with a defensive reaction to a falling power line."

"That," said Jones, "would be an explanation."

Seeking to establish Carrie's level of pain and suffering, Guerrini asked Jones about his own patients who had suffered severe burns. His answer: "Patients who survive these high-voltage injuries tell me that the pain they experience is excruciating and liken it to the worst pain they have ever experienced...Other patients have described to me when this occurs [as] an out-of-body experience in that they can hear and perceive what's going on and they want to move and talk but they can't."

Carrie must have experienced this for the 20 minutes in which the line was wrapped around her, evidenced by her writhing and moaning, Jones observed. He added that the medication administered after she was freed from the line's grip was not enough to relieve the pain and subsequent drugs would not have done so until she had suffered for a total time period he estimated at 43 to 47 minutes.

Levicoff's cross-examination was brief. First he established Jones' hourly pay for reviewing the records—$350. He also had Jones acknowledge that he had not treated "this particular tragic individual" and noted that four doctors who had been at her side—and were "all still here in Pittsburgh"—had not come to court.

The defense attorney asked whether the injuries Carrie suffered were to the "inside" of her left arm, suggesting something other than a defensive wound. But Jones responded that he did not "recall that there was a specific area."

"Now, doctor, I heard you testify about how long the current was entering this unfortunate individual, but, in fact, the truth of it is from the injuries that could have happened instantaneously, couldn't it?" Levicoff asked. He was trying to leave the jury with an impression that Carrie had perhaps suffered one quick jolt of electricity and no more pain after that.

Jones responded that the electrical burns and those created from Carrie's burning clothes could not have happened instantaneously. But that wasn't what Levicoff was asking.

"What I'm actually getting to is this: If she had several different points of electrical injury, it's impossible to look at that after the fact and determine how many minutes it was until this one occurred and that one occurred, you just can't tell, can you?"

"How many minutes between...no."

Guerrini didn't think the jury would believe that Carrie suffered one moment of instantaneous pain, but he sought on re-direct to erase that possible impression from any juror's mind.

"Dr. Jones, based upon your review of all the information, not just the medical records, how long do you believe that Mrs. Goretzka was continuously shocked?"

"Well, I believe that she continued to receive electrical shocks the entire time that the wire was in contact with her body."

"Twenty minutes?"

"Which was twenty minutes."

Chapter 62

While Levicoff had treaded gently with Dr. Jones and on the subject of Carrie's injuries, Mike Goretzka had been fuming throughout his cross-examination. Avrum Levicoff hadn't meant any offense, but Goretzka had taken it. He was probably being overly sensitive, but he objected to the defense attorneys' references to his late wife as the "patient" or, worse, a "tragic individual" or "this unfortunate individual."

Mike Goretzka cornered his own lawyer after the testimony. "I really object to Carrie being called 'the victim' or 'the unfortunate individual.' They should call her Carrie or Mrs. Goretzka," he told Specter. "She wasn't an 'unfortunate individual,' she was my wife."

Specter didn't necessarily agree that the terms the defense used were intended to be disrespectful. But he recognized that if his client felt that way, perhaps a member or two of the jury would also. "Let them go," he advised. "Let them do their own stupid things."

But Mike Goretzka was incensed. He wasn't going to listen to Carrie referred to in characterless terms, or worse, described euphemistically—she hadn't been "unfortunate," she had been wronged—for the whole trial. He insisted that Specter say something. Which he did later that day in an email notifying Levicoff of his client's sentiments. "Mike Goretzka was upset at your characterizations of her today with the words 'that unfortunate woman.' He respectfully requests that you refer to her as 'Carrie' or 'Carrie Goretzka' or 'Mrs. Goretzka.'"

Levicoff did not respond, but he did comply.

Chapter 63

Mike Goretzka had complete confidence in his lawyer. He trusted Specter with his family's financial future and to follow his wishes to make West Penn Power pay a high price for his wife's excruciating and untimely death. He trusted his lawyer to "do the right thing." What Goretzka lacked was an ability to pronounce his first name.

"Shannon said he'll probably...Shannon? Did I say it right," Goretzka would ask, laughing and shaking his head.

"Shay-nin," he'd be told.

"Jeez, why can't I remember that? Shay-nin, right?"

Then five minutes later: "Well, Shannon said...Oh, no, I got it wrong again. Sha-neen?"

Baldwin and Guerrini would laugh with him. "No, Shay-nin," they'd say.

And this was in the next-to-last week of trial, when they'd known each other for years. Mike's older brother, Chuck, didn't come as close as Mike to saying Specter's name correctly, pretty much giving up. The mispronunciation got to be a continuing inside joke, to the point where Baldwin and Guerrini started saying "Shannon" as well behind the boss' back. Mike Goretzka usually opted for the simple "Mr. Specter," though that seemed odd considering how well the two men had gotten to know each other by this time.

Specter didn't mind the mispronunciation. He was used to it and, in fact, rarely corrected it after the first time. His was an unusual name, actually a last name, given to him for his paternal grandmother, Lillie Shanin. Specter and his wife, Tracey, named one of their four daughters for Lillie, though spelling her first name without an "e." For such an outwardly staid guy, Specter's daughters had very informal names, all containing five letters and ending with "i"—Silvi, Lilli, Perri and Hatti.

Truth be known, Specter really didn't care what most people called him, to his face or behind his back. He had tough skin, largely inherited from his father, the son of a junkyard owner and door-to-door fruit peddler who—as if it wasn't hard enough being the only Jewish family in Russell,

Kansas—got thrown out of town after town by the local gendarme acting on the complaints of established grocery store owners. In his later years, Arlen Specter had survived—without complaint—a brain tumor (benign and successfully removed) and several bouts with cancer, the treatments for which made his hair fall out and sapped his energy. But he continued to work and work hard, attending Senate sessions and casting votes. (Asked how he was by a visitor to the hospital a few weeks before his death, Specter, short of breath from a walk around the hallway, replied, "I'm tough. That's how I am, I'm tough.")

Throughout his career, Shanin Specter experienced the same celebrations and tribulations with every one of his father's elections. He especially remembered the pain he felt when he was 15 years old and his father was rebuked by the voters in 1973 in his second re-election bid for district attorney. His father also lost elections for mayor, senator and governor. The younger Specter went on to help run many of his father's campaigns, including five elections to the Senate.

Chapter 64

Everyone gathered back in the war room on Sunday night before the next week of trial was to begin. Specter wanted to go over the exhibits and the examination of John Dagenhart, who had missed only one day of the trial. The session showed why a review was necessary.

"Look at page 10 of your report, please. It doesn't show the wires in the trees, and the splice is drawn too close to the pole," Specter pointed out during the prep session. Dagenhart responded that the drawing was not made to scale, that it was just done for the purpose of numbering the parts. Specter: "So I'm not going to show this one."

The group agreed that the expert would stand at one point the next day and make a drawing to explain one of his multi-line charts—until Dagenhart started to do it. Specter watched for a few seconds and then grimaced. "This is going to be too clumsy," concluded Specter, "Let's just move the chart to the screen and you can use the laser pointer." Kinks were being ironed out.

Specter questioned and Dagenhart answered. The witness wasn't told what to say—a prohibition under law—but he was helped along, such as when Baldwin advised that it might be too complicated for Dagenhart to use language such as "10 times five to the third degree," that perhaps just saying the actual number might suffice. The back-and-forth went well. Until near the end, when Specter got to the big finale.

"Were they negligent? Was West Penn Power negligent?"

"That's a legal opinion. I can't answer that," replied Dagenhart, the engineer.

Not the answer Specter was seeking.

"You can in Pennsylvania."

"Well, no I can't."

"You can...We've cleared it. We've spoken to the judge and you can answer," assured Specter, who waited a few beats, then continued, "Was West Penn Power negligent?

"Yes."

"Was it reckless?"

"Yes."

"Why?"

"They didn't do what I would expect utilities would normally. They didn't install it properly, they didn't do follow up. I can go down the list..."

Better.

Chapter 65

While George Westinghouse was seeing the success of AC current over longer distances, Thomas Edison was fuming. His 121 operating Edison power stations used direct current, which, while fine for densely populated areas and business districts such as those in New York City, tended to lose power when electricity was moved any appreciable distance. Its feasible range—before costs started to outweigh the benefits—was only about a mile and a half. DC was on the verge of becoming obsolete for most locations. Edison was in a pickle.

So he did what any businessman might do when faced with such a conundrum. He turned to public relations. And since Edison couldn't demonstrate in any way that his DC power was superior, in the parlance of modern politics, he turned negative. He began a smear campaign, focusing his attention on attacking the competition, spreading the word that the other guy's product was worse. In fact, Edison employed a ghoulish PR campaign to try to scare the world into believing that AC power was a danger.

Chapter 66

Stephen P. Schachner looked much younger than his 69 years despite his past physical troubles. He was a recent survivor of esophageal cancer. Schachner was short and thin with a full head of dark gray hair and earnest eyes that peered through glasses. He spoke in a soft, soothing voice. He seemed like a guy you'd want to talk to if you had problems.

Stephen Schachner was the psychologist Kila Baldwin had hired to evaluate the Goretzka family. He was experienced in counseling children, adolescents and adults. Schachner, who held a Ph.D. in psychology from the University of Pittsburgh but referred to himself simply as "a shrink," had examined family members of the Goretzka family several times since Carrie's death and had grown close with Mike. Schachner had come away after each session with the same conclusion: Each family member suffered severe psychological problems and would continue to suffer. Specter, Baldwin and Guerrini had read the doctor's written reports and traveled to Pittsburgh to meet with him a month before the trial to see how he might appear as a witness. They liked his unassuming demeanor.

Dominic Guerrini, who would question Schachner at trial, told the expert he needn't be nervous about testifying and that the defense planned no rebuttal witnesses on the question of the psychological effects on the family. "They may not even question you," he added.

Baldwin and Guerrini interviewed the doctor briefly in the pretrial meeting, careful not to suggest answers but occasionally telling him when he went on for too long or strayed into the realm of technicalities. Such as when Baldwin asked him about Chloe and Carlie.

"They lost not only a primary attachment but also a same-sex primary attachment," said Schachner, then looked at Baldwin. "Is it OK to say that?"

Specter, who had been fiddling with his Blackberry, jumped in: "If I were to testify, I'd say, 'A child needs her mother.'" And he went back to his emails.

Dr. Schachner's main concern at the moment was something Specter had said, that he planned to speak with the children the next day, or at least to try. The psychologist was worried that the lawyer might be too direct with them.

"I'm concerned about them being interviewed and if they go to court and testify in court."

Specter, who had four daughters, assured the doctor he would be gentle. He had not made a decision on whether to put them on the witness stand and wouldn't until after he had spoken with them. If he thought it would place them under undue stress, he would not have them testify.

"When you go tomorrow," Schachner advised, "you should talk to them after you play with them for a half an hour. Come in with toys, then begin to chat with them." He suggested a series of questions:

"What do you like to do with Dad?"
"Tell me three wishes you have."
"Can you show me your bedroom?"
"What would you do if Mom was here?"
"What do you remember about your mother?"

Specter suggested one of his own: "May I ask if you miss your mom?"

"Yeah, that's fine," said Schachner. "If you ask them about the incident, ask them about it last."

Specter wrestled with himself on whether he wanted to have the children testify in court. He had discussed it with his wife, Tracey, and she had advised against it, that it was "overdoing it." But Specter felt he could do it gently, without traumatizing the young girls. And without the jury feeling the testimony was gratuitous or, worse, making a public spectacle of their sadness.

"Just the opposite," he said, "I want to show that they're likable, and that there's hope for them."

Chapter 67

Mike Goretzka sat in the front of the courtroom and listened to Dr. Schachner describe what was going on inside his head: "Mr. Goretzka was and is experiencing what is referred to as PTSD, or posttraumatic stress disorder, as well as depression, major depression-single episode," the psychologist said, explaining depression caused by a single occurrence. He told the jury about the widower's constant flashbacks and the nightmares that woke him in the middle of the night. How he had trouble feeling pleasure, how he had a sense of helplessness and a "good deal of anger." Mike Goretzka, the doctor told the jury, suffered thoughts of suicide.

Several jurors glanced at Mike Goretzka, who looked straight ahead, his face reddened but expressionless as he listened to the psychologist talk about him as if he wasn't in the room, even though he knew the doctor to be a very compassionate man. On a couple of occasions when Mike Goretzka had met with Schachner and cried about what he was feeling, the doctor had cried also.

"His strength is in his ability to grin and bear it, to persevere under any circumstance. But where this is a value in terms of his employment, it does not benefit him at all in terms of his personal life. He is an unhappy and depressed man."

That same strength made it hard for Mike to open up and to share his feelings, and made him reluctant to seek counseling. "The prognosis for Mr. Goretzka," said Schachner, "is very guarded." He also diagnosed JoAnn Goretzka with depression and PTSD, a disorder he said is difficult to treat.

Guerrini kept the questioning brief, moving quickly to the children. From playing with and spending time with Chloe and Carlie on three occasions, Schachner said he noticed high degrees of anxiety and social anxiety from the older child. Chloe, he noted, suffered sleep and eating disturbances as well as difficulties with developmental milestones as simple as using the bathroom. Carlie, he said, experienced even greater signs of separation anxiety and fearfulness, noting that at school she was afraid to go to the bathroom alone and had to be accompanied by her Aunt Carol.

This anxiety, he said, was evidenced in how the children clung to their father. They did this, Schachner said, because they "have transferred from the fear of separation from the mother figure to the fear of separation from the only parent figure left to them, and they carry at some subconscious or unconscious level a tremendous fear that they could lose their father as well."

The problems the children were experiencing stemmed from the fact that with Carrie's death, the whole family "structure has been destroyed." The doctor added that their problems were just beginning. As they grew older, their lack of self-confidence could become more pronounced, and he felt certain they would need therapy well into adolescence. "This insecurity can follow them through their lives," Schachner noted.

"Now that it's more than three years after Carrie Goretzka's death, have the children suffered the worst of their psychological injuries?" Guerrini asked the witness.

"I would like to say it's true," replied Schachner, "but it is unlikely to be true."

"Is it fair to say, doctor, that witnessing their mother's electrocution is something that's going to stick with Carlie and Chloe Goretzka for the rest of their lives?"

"Absolutely."

The defense had no cross-examination.

Chapter 68

Specter had yet to set eyes on Ron Hindman, never mind question the cable splicer for Verizon Communications. Hindman had not sat for a deposition. He had had nothing to do with the case. Yet Specter hoped to have Hindman help him prove a basic part of the plaintiffs' theory of what had happened on that fateful day, namely that the electric line had fallen first onto Verizon's line, hanging there for some time before falling to the ground and striking Carrie.

Ron Hindman didn't bother getting gussied up for court. He wore jeans and a dark-green, long-sleeve T-shirt. Hindman, who had worked for Verizon for 15 years, explained to the jury the complex innards of the phone line at that location. Two lines each with 50 pairs of copper wires—200 wires in all—were wrapped in different color-coded plastic, then covered in a metal sheath and then wrapped again in a black plastic jacket. The Verizon cable was strung beneath West Penn Power's line.

Hindman had gone to the scene the day after the accident. Indeed, KDKA-TV, the Pittsburgh CBS affiliate, had aired a report on the incident that captured his truck in the background. "There's me in an aerial lift truck in their yard," he observed from the witness stand. He told Specter that his company's phone line had been badly damaged. It was "melted...it was all bubbled up" and the 200 strands of copper wire were fused together. Such damage, he testified, would come from very high heat. But on cross-examination, Levicoff, who had spoken previously with Hindman, used the witness to support his theory of the incident—that if the power line had struck other lines, it would have created a sight that Carrie could not and should not have missed.

Q: Tell the jury what it would look like.
A: You would see an arc, a loud flash. It would probably crack.
Q: Would you hear...you mean, you would hear it and see it?
A: Yes.
Q: Would it look a little like an instantaneous...like a piece of fireworks almost?
A: You could say that.

Levicoff had gotten his answer. Now he pushed it a bit more. He asked Hindman if the power line had hit the phone line, could he tell "whether that contact occurred before or after the unfortunate contact" with Carrie?

"I don't know."

"You would have no way of knowing that, would you?"

"No."

Specter leaped from his seat, riled.

Q: OK. Let's just deal with a little bit of grade school physics, not even high school physics, all right. Now, the power line—of the three things we're talking about, Mrs. Goretzka...and the cable line and the power line, the power line is up the highest, right?

A: Correct.

Q: And which is the lowest. Mrs. Goretzka or the cable line?

A: That would be Mrs. Goretzka.

Q: Mrs. Goretzka. OK. So if the power line falls and using basic laws of gravity, when things fall, they fall down. They don't fall up, correct?"

A: Correct.

Q: And if it hit both the phone line and then eventually hit Mrs. Goretzka, it would have hit the phone line first, because the phone line is up higher than Mrs. Goretzka, correct?

A: That's correct.

Chapter 69

The wire brush seemed to dominate the entire trial so far, primarily with the question: Was one used to clean the line before it was installed in the splice? Much of the reports and deposition testimony by the experts had focused on this issue. Yet there was no way to tell for sure since the line in question had been burned up. So the experts did what they felt was the next best thing—they looked at the other connection, the two other splices in the line and particularly the side of the burned splice where the wire had remained intact. The theory went like this: If the linemen had cleaned that side of the connection, wasn't it logical they—or probably the same lineman, either Jones or Falo—had cleaned the other side, the one that had burned out? So had that side been brushed? Hubbell's Chris Havlik said no. He had seen no evidence of brushing with his naked eyes and that, he testified, was the true test. West Penn Power's engineer Jill D'Angelo had said basically the same thing. If a line was properly brushed, you should be able to see it with your own two eyes.

The plaintiffs' second expert, John Dagenhart, had run tests and had not seen indications of brushing on the intact piece of line, yet he acknowledged under cross-examination that, after seeing further evidence in the case, his views were "evolving" on the issue. Maybe that line had been brushed after all.

But even if evidence of brushing existed—and there would be more testimony on the subject later on in the trial—it did not mean the brushing had occurred when the marks had been made. Perhaps they were remnants from an old repair job. Perhaps they had been made by another instrument as the line was hoisted from the repair job on the ground back up onto the poles.

Specter added another facet to the debate. How about the other two splices used to erect the line after it had fallen in 2004? Those were put up by the same two linemen at the same time on the same day. If they had been diligent in brushing wires before installing them, then those still-intact lines would show evidence of brushing. They did not. And no one said they did.

So in total, there were three splices and six connections in the line. One had burned down. Of the remaining five, four showed no evidence of wire brushing and one showed perhaps, maybe, debatably, signs of brushing only under magnification. What did logic say? He would ask the jury. Was it more or less likely that the failed portion of the line had been vigorously brushed before installation?

On top of all this difference of opinion—maybe confusion was a better word—the power company's own lawyer had said in his opening statement to the jury that it didn't matter. Avrum Levicoff had said over and over that cleaning the lines with a wire brush wasn't necessary, that the important thing was how the jaws of the splice bit into the aluminum wires and that even with oxidation on the lines, they bit deeply enough to hold the line in place.

So what were the jurors to think? Specter hoped they believed his theory that the line was not properly cleaned, that the linemen weren't adequately trained and that their supervisors didn't give a damn. But he worried that they might focus too much on this issue and not the most important fact of the case: that the power line should not have fallen on Carrie regardless of the reason, regardless of whether someone brushed the wire or not. Would that point become obfuscated because of so many details, so many magnified images and so much talk of wire brushing that was all coming up at trial? Would the jury fail to see the forest for the trees?

Chapter 70

Going to trial, especially out of town, was like going to war. It was an all-consuming experience.

The combatants left their families for weeks at a time. Lawyers and support staff worked long days in the trenches, preparing witnesses and exhibits and strategies. Barbara Carberry, one of Baldwin's legal assistants back in Philadelphia, backed up her boss with documents and information at all times of the day and night and early morning. It wasn't unusual for Diane Grimmie, whose bedroom was part of the "war room" suite at the Fairmont Hotel, to be laboring at a laptop until late at night, often wearing slippers and her pink pajamas. She had been working for Specter for seven years and accompanied him to every trial, occasionally sharing meals with him and voicing candid opinions about aspects of cases. She was also the only non-attorney back at the home office who called Specter by his first name. She got picked for the job by a friend, Specter's former legal assistant, who told her, "You're the only one I know who can handle him." And who, it turned out, could decipher his chicken-scratch notes scrawled in the margins of various documents. While Specter was a strict taskmaster, Grimmie was a strict task-follower. The pairing worked well. "We have a super working relationship," Grimmie declared. "He respects me and he trusts me. That's a good word for it, trust."

Mike Kutys worked for Nextgen Reporting and his duties included erecting televisions and a giant film screen in the courtroom and then flashing Specter's exhibits up on them in rapid-fire succession. But he did more than that, he became part of the team. At another trial, he worked with Specter; the attorney wanted to use a collapsible pointer and not a laser. Kutys went out searching for one. When he couldn't find one, he improvised. He found an auto supply store that carried parts for cars built 20 years earlier, cars that still used antennas. The antenna worked just fine as a pointer. The lesson was simple: If General Patton wanted a pointer, you found him one. Kutys, like everyone else who worked for General Specter, became inured to the ways of the boss and learned that there was only one answer he wanted and appreciated: "Yes."

Stories abounded from past trials of lawyers struggling to keep their eyes open during late-night meetings and even sometimes in the courtroom. Coffee was ubiquitous. (Guerrini personally preferred a daily diet of 5-Hour Energy drinks. He kept the little red plastic bottles lined up on a dresser in his hotel room like tiny trophies.) Meals were skipped, weight was lost. Families were missed, tempers sometimes frayed. Those working long hours together sometimes became closer friends or the strain pushed them farther apart. Lawyers for both sides battled through illness and fatigue. Once at Kline & Specter during a difficult medical malpractice case, a lawyer assisting Tom Kline worked herself into a hospital bed. Exhaustion set in after she had toiled for several days well into the early morning hours, once straight through until 7:30 a.m. Bed rest and a $42.9 million verdict would help to cure the patient.

The clients were not immune, either. They were thrown into a world to which they were not accustomed, civilians in the middle of the battle zone. Mike Goretzka was in court every day, usually early, dressed in a suit and tie that seemed to him to be more like a noose. He listened to every word of the trial. He discussed matters with Specter after court each day. He worried over testimony, grew angry over some, forced to relive the worst day of his life over and over again, his emotions taking verbal shrapnel on a daily basis.

For the lawyers, the days lasted from early morning—Baldwin was generally up at 4:30—sometimes late into the night. The case dominated virtually every conversation, even during meals and workouts. Specter might stray for a few moments to talk about sports or an item in the news, but never for long. A typical example: "I watched part of the Monday night game after dinner last night. The Eagles could have won that game. Kila, is Campbell ready to testify this afternoon?"

Yes, she would reply, Campbell Laird was ready. As usual, everything was ready.

Chapter 71

When it came to experts, few people in the world—yes, the entire world—could match up against "the professor," Campbell Laird. Though elfin in stature, Laird was a heavyweight in his field. Maybe the heavyweight champion. At 76, tan and with a bald pate framed by longish white hair, Laird was a leading figure in the field of metallurgy or, as he more succinctly saw his role, he was an expert in "figuring out how things break" and how accidents happen.

Specter had hired Laird and had success with him in a courtroom before. Laird helped Specter win a $153 million verdict against the Ford Motor Company in a Nevada case involving a parking brake. In that case, tried in a federal court in Reno, Laird had figured out how the parking brake broke—it was defective—and caused a pickup truck to roll down the driveway in front of a home where a three-year-old boy resided, killing the child.

Campbell Laird possessed the confidence, though not the cockiness, of a man whose résumé read like a novella. It was 27 pages long and chockablock with degrees, accomplishments, awards and the titles of hundreds of scholarly articles he had penned. Since 1968, Laird had been professor of material science and engineering at the University of Pennsylvania, the Ivy League institution whose law school Specter had attended. He was now retired and lived in Dearborn, Michigan, but he held the title at Penn of professor emeritus, which if asked, he would explain meant "that they're willing to accept my work if they don't have to pay me."

Laird had spent eight years earning his undergraduate and doctoral degrees at the University of Cambridge (where Specter attended one year of law school). He had also taught at a few other impressive institutions—the University of Vienna, the Sorbonne in Paris and the Governmental Laboratory for Research Materials and Standards in Helsinki, Finland. He had been published hundreds of times and had won 14 awards, including Cambridge's coveted Darwin Prize for his doctoral thesis. "Charles Darwin, the man who changed our lives, went to my college," he was fond of saying.

Laird had also spent some time in the corporate world, learning first-hand about products and companies. He had taken a leave of absence from Penn to spend five years (1963-68) at Ford's scientific laboratory in Dearborn, where he did research into the fundamental properties of materials.

All of Laird's confidence came through not in a haughty superiority but in a pleasant manner and gentle voice that still held more than a trace of his native Ardrishaig, Scotland, despite his 40-year residence in the United States. "I took a two-year leave to go to the United States and I expected to return," he told the jury with an impish grin, "but that, as you can see, never happened." Campbell Laird was an endearing—one might even say cute—fellow.

In addition to Laird's unsurpassed expertise and likability was his integrity. He was an honest fellow who took no sides. He had worked on hundreds of cases and had appeared in court probably 100 times, estimating that there was roughly a 50/50 split in the number of times he had testified for plaintiffs and defendants in trials. "Maybe I deviated more to the plaintiffs' side, but not by much," he would testify. He wasn't sure because "I stopped counting."

By all accounts, Laird was popular with juries. He addressed a jury as though he were teaching class, looking at them directly, using his hands to explain things and a pointer to note details in exhibits on a large screen. And he always included the jurors in his lectures: "We can see evidence here…" or "What this shows us…" He used esoteric technical language in some cases, such as a "catenary slope" (to describe the curve in a wire hung from two points) and two breaths later pointed to an exhibit of molten aluminum as "that glob of stuff." He mentioned the "allotropic" tendency of steel (its ability to exist in two or more different forms) and could spout from memory the different melting points of various metals, but he often preferred to use terms like "orange-hot," which, he would tell the jury, is "more than red-hot." The professor was deferential but never condescending.

Levicoff did not object to Campbell Laird as an expert witness.

Chapter 72

The plaintiffs' star witness took the stand as though he were stepping in front of a classroom of college students. Armed with his lengthy report and various scanning microscope and X-ray images, Campbell Laird got right to the point.

"Why did this line come down?" Specter asked.

"It came down," Laird answered, "because it was given a head start in degradation because it was not cleaned properly."

The professor, his voice rising slightly at the end of sentences, explained in detail that aluminum has "a very strong affinity for oxygen" and thus corrosion, which can cause overheating and the wire to melt, become severed and then fall.

"Is it important to brush the wires?" Specter asked at one point.

"Oh yes, because it gets all the oxides off all the surfaces," he said, adding that failure to clean the wires with a brush "can set off the gradual degradation process ahead of time...It gives it head start."

"As we learn a lot of interesting things," Laird began one of many mini-lectures, showing an X ray that peered into the failed splice while it still held one end of the wire. "You see that glob of stuff? That's molten aluminum."

Yes, he noticed brush marks on one part of the wire, "but we would expect less corrosion," he said, deducing the marks must have been made before 2004, when the wire was installed. Other connections he examined in the line had no brush marks at all. "This," Laird concluded, "represents an improper installation and I'm surprised it lasted five years."

He noted that one of the other splices, the middle splice which had not failed, also showed no brush marks and some evidence of overheating. "It shows that molten metal dripped out," he noted, injecting some drama by switching to the present tense, "It's in a race with the one that failed...and the incident wire won the race."

Specter asked his witness to comment on a report defense experts had prepared that purported to show evidence of wire brushing of the intact wire that remained in one side of the failed splice. Shown what could have been several brush marks, Laird pooh-poohed such evidence. "Two little scratches. They could have been made when the wire was removed."

"Should a properly installed and maintained line ever fall?"

"It should not."

"What does the fact that this line fell on a clear and sunny day tell you?"

"It supports the conclusion that an error was made in installing the line."

And later...

"Did you form an opinion of whether West Penn Power exercised the highest degree of care?"

"Yes."

"What is that opinion?"

"They did not."

"And what is your opinion as to the adequacy of the training with respect to cleaning of the wires?"

"It was nonexistent," said Laird. "They ignored the recommendations every time they opened a package containing a splice. There were many warnings to the potential danger that they ignored. The normal response is that splices are cheap—cut them down and put another one up. You must examine... "

"Was West Penn Power negligent," Specter asked next. This was the first question the jury itself would have to answer when (and if) it began deliberations. But Laird did not provide an answer. Instead, he skipped right to perhaps the biggest question the jury would face, which was whether to find punitive damages against the utility. The test for that was whether it had acted recklessly or outrageously.

"Well, that's a legal term," Laird said about possible negligence, "I would say they were reckless."

Chapter 73

There had been a nasty hacking noise emanating from the audience throughout Specter's opening speech. The noise, a loud and particularly sharp coughing, was coming from a heavy, bearded man sitting in the second row who was evidently suffering a bad cold. His constant coughing fired like a machine gun in sudden and piercing bursts. Cough drops, whose wrappers lay on the courtroom floor near his feet, didn't seem to help. The man, it turned out, was a representative from one of West Penn Power's insurance carriers who would be a major player in closed-door negotiations attempting to settle the case. But for now, he was an unnecessary distraction. The judge gave the ailing onlooker a stern lecture.

"Whoever is coughing," said the judge during a recess, "I can't tell who it is [but] I would like to get some water in you, get you throat lozenges, something of that nature. If you cannot overcome your cough, please don't return to the courtroom. I'm not trying to be mean, but these lawyers have a lot invested in this case. It's a big case. They're trying to get their points across. We don't want the jury distracted from any point they make. So, I'm asking…if you can't control it, do not come back, because I will stop and clear the room. Not clear the room, clear the room of that individual. I don't want to do that, but this is just too important to have these attorneys interrupted by it." The man got his coughing fits under control.

A few days later, Judge Della Vecchia, who could be alternately casual and strict, would stop the trial to expel one spectator, a young man who committed the crime of sipping a cup of coffee in the courtroom. The judge allowed water in his court but nothing stronger and no food. Signs were posted outside the court noting the ban.

As the trial dragged on, the rules would slacken as the testimony got longer and the courtroom warmer. Hunger and sleepiness began to set in. Spectators' heads could be seen bobbing from time to time. The same man who had been warned about his coughing was awakened on several occasions by the noise of his own snoring, which, luckily for him, went unnoticed by the judge. Food and drink were necessary just to stay awake during sometimes lengthy and technical testimony. Packages of gum and mints started to make their way around the courtroom, then candies. One specta-tor, seeking to avoid Della Vecchia's wrath with the sounds of crinkling candy packages, dumped the contents of two bags of M&Ms in an open jacket pocket for easy, and quiet, access. During some of the breaks, Specter wolfed down a cup of soup at the plaintiffs' table. Empty soda bottles and candy bar wrappers piled up in the sole courtroom trash can. By the trial's final days, many in the audience would munch on power bars, cookies and even concealed sandwiches consumed in little pieces broken off surrepti-tiously in paper bags kept under a chair or in a coat pocket. If Della Vecchia noticed, he had stopped caring.

Chapter 74

Campbell Laird was good, but he wasn't perfect.

For starters, the judge let it be known that he would not allow his courtroom to be steamrolled by the witness, interjecting when Laird began to launch into a lecture or lengthy detail. Such as when Laird, under cross-examination by Avrum Levicoff, was asked about where the high temperature came from that burned down the line. The witness mentioned the power line's steel inner wire, known as "the messenger wire," that was in the center of a series of coiled aluminum wires, then noted: "Unfortunately, the properties of the material that make it strong are antithetical to making it conductive. So it's a high-resistance wire and, therefore, under I-squared-R, it gets hot... "

"Professor," nudged the judge, "this isn't Cambridge; this isn't Penn. You will just answer his questions, OK?"

Laird agreed to try again.

"Where does that high temperature come from?" Levicoff asked.

"The current," answered Laird."

Generally, Laird held up well against Levicoff. The expert witness successfully disputed several hypotheses the defense attorney offered, such as the notion that the fallen power line would not have rested for any length of time on the Verizon phone line—which contained copper—before dropping to the ground, as the plaintiffs had asserted.

"And that," Levicoff queried, referring to the high temperature of the electric line, "would melt copper instantaneously, wouldn't it?"

"No!" replied Laird, seemingly astonished that everyone would not know the correct answer. "Copper is an excellent conductor. That includes thermal conduction. So it would take a while to draw current into it and heat it by the combination of the initiating arc and the high temperature in the messenger wire."

Levicoff moved on. However, he was laying a trap for Laird from which the professor would not escape.

Laird had done two separate reports for the plaintiffs about the accident. The first did not include an important fact that the second one did. It involved the splice from which the power line had failed, specifically the side of the splice in which the line had remained intact, which came to be known at trial as the "unfailed side of the failed splice." The defense contended that a lot could be learned from that part of the power line, namely that if the intact part of the line that remained inside the splice showed signs of wire brushing, it could naturally be assumed that the fallen side had also been brushed. Some installers tended to use the same technique for both sides that they installed.

> *Levicoff:* "When you examined that evidence under magnification, did you discover...the unfailed side exhibited evidence of wire brushing?"
>
> *Laird:* "I don't think I did."
>
> *Q:* "So you missed that?"
>
> *A:* "I did."
>
> *Q:* "You missed it, all right. It happens, even to someone who's a terrific metals scientist.

This last part was not a question, but Levicoff evidently could not resist rubbing it in a little. But Laird seemed to take it in stride, as if it were a compliment. He responded merely, "Thank you, sir."

Under further questioning, Laird said he first discovered evidence of wire brushing when he looked at the report performed by Hubbell Electrical Products for the plaintiffs. He explained, or tried to explain, that the folks at Hubbell had had the luxury of being able to take the pieces back to their laboratory and had had more time to inspect the evidence.

"But you had two years up to the time you wrote your report to look at that piece, did you not?" Levicoff asked.

"I did."

Levicoff didn't let it drop there. Didn't Laird know, he asked, at the time he issued his initial, 45-page report on August 3, 2012, that that part of the line had been brushed?

> *Q:* Did you know that as of that date?
>
> *A:* As of that date, I knew it.
>
> *Q:* You knew it. Now, in that report, you do not state that fact?"
>
> *A:* No. Correct.

Q: Did you not at that time think that fact might have some significance?"

A: I did.

Q: But you didn't put it in the report?"

A: No.

Chapter 75

Another concern for Shanin Specter was the cost of the trial. He wasn't afraid to spend a buck to win, but this case was getting pricey. He speculated that the Goretzka case could wind up eclipsing the law firm's record spending of $750,938.33 in the *Davis v. Motiva* case. In that case, the firm had launched an investigation into what had caused an explosion at the Motiva Enterprises oil refinery in Delaware that killed a worker and injured several others. The only thing remaining of construction worker Jeffrey C. Davis, who was vaulted into a vat of sulfuric acid, were the soles of his shoes.

After the explosion, state and federal probes of the incident found nothing to implicate the company on grounds of negligence. Absolutely nothing. Various government agencies had accepted Motiva's explanation that the conflagration had been caused by the ignition of airborne hydrocarbons—oil-related compounds—that were set off by sparks from welding equipment. In other words, the explosion was the fault of workers. But Tom Kline, Specter's partner, did not accept that explanation, and he and an associate went to work to try to get to the bottom of things. They hired 14 experts ranging from chemical engineers to metallurgists to an astrophysicist, took the testimony of 39 witnesses in depositions and reviewed more than 40,000 documents. At the end of his own investigation, they came up with a very different conclusion than what the government had found and the company had offered. *The Legal Intelligencer*, the Philadelphia-based legal journal, reported in part:

> ...Kline said his investigation showed that the explosion was caused by an ignition of hydrogen gas emitted from leaks in the tanks that resulted from years of neglect.
>
> That finding was significant, Kline said, because hydrogen, which is highly flammable, is produced when sulfuric acid comes into contact with the steel tanks. Only a tank that is corroded and leaking will release hydrogen, he said.

Kline said Motiva's internal documents showed that the company was warned just a few weeks before the accident that the tanks were badly in need of repair.

A June 2001 memo from an inspector recommended an immediate shutdown and repair of the tank that later exploded, Kline said.

According to court papers, another inspector's warning, issued just one day later, was more emphatic. He wrote: "This tank farm needs attention now!"

Confronted with these findings, Motiva surrendered. In 2003, two years after the deadly explosion, the refiner wrote a check for the largest reported settlement in Pennsylvania for a single victim in a wrongful death case—$36.4 million. The law firm's $750,000 expenditure turned out to be well worth it. But that wasn't the end of the matter. As the result of Kline's investigation, the federal government decided to take another look and, in March 2005, the oil refinery agreed to pay a $10 million criminal fine for negligence and environmental damage of the explosion, which had also spilled more than a million gallons of acid and petroleum products into the Delaware River. Six months later, Motiva agreed to pay a $12 million civil penalty, an additional $4 million for environmental projects and $170,000 to reimburse state and federal governments for response costs, for a total of almost $16.2 million.

Chapter 76

Thomas Jones was a good-looking, middle-aged guy who wore a striped dress shirt but no jacket to court. His dark gray hair was slightly long and more than slightly disheveled. He carried an unassuming presence to the witness stand. When Specter asked about his education, he replied, "just high school." Now in his mid-fifties, Jones had worked as a lineman for West Penn Power for 26 and a half years. He had been one of the two linemen who had erected the power line outside the Goretzkas' house in 2004, after the first failure. He didn't recall who—he or his partner—had installed the splice that failed five years later. The two men alternated on that facet of the job, so there was a 50/50 chance that he had.

Jones gave it up right away. At lineman training school, had he learned that it was OK not to use a wire brush to clean the line before installing it into a splice?

"Yeah," he answered.

And what could be used instead?

"It would be a knife."

The wire brush was "pretty much the norm," but there "may have been a time, two" when one wasn't used.

Specter walked over to the plaintiffs' table and picked up a dark-blue book about four inches thick, the book of standards for linemen.

Was Jones aware that "the Bible" said to clean the line with a wire brush and that an unclean line "will set up overheating and eventual failure of the splice?

"Yes," responded Jones.

Did he know that back in 2004?

"Yes."

Did he agree with that assessment?

"Yes."

Did he agree a wire brush was a "much better way" to clean the line?

"Yes."

Q: And did you understand, sir, that if you don't use a wire brush, you're increasing the risk that the conductor [power line] will fail and it will fall and it will fall and energize?

A: Yes.

Q: And did you understand that if a conductor falls and energizes that that presents a serious risk of public health and safety?

A: Yes.

Q: Because if the line falls and strikes someone, it could kill them. Is that correct?

A: Yep.

Q: And if not properly done, it can be dangerous...for anybody who's below a power line?"

A: Correct.

Q: Which would be all of us, right?

A: Yes.

Specter appreciated the forthright answers. He was trying to be gentle with Jones, aware that Levicoff in his opening remarks had predicted to the jury that the plaintiffs' attorney would be out to crucify the company man. Specter asked his questions not in an accusing manner but in a conversational tone, trying to appear relaxed. He even half sat on the wooden rail that separated him from the jury for part of his examination.

But he wanted more from Jones than his possible negligence in cleaning the power line. Specter wanted to put blame higher up the corporate ladder. Had Jones ever been told about incidents involving splices failing because of poor preparation of the lines before installation? He didn't remember being told something like that and, he told Specter, "I wouldn't have forgotten that."

Q: And would it be fair to say that you would have remembered that because that would be something that you as a professional lineman would see as a very worrisome thing? Is that correct?

A: Yes, yes.

Q: Because that would indicate that you've got live lines falling and that could be a serious risk to public health and safety?

A: Yes.

Specter asked if Jones' superior, Jill D'Angelo, ever talked to him about proper line installation.

"No."

How about Frank Gogol, D'Angelo's superior in the safety and standards department? Did Jones ever discuss a problem of falling lines with Gogol?

"No, not that I recall."

Specter also sought to note that the cause of the previous line failure in 2004 had never been sufficiently investigated or determined. He asked Jones if it was important to investigate such failures and why.

"Yes," said the witness, "to keep it from ever happening again."

Chapter 77

Jeffrey Falo did not look like someone you'd want to trust with your life. Someone to go to a punk rock concert with, maybe. A stocky fellow with a head of hair that was bleached white and gelled into spikes, he wore a long-sleeve polo shirt and a gleeful grin to the witness stand. He had wide eyes and a resonant voice that occasionally broke into a goofy laugh. His mouth hung open in a smile for almost his entire testimony. At 49, Falo was a college graduate and a lineman with 15 years of experience who had been partnered, though in a somewhat lower-status position, with Jones in fixing the power line outside the Goretzka home in 2004.

Contrary to Levicoff's prediction in his opening statement, Specter wasn't rough in handling this man who, despite his somewhat odd appearance, worked hard to make a living. In fact, Specter took pains to be nice.

Q: How old are you, sir?
A: I'll be 49 years old on Saturday.
Q: Best wishes to you.
A: Thank you.

Falo seemed to be having a good time, so far. But Specter quickly let it be known that this was serious business. He noticed the witness appeared to be looking at Levicoff before answering several questions.

Q: I see you're looking at defense counsel?
A: No. I was looking at the court reporter. I thought she had
   a question.
Q: OK.
Della Vecchia: You're innocent.

Unlike Jones, Falo stood fast to saying he always used a wire brush to clean a line before inserting it into a splice. Falo said he had been taught to use a wire brush and that he never failed to do so because he knew that it "makes the wire cleaner for the splice...In my opinion, it is the best method…a back of a knife does a very good job, but I feel a wire brush does better." Using a brush was "right out of our…manual," he added.

Specter picked up the "Bible" and walked it over to the stand. Did Falo also agree, he asked, with its caution that an unclean line could produce overheating and eventual line failure? "That's what it says," noted the witness. "I'm not sure I do…I'm just, it's a little beyond me, I think."

Now Specter whipped out another document—Falo's deposition. He showed the witness that earlier testimony and reminded him of his prior statements. Portions of the testimony flashed up on the big screen. Falo's smile faded.

Q: And then you were asked, "You were taught as part of your work that if you don't clean a conductor properly, the splice could fail?" And your answer was, "Yes. That's correct." Is that what you said?
A: Yes, sir.
Q: …because if you didn't, somebody could get hurt. And your answer was, "Correct." Is that right?
A: Yes.
Q: And then you were asked, "If you didn't, there was a substantial risk that someone could get hurt or killed?" And your answer was, "Correct." Did I read that correctly?
A: Yes.

Specter asked if Falo still believed those statements.

"Well," he began, taking a long pause as the jury waited for his answer. "You know, looking back and reading this, I realize the importance of it, but I'm not so sure if, you know, improperly cleaning would do the damage that they are saying."

Specter held his eyes open wide. "That *they* are saying? Who is they?"

"The manual," Falo said, adding with a touch of uncertainty, "That's the manufacturer of the equipment, isn't it?"

Specter raced to the plaintiffs' table and grabbed the thick blue manual again, waving it over his head this time, then holding it before Falo. "I think this has your company's name on it…This isn't the manufacturer of the splice's manual. This is *your* manual?"

"Correct," replied the witness.

One last thing. "Based on your experience, sir," Specter asked, "should a properly installed splice ever fail?" Falo's answer surprised him: "I do believe it could happen. I'm certainly not an expert."

Back to Jeffrey Falo's deposition testimony:

Q: Page 74…lines 11 through 14, was the question, "Based on your experience, sir, should a properly installed (splice) ever fail?" And was your answer, "If it is properly installed, no, it should not fail." Is that your answer?

A: Yes.

Q: Was that correct when you said it, sir?

A: I understand what I said that day, but after thinking about, I mean, there is so many different factors.

Specter: No further questions.

Della Vecchia: Any direct?

Levicoff: I have no questions.

Chapter 78

"Is that fair?"

Specter would pose that question, or some form of it, 54 times during the trial. It was no simple quirk of speech. It was a tactic, one tested many times in battle, with good results. The occasion called for its use when cross-examining a reluctant and experienced expert witness.

"Is that fair" was a way of eliciting a positive response from a witness who did not want to say, or acknowledge, what Specter really wanted—a simple "yes." Saying that something was "fair" set a lower threshold for an affirmative response. It offered a compromise of sorts for a witness who refused to fully capitulate. It provided a graceful way out: "All right, you don't want to give in on this point, but would it be 'fair' to say such-and-such?"

Specter found that often a witness who refused to concede completely would agree that a point made by the lawyer was at least "fair," which he knew translated to a jury in its basic form as "yes." It allowed witnesses to salvage some pride, providing a little wiggle room even though they were essentially surrendering the point.

Specter used several variations: "Would it be fair to say?" "Is that fair so far?" and "Fair enough?" And very often the answer came back: "That's fair." Or simply, "OK." As he explained, "A lot of times you will ask a question and the witness will hyperanalyze the question and something they would agree to normally, they won't agree to in court. They're overthinking or being defensive. Saying 'is that fair' prefaces the question with something akin to saying, 'Please don't be overly technical or defensive.'" Additionally, the phrasing was somewhat leading, though gentle and not so obvious as to warrant an objection from opposing counsel. "By saying 'is that fair,' Specter noted, "I'm suggesting that it would be fair to them to answer in that way."

There was a second reason he used the phrase—to give the jury a sense that he was, in fact, fair: "It's very important that the jury feels that I, as an advocate, am being fair with the witnesses." Not rude or mean-spirited when extracting a reluctant answer, just necessary—and fair. Such as when later in the trial, he would question Jill D'Angelo, a supervisor at West Penn Power, who had said during her deposition that brush marks made on a power line should be visible with the naked eye. The defense had agreed that magnified inspections showed some possible brush marks, but Specter sought to hold D'Angelo to her initial statement that no magnification was necessary if a line had been properly brushed. After reading a portion of her deposition testimony, he followed with:

Q: And you felt that they weren't cleaned with a wire brush because you would eyeball the connector itself, the wire, to see if you could see evidence with your own eye that it had been cleaned with a wire brush; is that fair?
A: That's fair.

Specter would use a similar approach in his cross-examination of another defense witness, Dr. Catherine Corrigan, a brainy and skilled expert who had earned a combined Ph.D. in medical engineering and medical physics from MIT and Harvard Medical School. Corrigan had testified at many trials and was good at what she did for $600 per hour. Corrigan espoused her theory of how Carrie had come into contact with the power line. Specter sought to debunk, or at least raise a question about, Corrigan's professional qualifications to give such an opinion. He asked several questions on the subject, but Corrigan refused to give him a yes or no. So finally he sought to at least get her to acknowledge that she was indeed being a bit cagey. The exchange ended with a "fair" question and a bit of humor.

Q: Do you hold yourself out as an expert in accident reconstruction?
A: Only to the extent that it's biomechanical. Biomechanical reconstruction, I think, was the phrase I had used for Mr. Levicoff.
Q: Can you answer my question yes or no? The question being: Do you hold yourself out as an accident reconstructionist? Can that be answered yes or no?
A: Generally, no. If it's biomechanical—some might refer to biomechanical reconstruction as accident reconstruction. In that instance, they would be the same thing, but if it's vehicular, no.

Q: Would it be fair to say that in answer to my last question, that was not a yes or a no?

A: That would absolutely be fair to say.

Chapter 79

To demonstrate that Carrie's death was due to more than simple negligence, Specter needed to show that fault for the incident extended beyond just a lineman perhaps doing a lousy job. It would help to demonstrate to the jury that liability extended to the people of authority at the power company. Robert Schellhaus was the first step up that corporate chain.

Schellhaus trained linemen. In fact, Jeffrey Falo had testified in his deposition that Schellhaus was one of the men who had trained him. He had started with West Penn Power in 1980, and had served as a trainer for more than 20 years, rising to become one of the employees who ran the utility's training school. What Schellhaus had taught back in 1996, his last year as a trainer, was that it was perfectly fine to use the back of a knife or pliers as well as a wire brush to clean a power line before installation. He kept teaching that, he told Specter, even though the manufacturer of the splice had recommended using a wire brush. Did he know of the manufacturer's recommendation back at that time? To this question, Schellhaus gave three different answers—no, yes and "probably."

"When did you learn that the proper method was actually wire brushing and not these other methods," Specter asked.

"Through these proceedings."

"Through this litigation?"

"Yes."

All these years, and the trainer of linemen did not know until the Goretzka lawsuit that a wire brush should be used to clean a power line? Specter popped Robert Schellhaus' deposition testimony on the big screen, then pointed to a passage in which Schellhaus clearly indicated he knew a wire brush was recommended. The question had been: "Once you became aware that the manufacturer recommended that you use a wire brush to clean a conductor, did you then stop teaching your students that they could clean a conductor with a skinning knife or lineman pliers?"

Schellhaus' defiant answer at the time: "No, I did not."

He tried to explain that he had been aware that a wire brush was recommended, just not that its use was mandatory. Specter wasn't buying it. He pressed further.

"But did you know it back when you were doing training? Did you know that the manufacturer recommended a wire brush?"

"Probably," Schellhaus acknowledged. "I can't be certain, but I'll say yes. I probably did."

"Just so we're clear," Specter continued, "in the '90s, when you were doing the training, you knew the manufacturer was recommending wire brushing, but you were telling the men they could use wire brushing or skinning knives or pliers. Is that fair?"

"That's fair."

Chapter 80

Was Robert Schellhaus aware that his company itself had stated in its book of standards that an unbrushed wire "will set up overheating and eventual failure of the splice?"

"If that's what it says in there. If that's what it says, then that's what it can do."

But when all was said and done, the former trainer felt that the requirement that a wire brush be used was essentially a bunch of malarkey.

"Like I said," he told the jury, "nobody has still shown me where the other ones aren't acceptable...."

> Q: Do you still believe that a lineman's pliers and a skinning knife can do just as good a job as a wire brush?
> A: "I believe you can use them to get it as clean, yes, sir."
> Q: As clean?
> A: Yes, sir.

Levicoff kept his examination brief. He wanted to prove just one thing: that even if Schellhaus had acknowledged teaching the wrong cleaning method, there was no evidence whatsoever that he had trained the linemen who installed this particular line. In fact, the odds were that he did not. He asked how many trainers there were back in the late 1990s when Thomas Jones and Jeffrey Falo had received their instruction. Schellhaus recalled that there were "dozens" of trainers.

Did he teach either Jones or Falo?

"I can't recall exactly who I taught and who I did not."

Chapter 81

Thomas Edison didn't spare any lengths in his propaganda war against the alternating current of his foe George Westinghouse. He did so in public spectacles of the most macabre kind. Edison's employees would occasionally gather groups of citizens, then bring forward stray or unwanted animals they had rounded up. And they would electrocute the animals, using alternating current in an effort to demonstrate that it was unsafe compared to direct current. Edison's men put to death dogs and cats and also larger animals such as cows and horses.

On January 4, 1903, Edison carried out a particularly cruel demonstration. In front of 1,500 witnesses, handlers led an adult female elephant named Topsy from the Luna Park Zoo at Coney Island, New York, to an open area. The elephant had killed three zoo workers—there was no mention of rumors that the creature had been tortured, including being burned in the mouth with a cigar—and her owners wanted her put to death. Edison was only too happy to help out. Copper electrodes attached to her feet atop wooden sandals, Topsy was hit with 6,600 volts of AC power from Edison's generating plant, slightly less voltage than the maximum 7,200 carried in current distribution lines. Smoke billowed and the large mammal fell over onto her side, dead within seconds. Edison filmed the episode and showed it to other audiences. The film still exists and is hosted on youtube.com.

The Goretzka family at Disney World.
From left: Chloe, Carrie, Carlie and Mike. (Courtesy of Mike Goretzka)

Top: The Goretzkas' house. *Middle:* Carrie's shoes on the ground after the incident. *Bottom:* The burned ground where Carrie was struck. (Trial exhibits)

Top: The pole and lines adjacent to the site from which the power line fell. *Middle:* Closeup of the automatic splice that had held the power line. *Bottom:* The burned end of the line. (Trial exhibits)

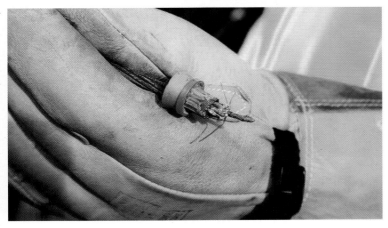

Top: Shanin Specter appearing outside the Allegheny County Courthouse. (Author photo). *Bottom:* Kila Baldwin (left), Dominic Guerrini and Shanin Specter in pretrial preparation at the Kline & Specter offices. (Author photo)

Top: Defense attorney Avrum Levicoff. (Courtesy of Avrum Levicoff).
Bottom: Allegheny County Common Pleas judge Michael Della Vecchia.
(Author photo)

From: D'Angelo, Jill A.
Sent: Wednesday, February 11, 2004 7:24 AM
To: Renner, Larry W.
Cc: Gogol, Frank A.; Bearley, Haven L., Jr.
Subject: Copper Automatic Failure

not yet seen a sample that definitely indicates that being the case, and I'm not sure that was the case for this one.

When I received the splice, the first thing I did was insert a clean piece of copper in the failed end. It inserted properly ar
held. This just means that the jaws were intact and not defective upon installation. Frank Gogol then cut open the splice
Attached are a few snapshots.

Outside of   Inside of   Aged Copper.JPG   New Copper.JPG
Splice.JPG   Splice.JPG

The following observations were made:

The importance of thoroughly cleaning the conductor prior to installation of an automatic splice or any other connector
cannot be over-stressed, ...

clean it, but that is not enough to remove the oxidation. It also shows that the jaws were not able to bite into the copper

Frank often cuts samples open that we receive back from the field to reveal more about what actually happened. Even
though we were able to see that the conductor was fully inserted into the good end of the splice, we could not determine

Based on our experiences, lack of full engagement and/or not cleaning the conductor (especially a solid conductor) can
result in a weak contact point electrically and mechanically. While an installed connection that does not meet the
manufacturers' recommendations can sometimes hold upon initial installation, when left under full-tension for a period of
time, especially with increased tension and conductor movement, the splice may eventually fail.

Top: Almost two years before the fatal accident, an internal West Penn
Power email notes that the power line has fallen twice. The earlier incidents
caused Mike Goretzka to be concerned about his family's safety. In one fall,
the Goretzkas' lawn was burned. Mike had been told about the other fall
by a neighbor, but it was unsubstantiated and never reported. (Trial exhibit).
Bottom: Part of an email from Jill D'Angelo to her boss and others noting
that the proper cleaning of lines "cannot be overstressed" and that
improperly cleaned lines "may eventually fail." (Trial exhibit)

Top: Chloe and Carlie outside the courtroom. JoAnn Goretzka is in the background holding a shopping bag. (Author photo). *Bottom:* Plaintiffs' experts Bill McHugh, John Dagenhart and Campbell Laird. (Author photo)

Chloe, Carlie, Mike and their dog Jackson enjoy a moment in their new home in 2015. (Author photo)

Chapter 82

Frank Gogol was a little higher in the command chain at West Penn Power than the previous witnesses. He had started as a lineman in 1979, moved to a construction lines coordinator and then was promoted to a construction specialist, a job in which he worked with standards and safety.

Gogol, a thin, middle-aged man with a shaved head and salt-and-pepper moustache, admitted that there had been times when as a lineman a wire brush might not be available, and so he didn't use one. Maybe he was out in the field and there was a storm and the brush got lost or maybe he just didn't have one on his belt. "You can only hang so many things on a lineman's belt, is that right?" Specter suggested, and Gogol agreed.

"Me personally, I have used the back of a skinning knife, and I have used a piece of emery cloth, the grit paper, to clean a conductor, and I have used the side cutter on my pliers...It was a few occasions I didn't have a brush available." Gogol acknowledged that doing so violated the company standard, but when necessary, he said, he used "whatever means I had available."

Later, Gogol became a safety manager and a safety supervisor. He worked from 2002 to 2011 with Jill D'Angelo in the company's standard's department when he noticed three splices had been brought in showing characteristics of overheating. That "caught my interest," he said, adding that he and D'Angelo discussed the splices. Gogol knew that such splices presented a potential danger. He agreed with Specter that it was important to determine the cause "because if it comes down once, it could come down again.... "

Yet Specter had established, in one case involving a failed splice, that West Penn Power had not investigated fully enough to find a cause, and that was the first line failure that had scorched the Goretzka property in 2004.

Q: A line comes down, you need to try to figure out why the line came down?

A: Correct.

Q: Is that correct?

A: That's correct.

Q: That's very important?

A: That's correct.

Why was that important? Specter wanted to know. Because, replied Gogol, there were many causes for a line to fall and the power company would want ascertain that cause. He ticked off a number of them, including a storm, a tree, a lightning strike, high winds, an overload.

"Right," said Specter, "but a line certainly just shouldn't fall out of the sky on a clear and sunny day?"

"I agree," said Gogol.

Levicoff had no questions for the witness.

Chapter 83

The audience and, presumably, the jury, had been awaiting the testimony of members of the Goretzka family who so far had sat silently in the courtroom, save for the occasional sniffling and stifled sobs. JoAnn Goretzka, the initial witness to see Carrie being electrocuted, was the first scheduled to testify. Slightly stooped, she walked slowly yet steadily to the witness stand. A nervous smile was etched across her face, making it look like she was happy about something when, in fact, she was not happy about anything. Her early answers came out flat and almost matter-of-fact. To Specter's questions she gave one-word replies, forcing him to draw her out. His first was a simple one.

"How are you doing?"

"OK."

"You sure?"

"Yes."

And later:

"You're Mike's mom?"

"Yes."

"Are you proud of Mike?"

"Yes."

JoAnn related the facts as she saw them, from the incident that killed her daughter-in-law to its current-day aftermath to what she foresaw of her family's future. Her testimony seemed unemotional. She suppressed her feelings. JoAnn's voice did not crack. No tears showed behind her thick glasses. In a way, her calm, unadorned and unrehearsed testimony made it clear she was not playing to the jury, giving her words perhaps greater impact. But maybe not: a flat affect could also simply fall flat.

JoAnn, 69, who wore her blonde hair short, said she was proud of Mike because he had accomplished a great deal in his career and was "a very good son." Period. She described Carrie as "a loving, caring person and she was an awesome mother" whose children "were her whole life." She told the jury: "I mean, Carrie was almost like a daughter to me. I really loved her a lot."

JoAnn recalled the events of June 2, 2009. She and Carrie and Carlie and Chloe were sitting on the couch watching cartoons while dinner was cooking. Then "all of a sudden the power went out." When that happened, JoAnn said, "the girls got antsy because, you know, when television goes out for them, that's it." She smiled as if not knowing what happened next. Several jurors smiled back at her.

With the help of photos—the couch they were sitting on, the dining room, the kitchen, the kitchen window, the garage, the side of the house— Specter took JoAnn back to her movements on that day. She stood from the couch and went to the window where she saw two large pine trees on fire behind the house with a wire hanging in the trees. She remembered Carrie picking up the kitchen phone to call for assistance, but it didn't work. She went to get her cell phone, which she kept in her car in the garage.

"And the girls were anxious, you know, 'Where is Mommy? Where is Mommy? What is going on?'"

So JoAnn went to check. She went out the front door and called for her daughter-in-law.

"'Carrie, Carrie.' And I happened to look, went down to the steps and looked over to my left and Carrie was lying there engulfed in flames."

JoAnn jumped down the steps and ran out onto the grass on the side of the driveway, she recalled, "and I took two steps onto the grass, and when I took those steps, it shocked me and I was thrown backwards and I burned the tips of my fingers. And I'm yelling, 'Carrie! Carrie! Somebody has to help her. Somebody has to help her!' And the girls heard me and they ran out on the porch and they are yelling, 'Mommy! Mommy! Mommy is on fire! Mommy is on fire!' And I'm yelling to them, 'Please get in the house. Please get in the house!' And I'm trying to yell for help."

Then a neighbor who was a fireman came over, then a woman who lived nearby also started screaming for help. More and more neighbors ran to the Goretzka house.

"And I'm sorry, but after that I don't remember anything. Everything just...I don't remember how I got in the garage. I don't remember how I got on the steps in the house to sit with the girls to try to comfort them. Everything just went from my mind at that point...and after that, I'm sorry. I just can't remember anything. It just, the sight of seeing Carrie on fire I'll have in my mind for the rest of my life."

Chapter 84

The stakes were high, and the hours of effort and the gravity of the circumstances started to take a toll on the combatants. It wasn't only the pressure of the trial, but also, for the plaintiffs' lawyers, being away from the comforts of home, missing husbands, children, pets, one's own bed. Signs of wear were beginning to show.

For Kila Baldwin, apart from her husband and two small children and sleeping fitfully most nights if at all, the stress had been mounting since the first day of the trial. At home, she was used to getting up most mornings at 4:30 for a leisurely run or workout at the gym and then showering and heading to work, but she had also gone to bed by 8 or 9 p.m. the nights before. At trial, she stayed up usually until midnight or beyond getting things ready for the next day (with her staff back in Philadelphia working some days until 3 a.m.), gathering documents and exhibits, anything Shanin Specter felt he might need for trial. Her only respite was dinner, generally with Specter and Guerrini, where the conversation inevitably turned back to the trial, and Baldwin jotted more items onto her ever-growing to-do list. Guerrini helped take some of the load, but the case had been largely Kila Baldwin's baby since the beginning, and she felt ultimately responsible for every minute detail. Most trial days, Baldwin tried to sneak in an hour at the gym before dinner, but often time ran out before she could put on her sneakers. She tried to sleep a little later than usual, but no matter how tired her body was, her internal alarm rang each morning at 4:30, and she would sit up in bed, her mind racing. Each morning, she arrived in court by 9 a.m., appearing, at least on the outside, buoyant and in good spirits. Until one day.

The last straw for Baldwin came on the Wednesday before Thanksgiving. The previous night, she had chosen to skip dinner with Specter and Guerrini. While they were at a steak house, Guerrini mentioned to Specter that he was scheduled to question several witnesses during the course of the trial, but that Baldwin had none to examine. He suggested that she take one of his. Guerrini knew that the original plan had been for Baldwin to examine three expert witnesses at trial, but that Specter had dropped one from the list and later decided that he would question the other two himself.

Specter had considered but never promised the witnesses to Baldwin. He trusted her skills, but as the trial began in earnest and the financial stakes escalated, he concluded that he would rather have the task done by the person he trusted most—himself. No offense intended, but that was the way it would be. The first major witness, Chris Havlik, had been critical. He was inexperienced at testifying and it was unknown how much latitude the judge would allow or how aggressively Levicoff would cross-examine Havlik. Specter felt his experience was needed.

With the second of Baldwin's possible witnesses, John Dagenhart, he recalled, "I don't know why I didn't have Kila examine him. Maybe I should have." But again, he felt Dagenhart was an important witness, and Specter's nearly 30 years of experience dictated that he do the questioning. Also, Judge Della Vecchia had been rough on Baldwin during her examination of a witness in a prior case. Specter didn't realize that Baldwin, whom he respected and liked and had entrusted with a great deal of responsibility in this and other cases, was unhappy about her diminished role. To say the least.

Guerrini knew this and assumed Baldwin would gladly take one of his witnesses. Even though she would be pinch-hitting, it was still a turn at bat in the big leagues. He also strategized that it would be a plus for their side if the mostly female jury saw Kila Baldwin holding the reigns for a time. Specter had no objection, but he was concerned that the gesture by Guerrini, who, at 34, was only a year older than Baldwin and held an equal position with her at the firm, could be taken as condescending. Guerrini considered the possibility. But he and Baldwin had become close working the case together. In fact, they had spent so much time together during this and a previous case tried in Pittsburgh that waiters in some of their favorite restaurants had come to believe they were a couple. Guerrini considered Baldwin a friend, and he was willing to take the chance. He asked that Specter make the recommendation, which he did at the end of an email to Baldwin about another subject that night.

"BTW, would you please examine Lally?" he asked about the expert who would testify about the economic loss of Carrie's death. The testimony would be largely mechanical and unchallenged.

The response was quick and curt: "Dom is already prepped on this; he can do it."

Specter suggested, "It would be good for you to call a witness. Dom agrees… :)"

Whether it was the fact that the two men had discussed this without her present, or "Dom agrees" or the email Smiley Face, Baldwin found it all patronizing. A match had been lit.

When Guerrini broached the subject the next day during the lunch break (and fortunately after almost everyone had left the courtroom), Baldwin's Irish temper ignited. Her face reddened, tears flooded from her eyes and her voice burst from her as a shout.

"I'm not taking your witness! Why should I take your witness? I've had it! I'm done with this. I'm going home. I'm quitting the case and I'm quitting the firm and I'm going home. I don't need this! My husband makes a good living. I'm getting the hell out of here!"

And she meant it. Unbeknownst to the stunned Guerrini, Baldwin had already packed up her room and had her bags ready to be taken to her car as soon as she checked out. If she even bothered. She was still seething at learning that she would no longer be examining Havlik and Dagenhart, but the latest jab had been too much. "Then why the f--- am I out here? I've wasted my time," she recalled thinking at that point. "I could be home breast-feeding my son."

This was another element of her rage. Baldwin had given birth to her second child, Liam, only three months earlier. She had returned to work a week and a half after giving birth. Perhaps too soon. And it had been a difficult delivery, with the umbilical cord wrapped around the child's neck, and it was preceded with a number of false labors. During this stage, Guerrini had called her cell phone. "I was actually pushing when he called. I stopped for a minute, answered his questions and went back to pushing," she remembered. She had also had some tough times before her baby was born as she worked on a case involving a number of hospital staffers and doctors. It was a tragedy in which a baby had suffered a serious brain injury during delivery. The deposition process had been so antagonistic that an opposing attorney had screamed at Baldwin and even gave her the finger. The episode had caused her blood pressure to spike and her doctor to confine her to bed rest until her own delivery.

Now, out in Pittsburgh, Kila Baldwin missed her young family. Even though she and Guerrini made the trip home on weekends, Friday nights were basically spent in a tired stupor, most of Saturdays working in the office and most of Sundays traveling back to Pittsburgh. There was precious little time for family life.

"I was furious," Baldwin would recall with a small laugh months after her tirade in the courtroom, feeling bad about directing her ire at Guerrini. "I was already mad at the email from Shanin the night before, and when Dom told me he was willing to let me take a witness, I got even madder. It was like, 'We'll let you take one stupid witness.' I was really ready to go home."

But she didn't. "I just calmed myself down. I didn't want to leave the Goretzka family. So I stayed. I unpacked my bags." Later, she would examine one of Guerrini's witnesses.

Chapter 85

Specter did all he could to have the jury relive the moments along with JoAnn Goretzka. He flashed up photos of the lawn, showing the charred spot where Carrie had been felled. He showed photos of the teal Crocs shoes she had been wearing that flew from her feet and were left lying near the burn marks. He presented the hair clip she had worn that day as evidence—a physical connection to Carrie—and gave it to the jurors. He also handed them Carrie's scorched pink cell phone to pass among themselves. The jurors studied the device, turning it over in their hands, feeling the melted plastic. Specter also showed them the clump of hair, Carrie's hair, which Mike Goretzka had taken from the lawn after the rescue team lifted her from the ground. Specter did not hand them the hair, contained in a clear plastic bag, but held it out and walked in front of the members of the jury.

JoAnn, also a claimant in the case, told about her burned fingers. She was used to getting little burns, she told the jury offhandedly. "Everybody knows, if you're a housewife, you practically burn yourself all the time. I usually burn myself once a week ironing clothes or cooking, something like that," she said smiling, then added, "But these burns were so painful that I can't explain how painful they were." If the electrical burns to JoAnn's fingertips were so distressing, the jury was left to wonder what Carrie must have felt.

There were also psychological scars, she testified, both to her and her granddaughters.

Q: How often do you think about it?

A: I think about it every day. I mean, I get up thinking about it. I go to bed thinking about it. And really, I have a dog and I take my dog for a walk every day, and I study wires all the time. I mean, I have never done this before, but I'll actually stand there and look at the wires and think to myself, How could that have happened? How would that have come down and landed on Carrie? I mean, you just take it for granted when you go outside and you're walking and you're walking under a wire, you never think it is going to fall.

And I mean, I have been doing this for three and a half years, studying wires.

Q: When you think about what you saw, what do you think about?

A: Just how much pain she must have been in. How she had to suffer. And it just shouldn't have happened. She was a good person. She had her whole life to live, and it was all taken away with just one split second.

JoAnn Goretzka testified that her grandchildren were still having a difficult time coping with life without their mother. Especially Chloe, who was four years old at the time and had known Carrie twice as long as her younger sister. Chloe also had a clearer recollection of the awful event that had taken her mother from her.

Now eight, "Chloe is really just starting to come around. She is starting to make friends in school," testified JoAnn, trying to be upbeat. It didn't last long.

So many reminders would make Chloe sad or set her off, JoAnn reflected as Specter flashed a photo of Chloe on the big screen and monitors in the courtroom. At parties at school attended by parents, JoAnn related that Chloe would pull herself away from everyone else and look in envy at the other children's mothers. "I know one day at school she said to somebody, she says, 'You're lucky. You still have your mommy...I don't.'"

"It just breaks my heart to see her like that because she is such a good little girl...she has gone through so much pain and everything, and I don't know if Chloe is ever going to be the same. I really don't." JoAnn shook her head as she said the words, letting out a soft sigh. In the first row of the courtroom, her older son, Chuck, a muscular man with a chiseled jaw and broad shoulders, began to cry.

JoAnn, in her perfunctory manner, related how Chloe was now prone to outbursts. One minute she would be happy and then, out of nowhere, "She will just have an outburst and she just can't control herself. We can't talk to her. She will cry and she will carry on and she just goes in herself. We just can't get through to her.

"And I try to give her as much love as I can because I know she wants that love. I know she needs that mother." Now Mike's sister Carol began to cry.

JoAnn told the jury that Chloe had only started talking about her mother in the past year. Specter asked what Chloe talked about.

"Well," replied JoAnn, "she knows her mommy is her angel." She said the children visited their mother's grave and left cards at the site. For a long time, all Chloe's drawings were in black, but she later began using colors. JoAnn held up two of the cards and read them aloud for the jury: "I love you, Mommy. You're an angel...I miss you. Love, Chloe."

JoAnn said the children frequently looked at their mother's photographs around the house, particularly one stuck to the refrigerator door. "The only thing they're afraid of now is they know they can't remember Mommy's voice anymore. And that bothers them. They know what Mommy looks like but they don't know what Mommy sounds like anymore." And then Mike Goretzka, his face red and eyes teary through much of the testimony, for the first time at the trial gave up on trying to fight back his emotions and sobbed openly. The jurors glanced from JoAnn to Mike and his siblings, Carol, Amy and Chuck, the family all crying and blowing their noses. John Salandro, Carrie's father, who attended much of the trial with the Goretzkas, sat silently. A photo of the girls in blue dresses, both smiling, Chloe with her arms around her little sister, appeared on the courtroom screens as the testimony and the sobbing went on.

Specter took it a little further, asking about the girls' feverish attachment to their grandmother and their father. JoAnn explained she could never go far from the girls without their calling out for her. "Grandma, where are you? Grandma, where are you!" they would say loudly, worry in their voices. She would shout back that she had only gone to the kitchen. They did the same with Mike when he was home, even insisting on sleeping in his bed every night since the tragedy.

JoAnn explained. "See, when this happened, they never really got to say good-bye to their mommy. And I think now that anybody they can't see, they are afraid they aren't going to come back."

Judge Della Vecchia recessed the jury for the Thanksgiving weekend.

Chapter 86

By the time Thanksgiving rolled around, everyone needed a break. Della Vecchia had sensed this and adjourned in the early afternoon. Specter raced to his hotel, grabbed his pre-packed bag and got a ride to Pittsburgh International Airport, where he hopped aboard US Airways Flight 587 to Phoenix. There he rendezvoused with Tracey and the children at his in-laws' home in Arizona.

Except for a brief conversation with Tracey, Specter did not discuss the trial with his family—"It was too gruesome to discuss around others"—and he tried not to reflect on it, though he was unsuccessful. Thoughts about the case banged around in his head—the upcoming witnesses, his strategy, negotiations over a possible settlement. Emails went back and forth among him, Baldwin and Guerrini. But going out West did help him relax. Specter played squash most days. And he made the time to play one round of golf, though just one. "I made it a point to stay out of the sun," he said. "I didn't want to come back with a tan. I didn't want the jurors looking at me and thinking, 'That Goretzkas' lawyer was somewhere nice for the holiday.'"

Specter played his sole round at the Estancia Club, a verdant, 640-acre oasis that rose miraculously from the desert in 1995 in northeast Scottsdale. Afterward he went back to the clubhouse, took a seat at a round table at the bar and ordered a cold beer. A college football game was on the large-screen TV that stood watch above the rows of liquor bottles. Another golfer took a seat at the table. The two men exchanged greetings and went about watching the game. Specter thought he recognized the younger man, who wore his dark hair on the long side, but he wasn't sure and resolved to leave him his space. After a while, the other golfer asked Specter how he liked the course and mentioned that he played a lot at Estancia, that it was his home club. Specter asked what was the best round he'd ever shot there and was startled by the response. It was a 58, from the back tees. The score was a course record. Specter introduced himself and learned the name of his new acquaintance. It was Gerry Lester Watson, Jr., though most people knew him as Bubba. Earlier that year, he had won the Masters Tournament in Augusta.

A few days later, Specter kissed his family good-bye and headed for the airport. He arrived back in Pittsburgh on Sunday afternoon. Baldwin had returned on Saturday. Now the team gathered in the war room. The candy bowls had been refilled and the refrigerator replenished with cold beer. Everyone looked rested and ready to go.

Specter wanted to walk through the coming week. First, he would continue with JoAnn Goretzka on the stand. He had told the judge before court recessed that he had only anticipated five more minutes, but Della Vecchia had called the break anyway.

"I question whether we should bring her back at all," Guerrini told Specter, feeling that JoAnn had already done well as a witness, the jury had seemed receptive and there didn't appear to be much more to accomplish with her testimony.

Specter disagreed. "The defense is going to cross-examine her, so I might as well ask her some questions," he said. "I want to ask her how her Thanksgiving was, about Mike's relationship with the girls."

From there, Specter planned to question several experts and West Penn Power employees, but he had decided to pass on several other potential witnesses. He was growing concerned about the length of the trial, now two and a half weeks old. He wondered how much the jury could, or would, take. "This is borderline too much. This is turning into a hell of a long trial," Specter told his colleagues.

Baldwin asked about Mike Goretzka's sister Carol, who had a quit her job as a pharmacy technician to help take care of Chloe and Carlie when her brother went to work. She went to school with the girls every day at 7 a.m. to help get them situated and, later, to take Carlie to the bathroom. When did Specter plan to call her to testify? His answer surprised those in the room. "I'm not going to put her on, and I'll tell you why."

Specter was concerned that testimony from Carol, a vivacious blonde who seemed caring and happy, might give the jury a wrong impression. "If she testifies, the jury can think that she's a mother replacement, a replacement for Carrie," he said. "Why do we want to give that to the defense?"

"OK," said Baldwin, though she looked more resigned than convinced. "Are you sure?"

"Yeah."

"If you disagree, tell me." Specter always made the final decisions, but he often solicited and considered the opinions of others before deciding to follow or disregard them.

"No," said Baldwin, "you're right."

Chapter 87

"JoAnn, good morning. Did you have a restful holiday?"

"So-so." Unknown to Specter, more sadness had visited the Goretzka family over the weekend. Chuck's dog, a Jack Russell terrier named Dakota, the same dog JoAnn had mentioned walking only a few days earlier, a pet that had been with the family for 17 years, had died. "So it was hard on all of us."

Specter offered his sympathies. The looks on a few of the jurors' faces also seemed to convey the same.

"You know," mused JoAnn, whose husband, Carl, had died eight years earlier, "the older you get, you realize that people are leaving you." She said it without emotion, merely recognizing the nature of things. But then, looking toward the jury, she added: "But we really didn't expect Carrie to leave us."

She had talked about Chloe before the holiday recess; now she spoke of her younger granddaughter. "Carlie really doesn't remember too much about Carrie because she was only two years old at the time. She was just starting to talk," JoAnn said, yet she noticed a "sadness" in the child's eyes.

Perhaps the most profound change she saw was in her son. "He's not the same," JoAnn stated. She told Specter about Mike's wonderful marriage and life with Carrie, how they had met in high school and how they had done everything together. "But now I can see Michael, when he comes home, he doesn't say anything. He'll just go sit on the couch in the living room and he's like a thousand miles away. I mean, I can see how much he's hurting inside, and you just don't know what to say to him. What do you say to him? He lost the love of his life. He lost the mother of his kids."

JoAnn Goretzka's testimony had been long and sad. But Specter had taken pains to try to make sure it hadn't been morose or tiresome. He also didn't want it to be without hope for the Goretzkas. He had learned over the course of many other trials and much thought that people, namely jurors, responded better and more generously when they thought their actions could provide help. They appreciated victims with good attitudes, those willing to imagine a brighter future and motivated to make one happen. They did not respond as well to those who appeared as "hopeless cases."

In another case that Specter tried years ago, he had made the point that even a young man in a vegetative state was not without hope. At that trial, in which Specter represented David Caruso, who suffered severe brain injury as a result of a hospital error involving his breathing tube, he had cross-examined a defense witness and gotten him to acknowledge that even vegetative people can occasionally regain their health. He had cited the case of a police officer who regained his senses after 12 years in a vegetative state. "The point is that where there is life, there is always hope." Specter then went on to deliver a closing speech in the first-person as David Caruso, letting Caruso speak through him, telling the jury of his family and his fiancée, of future plans, of dreams and aspirations that would never be. The jury handed down a verdict of $49 million.

There was hope for Mike Goretzka and his children, too. It might be hard to see it now, but it was there. "Do you have hope for Mike?" Specter asked JoAnn Goretzka.

"Oh yes, yes."

"Why is that?"

"Because he's a strong-willed person, and I know he can handle anything that's put on his shoulders. So I know he'll move ahead."

"Do you have hope for those girls?"

"Oh yes," said JoAnn, for the first time showing a smile that was real and not tinted with tortured memories.

"Tell us why."

"Well, they're both strong, and I know they're going to, you know, succeed in what they do," she said, though adding that they would always miss their mother. "She's not going to be there when they go on their first date. She's not going to be there when they get married, when they go to the prom. She's not going to be there…I mean, do you know how important a mother is to two little girls? I mean, a dad is great with them, but a mother? Nobody can replace a mother." Specter thanked JoAnn Goretzka for her testimony.

The defense had no questions.

Chapter 88

John Dagenhart and his firm, Clapp Research Associates in Raleigh, North Carolina, had proven indispensable to the plaintiffs throughout the discovery process. The firm had top-notch expertise when it came to electrical devices. Dagenhart was an authority in the field of electric power, one who had not only worked in all facets of the field, but had also written papers and delivered addresses to conferences on the subject. Getting him in the plaintiffs' camp was also considered a coup since he had gone to bat in the past for the enemy, doing about 80 percent of his work for utility companies' legal defenses and sometimes for West Penn Power itself.

When asked about this on the witness stand, Dagenhart said he believed "there might even be a project in the works that's currently under way" with Avrum Levicoff's law firm. Just getting Dagenhart away from the power company was a minor victory. Yet as knowledgeable and helpful as Dagenhart was in the lead-up to trial—and considering his steep fee—he wouldn't be so terrific when it came to testifying in court.

Tall and bearded, Dagenhart was a nice man. He had a soft voice and a softer manner, and he projected a country boy sincerity. Gomer Pyle with an engineering degree from the University of North Carolina.

"Would that explain your slight accent?" Specter asked.

"Yes, sir."

To which Judge Della Vecchia cracked: "You should have said, 'What accent?'"

So Dagenhart said, "I don't know that I have one, actually."

"We all do," Specter replied, continuing his examination without missing another beat, "And following the university..." Dagenhart had put in 12 years in all sorts of jobs—even reading meters—with Charlotte-based Duke Power Company, the largest electric power holding company in the United States. Then it was on to Clapp, a consulting firm that also conducted training courses for those who worked in the field of electricity. However, in his 32 years in the industry, Levicoff ascertained, John Dagenhart had never actually investigated one incident such as that at the Goretzka property, nor did he have experience installing an aluminum cable splice. He'd never even seen it done.

But Dagenhart had examined all phases of this particular case, 132 different items in total—physical evidence, photos, TV coverage, cell phone records, deposition transcripts of virtually everyone involved, right down to the first responders and the Goretzkas' neighbors. His file on the case was "so big that I had to have it shipped," he told Specter from the stand. And except for one day, Dagenhart had also sat through the entire trial to date. That was on Specter's insistence. He liked his expert witnesses to be in the courtroom for a time before actually taking the witness stand. Sometimes they stayed for a week or more. This was done at great expense, but Specter wanted his experts to hear some of the other witnesses and to get a feel for the place, for the judge and the opposing attorney. It made them more knowledgeable and more comfortable when it was their turn at bat. But Dagenhart, Specter was about to learn, had trouble with the curve.

Chapter 89

John Dagenhart's report and his testimony comprised, basically, several assertions. "In my opinion, the conductor was not prepared appropriately," he told Specter from the witness stand, "nor was the conductor properly installed from a physical standpoint." The line wasn't brushed before insertion into the splice, and there hadn't been enough pressure applied after it was inserted to make the teeth bite down deep enough into the aluminum wires. Also, he said, the fuse used on the line was too large, so "you don't have as good of an opportunity to blow the fuse when something does happen."

But there was a problem. In his written reports, Dagenhart had stated that the power line had been brushed at the site of the splice that failed. He couldn't tell on the destroyed side, but the other side did show evidence of brushing. It was logical that the other side had also been brushed. But now Dagenhart said he didn't think so. Specter gave him a chance to explain his change of opinion.

"It's clear in my report that I felt there was wire brushing…And I really thought there was wire brushing. But at the time that I physically looked at it with my naked eye, I didn't see any. And this week when I looked at it again—excuse me, last week when I looked at it again with the naked eye, I couldn't see any evidence of wire brushing. So, from looking at it from a magnified standpoint, it looked to me that there was [wire brushing] at that time."

"OK. Well, how about now? What do you think?" Specter asked.

Dagenhart gave a nebulous response: "My views on that are evolving. I'm leaning toward that not being wire brushing at this point."

An "evolving" opinion? "Leaning" toward the wire not being brushed?

Specter plowed on. He concluded with a straightforward line of questioning.

"Did West Penn Power fail to use the highest degree of care applicable?"

"Yes, they did," Dagenhart testified.

"How so?"

"Well, they didn't appropriately prepare the conductor. They didn't use the proper techniques. They didn't have the right fuse for the installation."

"Was West Penn Power negligent?"

"Yes."

"And how so?"

"Well, they just didn't do what a power company would be expected to do under such circumstances, under normal conditions."

"And were they reckless?" This was the test for proving punitive damages. It wasn't enough for the power company to have been negligent. Its conduct had to be "outrageous" or "reckless."

"Yes," Dagenhart responded.

"How so?"

"Same reason."

It was not the strongest testimony. And now Dagenhart would have to face Levicoff. The cross-examination wasn't going to be easy.

Chapter 90

Avrum Levicoff would seek to make John Dagenhart seem inept, or worse, deceitful. He noted repeatedly that the witness had stated in his reports—he had filed two, one initial report and another after seeing the defense team's expert report—that he believed the intact side of the failed splice had been wire-brushed. Then, only a week or so before trial, he had reversed that opinion.

"How did you inspect it? With your naked eye?"

"Yes."

"Did you use any magnification?"

"Personally, no."

"Did you ask for magnification devices?"

"I don't recall asking."

Levicoff showed Dagenhart two pieces of the wire from the unfailed side of the splice. "That splice was put in presumably by the same individual, both sides, right?"

"I presume," said Dagenhart. This meant that if one side had been had brushed, probably so had the other.

Levicoff chided Dagenhart that in his second written report, "You didn't say, 'I'm not sure.' You didn't say 'I don't know.'" He added later: "And you stated it was clear that the conductor was brushed?"

"Yes, I did write that."

"And that was just October, a month and a half ago, isn't that correct?"

"Yes."

Levicoff at one point interjected a standard question: "You understand it was important that the statements you made in this report were true and correct to the best of your ability, did you not?"

"Yes."

The defense lawyer also attacked Dagenhart's second assertion, that the wire had not been installed properly into the splice. The witness had based this view on seeing Thomas Jones, the lineman, demonstrate in court how he inserted a line into a splice, then pulled it straight out to tighten the grip. But, Dagenhart testified, the proper procedure was to pull the wire sideways out of the splice, creating greater tension and thus a deeper bite of the teeth.

Levicoff asked about what happened after that. Was Dagenhart aware—"I understand you've never put these in. In fact, you've never seen one put in," was how Levicoff prefaced his question—that during installation the wire (or conductor) was supported by a hoist. Did Dagenhart realize that the line was 200 feet long? That would amount to a fair amount of weight.

"When you let off the hoist, does your engineering mind tell you what would happen to the conductor," Levicoff asked. "What would happen?"

"Well, in my mind, the teeth would begin to dig into the conductor...."

Levicoff didn't say so, but the implication was clear—the weight of a 200-foot, seven-stranded metal wire would likely exert greater pull on the line than a lineman tugging it, whether straight or sideways.

Dagenhart's third assertion stated that the fuse used on the line had been too large, and that a smaller fuse would have tripped the power off sooner and prevented the catastrophe. Levicoff knew a few things about fuses. One was that the devices—no matter their size—have the capacity to distinguish a difference from normal current.

"Is that correct?" he asked Dagenhart.

"Yes."

"And that would be true of any size fuse, be it a 25-amp, a 65-amp, a 100-amp, or a 140-amp. Isn't that correct?"

"With the exception that they operate at different times for the same current."

In other words, one worked faster to shut the power down. Levicoff wanted to explore this. He put up a chart on a large screen on the other side of the courtroom showing "Total Clearing Time Curve Characteristics" and asked Dagenhart to use a red laser pointer to note various places on the chart. The witness did as he was asked, but the red dot on the chart jumped about like a flying insect.

"I'm sorry about my hand shaking," Dagenhart said to the jury, explaining that medication he took since a kidney transplant four years earlier left him trembling slightly.

"God bless you, sir," Levicoff replied. "That's all I can say."

But Dagenhart continued his thought: "If I was having to shoot my dinner during deer season, I'd starve."

That got a few smiles from the jury, but Levicoff kept his focus on the chart. How long would it take a 1,000-amp fuse to blow? he asked.

"One second."

He pointed his witness to the chart and asked about a far smaller fuse. "How about a 25-amp fuse? How quickly would that blow? You said it blows quicker. How much quicker?"

Dagenhart fumbled for the answer, saying he was having difficulty reading the chart. Levicoff tried to help, taking the witness step by step down the chart.

"Half a second?"

"I think it says a tenth? Tenth of a second."

"So one fuse blows in a second. One fuse blows in a tenth of a second. Is that correct?"

"Yes," Dagenhart finally acknowledged, "that's correct."

The answer seemed to negate the theory that a more properly sized fuse could have prevented the incident. Could nine-tenths of a second really have made much of a difference for Carrie?

The plaintiffs' trial team didn't say the word out loud but they felt it: "Ouch."

Chapter 91

Specter used a tactic at trial that he felt was very useful strategically—not one you saw in the movies and not one that other lawyers often employed. Generally, the plaintiff's side, which got to present its case first, started with witnesses supporting its side and then the defense followed with their witnesses. But Specter made it a practice to call to the stand some witnesses who were on the defense list. Rather than wait for the defense to question the witnesses and then cross-examine them himself, he called some defense witnesses before they had a chance to answer the beneficent questions of the defense team and help tell the story from its perspective. This tactic, called examining a witness "as of cross," was allowed and perfectly legal.

Specter did this for two reasons. One, by getting to a witness first—and deducing the gist of what a witness was going to say at trial from prior depositions or expert reports—he hoped to take some of the steam out of the planned defense testimony. He was, in a sense, rebutting the witness' argument before the witness even had the chance to make it. Two, if Specter did not call the witnesses to the stand first, which was his right as plaintiff's attorney, the defense was under no obligation to call them later. He knew from prior depositions that Baldwin and Guerrini had elicited important information from some witnesses that Specter wanted to come out at trial. He could make the same points with his expert witnesses, but it would be less dramatic than if the words—and in some cases the admissions—came from the mouths of West Penn Power employees themselves.

The strategy could strike a touch of fear in a witness, especially non-expert witnesses who were not used to testifying in court. Specter knew that calling a defense witness first took skill and care. He wanted to avoid being too aggressive, at least initially.

"I had Levicoff's words from his opening statement ringing in my ears, that I would be trying to make the defense witnesses look foolish," he recalled later. "I didn't want to be that aggressive lawyer."

Specter also was wary not to ask leading questions, as much as he might want the control that leading questions provide. If a witness didn't give the answer he expected or wanted, he could refer back to their deposition.

"Remember when you said in your deposition testimony…" Specter wanted the answers to seem as if they were not coerced.

"I don't want to ask them, 'Did you see the red light when you approached the intersection?' and just have them say yes. I want to ask them, 'What color was the light when you approached the intersection?' I want the guy to say, 'Red. The light was red.'"

Chapter 92

Jill D'Angelo, a standards engineer and manager at West Penn Power, was used to giving orders to working men. She was a large woman, stately and imposing, seeming taller than the six-foot-two Specter as she made her way to the witness stand. She appeared stern in a gray jacket worn over a mauve blouse. But when she entered the courtroom from her seclusion in the outer hallway, D'Angelo seemed taken aback.

"Oooh," she sighed somewhat loudly, like a releasing pressure valve, when she came into the courtroom and was struck by the heat and the crowd. A patina of perspiration on her forehead, she walked tentatively to the stand as if trying not to spill the considerable weight of the testimony that rested on her shoulders. When she spoke, it was with the timbre of a little girl.

With D'Angelo, Specter sought to link the blame for Carrie's death from the apparent negligence of linemen working out in the field to what he contended was the "reckless disregard" of those working in the executive offices of West Penn Power. Jill D'Angelo was Specter's bridge from compensatory to punitive damages. But she was, in her fifties and after 31 years with West Penn Power, a veteran and fervent company soldier who would not go down without a fight. She also struck, at least initially, with her soft, tiny voice and blonde hair worn in short bangs, a sympathetic pose. She seemed emotionally vulnerable, almost fragile, and Specter knew—especially with a male attorney questioning a female witness—that he would have to tread lightly to avoid alienating the jury. But Specter was determined to elicit what he needed from Jill D'Angelo—an admission that the company had not done what it could have done to prevent Carrie's death. Armed with D'Angelo's deposition, Specter would not let his witness stray from the truth of her prior testimony. "If she varied, I would impeach her," he would recount later. And he would be polite but firm in doing so.

D'Angelo's testimony would span two days, two grueling days. She would resist surrender on even minor points. And Specter would not relent, trying his best to remain even-tempered, to keep his voice regulated, to be respectful and courteous, but to keep his witness' back against a wall, leaving no escape routes. From the start, the tension was palpable.

"Now Ms. D'Angelo, good afternoon. Thanks for waiting today," Specter began, smiling lightly as the afternoon session got under way. "I know it's been a long day for you."

D'Angelo looked straight ahead, not returning the salutation or the smile.

"Ms. D'Angelo, may I trouble you to pull your chair closer to the microphone, please?" Specter asked. Even on this point she put up a fight.

"Are you having trouble hearing me?"

"Just keep your voice up if you could."

"All right."

"The closer you speak into the microphone, the better." Specter stated, establishing control.

D'Angelo, who had a degree in engineering, was in charge of standards at West Penn Power. This included the standards for splices, also known as connectors.

"And are you the person at West Penn who's most knowledgeable on the subject of the standards with respect to splices?" Specter asked.

"I'm not sure that I can say I'm the most knowledgeable," D'Angelo replied, unwilling to give any ground.

"How about one of the most knowledgeable, would you go for that?"

"I'll go for that, yes."

It was going to be a long couple of days.

Chapter 93

Much of Jill D'Angelo's testimony would revolve around two documents. One was an email that D'Angelo testified she remembered sending to West Penn Power employees—a notice about the importance of wire-brushing power lines before installation—but which she could not produce. The other was an email—detailing three burned power line splices and the discussion about them among herself and several other managers—that West Penn Power had failed to reveal to the plaintiffs and that was produced only the night before her second day of trial testimony.

Specter started by building a foundation for the jury. He flashed a blow-up of the standard in the company manual regarding splice installation. An update had been made in 2000, new language that D'Angelo herself had contributed: "Unclean conductor will set up overheating and eventual failure of the splice." She said the sentence was added at the suggestion of one of the manufacturers after a splice had failed. Another splice had also failed, she acknowledged upon questioning, and "there may have been others" as well. That's why the standard was strengthened.

To communicate the change, to make it known and thus stress its importance, Specter asked, "You need to do more than just put them in that book, I would assume, would that be fair?"

"That's fair."

As an example, Specter asked whether a newsletter was sent out. D'Angelo gave a response dealing with standard changes and cover letters. Specter let her finish, then said, "OK, let's just stick with my questions for a second, which is the newsletters." Did she send one out? he wanted to know.

"I'm not sure that I did," D'Angelo responded.

Not good enough. To Specter, that answer implied that she may not have sent one.

"Well, Ms. D'Angelo, I respect what you're saying when you say, 'I'm not sure that I did,'" though he really did not respect that answer one bit. He handed her a stack of all the company's newsletters from 2002 and defied her to find the one regarding wire installation she might have circulated. She leafed through them slowly. Very slowly. Specter folded his arms and rested against the wooden railing of the jury box as he waited patiently. The jurors watched D'Angelo.

After several long minutes, she looked up. "I don't see one in 2002."

D'Angelo said she thought she had sent a prior newsletter or email in 1999 instructing linemen on proper wire installation. Again, such a newsletter did not appear in the stack Specter had been given before trial. Well, she said, perhaps it had been a cover letter or an email.

"As you sit here today, Ms. D'Angelo, do you recall a specific email that was sent out to all those concerned with…proper conductor preparation in this time period to tell them what they should be doing?"

"I thought I had," she answered in a small voice. She told Specter she had handed over all her emails to Levicoff.

"May I ask you," Specter pushed further, "overnight to take a look at those emails and tab the one that you think refers to that subject, please?"

"That was going to be my idea," Levicoff interjected.

Judge Della Vecchia added: "You go through them and see if you can find this email that you've referenced a couple of times that you believe was sent out on this topic.…"

Specter switched gears for a moment. He asked whether as head of standards and safety, D'Angelo was concerned that several splices had burned and failed. She answered that she had been. Specter pushed.

"Why?"

"Because of the fact we were told [by the manufacturer] that they could fail if they weren't cleaned properly."

"And why would the failure…concern you from a safety perspective?"

"Because if it's in the air, it can come down."

"And if it's energized, it can kill somebody. Is that fair?"

"Yes."

So there had been a potential danger caused by failing splices resulting from improper preparation of wires installed into splices, caused perhaps by failure to clean the wires with a wire brush. The company installation standard had been changed with several new lines in the thick standards book, yet no newsletter or email had been circulated, at least any that could be found.

Specter next asked if the linemen who had installed the failed splices had been identified. No, D'Angelo responded, they had not.

Had the company used the incidence of these failed splices as an opportunity for a "teaching moment"? Specter seemed to dip slightly into condescension with his next question: "Do you know this concept of a teaching moment? Have you ever heard that phrase, a 'teaching moment'?"

D'Angelo made a face. "I can understand what you're saying, yes."

"OK. In other words, something bad happens. You bring the person in front of you and you tell them the bad thing that happened and maybe there will be a consequence, too, is that right? That would be a teaching moment."

"OK."

"Did you see to it that the linemen were told that the splices that they had installed had failed because apparently of improper installation technique?"

"No."

Enough for one day. It was 4 p.m. and the judge agreed to pick things up the next morning.

Chapter 94

At dinner that night, Guerrini asked Specter what kind of a settlement offer he'd like to see from West Penn Power—how much the utility needed to put on the table to get him to play ball.

"What would it take to get your serious interest?"

"Thirty million."

"I agree," the younger lawyer responded, "but I don't think they're going to get there."

Specter raised one eyebrow and answered with a wry smile. "Right," he said, but the word did not mean that he agreed, just that he had heard what Guerrini had said, which he then pretty much ignored.

"If they offer somewhere in the $30 million to $40 million range, then Mike Goretzka would say, 'What do you think, Mr. Specter?' And I would say, 'Let's see what the remedial steps are.'"

In other words, the monetary range was one that Specter believed the power company would eventually get to. And one he was willing to consider.

He could not have predicted at the time, not remotely, the crazy ride the settlement talks were going to take. Never mind the ultimate conclusion.

Chapter 95

"Ms. D'Angelo, good morning."

Whether she had softened or had been advised by counsel, this time the witness returned the greeting. Specter reminded D'Angelo of where they had left off the day before, with her promise to search overnight for the email she said she may have sent alerting linemen about the importance of proper wire-cleaning using a metal brush. He wanted to know—"and please keep your voice up," he instructed—if she had been successful in finding it.

"And was there any such email?"

D'Angelo replied that she had not found one, but that she did discover an interim update to the company manual. Specter stopped her.

"Let's just deal with the first issue of this alleged email, if I could, all right?" Specter emphasized the word "alleged" only slightly, but perceptibly. "Was there any such email of the type we've been discussing?"

"I did not find any mass communication specifically about that statement letting everyone know that this is a change."

"OK. And this was the document that yesterday you did think you sent out, correct?"

"Well, I thought I would have sent something out close to that time."

"Because this was a very important issue, the issue of making sure there's proper conductor preparation was a very important matter for public safety, correct?"

"It is an important issue."

"Yeah," finished Specter. Not a question.

He moved to another issue, the fact that in 2004, West Penn Power received three failed splices from the field. All had apparently overheated. The splices were made by Hubbell, the same manufacturer of the splices that fell on the Goretzka property. They had been sent to Hubbell for inspection, and the manufacturer had reported back that poor cleaning of the wire probably started the problem that caused at least one of the splice failures and possibly all three. From the witness stand, Jill D'Angelo acknowledged that this information had been shared with her and others at West Penn Power, including Haven Bearley, her boss and the manager of the standards department at the time, now retired.

Specter quoted Bearley in an email as saying: "The majority of our automatic splice failures have been attributed to poor conductor preparation and improper splice installation."

Despite her boss' statement and Hubbell's assessment that poor cleaning likely caused the splice failures, D'Angelo still stubbornly refused to say that improper cleaning resulted in the three splices failing.

"Did you think they were wrong?" Specter asked, referring to Bearley and Hubbell.

"Well, I don't know if they were absolutely correct."

"OK. Well, did you send the evidence to somebody else for them to assess it?"

"No."

D'Angelo did agree with Specter that getting word out about properly cleaning wires before installation would have been important. Specter ticked off what she could have done to ensure that occurred—updating the standard in the "Bible," sending out a newsletter, having a training video for the linemen to watch, and then he ran out of things. Nothing else had been done. But steps could have been taken, couldn't they? Couldn't a meeting of the company's linemen, all 800 if necessary, have been convened to stress the critical nature of proper cleaning and installation? Did D'Angelo ever address the linemen?

"No, I haven't," she said.

Did she or Bearley address the employees at the company's service centers? No. Could they have tested the linemen on proper cleaning and installation procedures? Yes. And did they? No.

The email conversation among D'Angelo, Bearley and two other company managers—Frank Gogol and Larry Renner, a linemen manager—took place about two months before the power line fell at the Goretzka property in June 2004, burning the lawn. D'Angelo had been apprised of the incident.

Before going any further, Specter wanted to know about the Notice to Attend that the plaintiffs had sent to D'Angelo, a document ordering her not only to show up for court, but also to turn over all relevant documents in her possession before that appearance. The emails involving her, Bearley, Gogol and Renner had not been among the documents.

Q: OK. Now, did you produce this document to your attorney?

A: Yes.

Q: When?

A: Some time ago.

Q: Can you give me an idea as to when that was?

A: A couple months maybe.

Q: A couple months ago. Do you know when we got it?

A: When did you get it?

Q: I'm asking you. Do you know when we got it?

A: Last night.

Q: Yeah, last night...right. This should have been given to us when you appeared yesterday in court. Correct?

(The witness nodded.)

Q: You have to answer verbally, ma'am.

A: Yes.

Back to the emails. In one sent by Jill D'Angelo to three people—Larry Renner, a lines manager, and copied to her supervisor in the Safety and Standards Department, Frank Gogol, and the manager of the department, Haven Bearley—she noted that one failed splice they looked at, a relatively new device made in 2003, "was not cleaned properly prior to installation." She also noted that "the importance of thoroughly cleaning the conductor prior to installation of an automatic splice or any other connector cannot be overstressed...." Specter seized on the word.

Q: And you say: It can't be overstressed. Right?

A: Correct.

Q: It can't be said too many times, right, especially to the men?

A: Correct.

Q: They have to know that?

A: Correct.

Q: Because if the line fails, a live energized line can kill somebody. Right?

A: Correct.

Q: It would have been very easy to figure out who were the men that installed that splice, wouldn't it have been?

A: I suppose so.

Q: Right. And get them in front of you and tell them, "Gentlemen, you installed this splice, you did so incorrectly. This splice failed. We're lucky that nobody died as a result of that, but somebody could have." That all could have been done, correct?

A: Correct.

But it wasn't done, as D'Angelo had to acknowledge. That was not her job, she told Specter, though she acknowledged it would have been, should have been, someone's responsibility.

Specter had more questions for this witness, but he felt that D'Angelo, her answers less combative now, might be nearing a breaking point. He felt that she had been a "bad actor" in this incident, that her actions—inactions, really—and those of other West Penn Power managers had caused Carrie's death. And now she was the company point person to defend West Penn Power in court. Specter felt the jury would see D'Angelo the way he did. Still, as he looked at her now, glassy-eyed and her voice muted, he did not want the tables reversed. He did not want those eyes to spill over or the voice to crack. He did not want to seem mean to the jury. He asked the court for a brief recess.

After the break, Specter moved to the incident at the Goretzkas' house. He wanted to know Jill D'Angelo's actions after the tragedy. Yes, she responded to a question, she was aware that the wire had fallen on a clear and sunny day and that the failure was not the result of a storm or a car crash or other traumatic event. And she agreed that the incident was of "the utmost seriousness"—Specter's words—because West Penn Power had never had someone killed as the result of a fallen line since she had started working there. And yes, as the person in charge of splices at West Penn Power, she had seen photos of the splice where it had remained on the wire near the top of the pole.

Q: OK. And what did you think...?

A: I just wondered what exactly happened.

Q: Did you ask?

A: I don't think anyone would know at that point.

Q: You were in charge of splices at West Penn Power. Correct?

A: Correct.

Q: It appeared that a splice had failed. Correct?

A: Correct.

Q: One of your splices?

A: One of the splices that we saw, yes.

Q: Does that mean one of yours, right?

A: If you want to call it mine.

Q: Did you investigate what happened?

A: No.

D'Angelo said she never inspected the splice, and that she never asked to see it. But at one point she finally did see the failed device. And when was that?

"When we met with counsel for the first time," she told Specter. The inference was clear: not until after her company was sued over Carrie's death.

Chapter 96

Levicoff injected some levity into the trial whenever he got the chance. Perhaps it was an attempt to nudge the jury on a personal level, to get its members to like him and, by extension, his client. Or perhaps it was simply a good-natured, keen sense of humor that even the sober proceedings couldn't suppress.

One such opportunity arose when Specter questioned D'Angelo about whether she had sent the email about proper splice installation to "the broad diaspora of the folks in charge of the linemen and the linemen themselves."

Levicoff couldn't help himself. He rose from his chair.

"Your Honor, I have to object," he said, chuckling. "All my career, I've been waiting to object to a question with the phrase raw diaspora."

"Broad diaspora," Specter corrected him, smiling too.

"Broad diaspora. And I seize the opportunity! I'm not sure what that question means."

Judge Della Vecchia knew the meaning. "Diaspora means the spread, you know...People spread out," he said, then looked toward Specter. "I understand your question to be saying all the employees, something like that."

"All the employees for whom this would be a relevant topic, yes."

Levicoff took his seat. "That's better," he said.

Chapter 97

Avrum Levicoff kept Jill D'Angelo on the stand only a little longer, a matter of minutes compared to the many hours over two days that she had spent answering questions from Specter. By this time, D'Angelo seemed worn out, her voice trailing off into a whisper at times.

"My hearing is very poor," Levicoff told her, imploring her to speak up. "If I can hear you, I know the jury can hear you."

His goal appeared to show the jury that, despite the obvious hindsight, it would have been hard, at least in the early 2000s, for D'Angelo to have foreseen the tragedy to come.

Levicoff's first question went to the failed splice that had prompted her newsletter. He established three things right off: (1) that the splice was made by MacLean/Reliable, not Hubbell; (2) that the line was copper; and (3) that the manufacturer had acknowledged a defect in the splice, and that the profile of the clamping metal jaws, or teeth, had been out of specification. He also established that the failed splice that had inspired the 2000 company manual change had been a failure involving a copper wire and a splice used for copper wires. And that copper wires can form "very, very hard" copper oxides that make it difficult for the splice teeth to take hold. The implication: All these factors pointed to a situation very different from what occurred at the Goretzkas' house, where the line was made by Hubbell and was aluminum.

"Had we had any...failures to that point in time of the aluminum automatic cable splice?" he asked.

"No."

And later: "Have we had any burndown failures of aluminum as of 2000?

"No."

Levicoff asked if there had been any burndown incidents between 1999 and 2004 involving aluminum stranded wires.

"No."

In fact, the only evidence of a problem was the three burned splices that showed up in the office and had become the subject of emails among

D'Angelo and other managers, and nobody said they knew where they had come from or if they had even caused a wire to fall.

While Specter had sought to stress that company managers should have done more to investigate and prevent splice failures, Levicoff sought to stress that failed splices, and especially burndowns, were a rarity that managers could hardly be expected to anticipate, never mind prevent.

"By the way," Levicoff asked, "do you know on an order of magnitude—I don't mean the precise number—but do you know how many of these [splices] we have obtained and put in use?"

D'Angelo did not have a precise number, but she had searched the utility's purchasing information from 1997 to 2007 and had come up with a pretty good idea for the 10-year period. The number was quite large.

"It was, I think, over a million."

"A million?" asked Levicoff, evidently wishing the jury to hear the number twice.

"Yes."

Chapter 98

Killing animals wasn't enough for Thomas Edison and his crew. The New York legislature had approved the use of electricity to execute prisoners, and Edison set out to facilitate the state's death penalty. In 1888, he hired an inventor named Harold Brown to create an electrical device to kill humans with alternating current. Brown and an assistant came up with the electric chair.

Edison's goal was, as always, to show the public the dangers of the AC power being developed by his competitor George Westinghouse and the relatively safe nature of direct current power. He had already demonstrated this with public executions of animals, using a Westinghouse AC generator attached to a metal plate to kill strays. These executions resulted in the coining (by reporters who covered the killings) of a new word—"electrocution." Brown and his team sought to show that alternating current would also quickly end the life of a human being. The assumption was that people wouldn't want the same power source in their homes that was used to put convicted felons to death.

The first law providing for execution by electricity went into effect shortly afterward, on January 1, 1889, after Edison and Brown had testified before a government committee that the electric chair provided a form of death that was painless. George Westinghouse protested, even funding appeals by inmates. But the electric chair became New York's means of execution and, despite the opposition of the namesake himself, the act even became known for some years as being "Westinghoused."

Chapter 99

Unlike all the other experts at the Goretzka trial, John Lally had no opinions. Just facts. Lally was a certified public accountant who owned his own firm in nearby Sharon, Pennsylvania. In his mid-fifties, he often testified at trials to offer a cold and calculating assessment to one question: What is a person's life worth? Literally.

In this case, Lally's job was to determine not the pain and suffering felt by Carrie or the emotional loss suffered by her family, but the economic loss resulting from her death. How much would her net earnings have been worth over the course of her lifetime? Lally eschewed emotion, using only numbers and mathematical equations to arrive at his conclusions. He based his estimates on four things. The first three were the loss of Carrie's potential lifetime income, lost fringe benefits and the value of her household services. He added those three factors and then subtracted the fourth, which was the cost for her personal maintenance—basic food, clothing, utilities, transportation and the like. He made three models based on how long Carrie might have been expected to live. Which model the jurors accepted, if any, was up to them.

Questioned by Baldwin, Lally told the jury that Carrie had earned an associate degree at Allegheny County Community College and had worked for a few years at a post-hospital nursing care facility and later for nine years at Omnicare, a nationwide provider of medication, nursing and assisted-living care. Carrie had worked in the billing department, starting at an annual salary of about $19,000 and working her way up to a supervisory position that paid $62,000. She had had a bright future, earning "exceptional" performance reviews from her bosses, before leaving to take care of her young children. She had planned to return to work when her youngest started school.

John Lally seemed to have constructed a fairly conservative estimate of Carrie's future income. He had her not returning to the workforce for six years and then at a salary of only 80 percent of what she had earned when she left Omnicare. Baldwin had Lally run down all his calculations and concluded by asking him to give his three different totals for Carrie's economic loss. The first was based on the supposition that she would have worked until she was about 60. The amount was $2,630,533. The number rose to $3,362,583 if she had worked until age 65. And had she worked until she reached 70, the value of her lost earnings, benefits and household services minus personal costs totaled $4,359,816.

Lally's testimony went uncontested. The defense had no questions.

Chapter 100

Specter decided not to call the Goretzka children to the witness stand. Carlie was too young. He felt that Chloe could handle the experience and that it would be helpful to have the jury experience her pain firsthand. But it was also a possible hazard to the children's well-being. He didn't want to cause them any more harm—and he didn't want the jury to think he was willing to take that chance. Their testimony could do more harm than good. "The jury might resent me and even Mike Goretzka for putting a child on the stand," Specter explained to Kila Baldwin at one point. "They might think, 'why put a child through that?'" But he didn't want them to go entirely unseen either. The children were at once cute and sorrowful. Chloe especially appeared to carry a burden on her small shoulders, her sorrow captured in her reticence, the way she withdrew slightly from strangers, her eyes wary.

Specter had discussed his quandary with Don Matusow, a veteran lawyer in his firm. Matusow proposed a middle ground: show the jury the children, but do not put them through the rigors of testifying. Specter decided to bring the girls into court very briefly when their father began his testimony. He would ask Mike Goretzka first about his children.

Chloe was eight years old now with brown hair, brown eyes and a serious countenance. Carlie was blonde with brown eyes and, at six years old, more of a carefree spirit, full of energy and a bit of a rascal. She smiled a lot more than her sister, perhaps because she had been younger at the time of the tragedy and had remembered and understood less of what her eyes had seen.

On this day, the children had been waiting since 10 a.m. to make their appearance in the front row of the courtroom while their father took the stand as the plaintiffs' last witness. It was now 2 p.m. and they were still waiting, Chloe in a black dress with a shiny silver headband and Carlie in a gray dress with her hair done up in a bun. To fill the time, they had been taken a few blocks from the courthouse to a Macy's department store to see Santa Claus. They both told him they wanted a puppy for Christmas.

"Tell us about Chloe," Specter said to Mike Goretzka. As he spoke, the jurors looked at the children.

"She's a little bit of a wild spirit. She gives Daddy a little bit of a run for his money," answered Goretzka, smiling at his older daughter, who smiled back. "She likes to go into Daddy's work on the weekends and play on the copier and make a nice big mess for Daddy. She's also my helper. She helps me with Carlie. She helps me to get Carlie ready, helps me get Carlie dressed, helps me get Carlie's hair done, and Daddy really counts on her."

Carlie, he said, liked to play, to color, and to sing and dance. "She loves Sunday dinner. That's steak night at our house. She gets all excited on Sundays. She loves to cuddle, loves to lay with Daddy. I love her to death, both of them." He looked at his children and smiled at them.

"Did you feel it was important to have the jury meet your girls?" Specter asked.

"Yes."

"Why is that?"

"They're more affected by this than anybody, you know. They don't have their mother. Nobody sees a lot of what we go through, what we've been through the last three and a half years."

A relative took the children out of the courtroom at this point. Specter didn't want them present for what was to come next.

Chapter 101

Mike Goretzka, dark-haired, medium height with a solid build, and Carrie, a blonde with a radiant smile, had met in high school. He liked her and thought she was pretty, very pretty. But he was too shy to ask her out. Then luck intervened: Mike needed hernia surgery.

"I asked her if she could pick me up and take me home till I was able to drive again" since Carrie lived near his house, Mike told the jury, grinning at the recollection of his ploy. "I thought that would be an opportunity to get to know her better." He eventually got the courage to ask Carrie on a real date. They dated through the end of high school and throughout college and, five and a half years after that first date, Mike asked Carrie to marry him, which she did three years later.

"So you had a long engagement?" Specter noted.

"I'm sort of a planner," said Mike. He explained that first he had wanted to get his finance degree from Duquesne University, pay off his student loans and have enough money to put 20 percent down on a house. Since high school, he had labored part-time side by side with his father, a working man of German descent, doing custodial work—scrubbing floors, painting, shoveling snow and whatever else was needed—at the 170-employee Family Home Hospice. Mike later got a job with the company's accounting office, then was promoted to head the finance department and eventually was named senior vice president. He and Carrie married on May 4, 1996, and moved into their new home in West Hempfield.

"It just took a little bit of time," Mike told the jury. "I'm glad she put up with me."

It was a nice story. But everyone in the courtroom knew it had an unhappy ending.

Specter shifted slowly into unpleasant territory, asking about the power line and the previous time it had fallen, in 2004, when it burned the Goretzkas' lawn. Mike recalled how he came home from work one day, looked out his kitchen window and saw an eight-foot-long burn mark in his lawn in the shape of a fish hook. (Specter flashed up a photo showing the scorched lawn.) The line had been repaired but not his property, nor had he been given any explanation. "Nobody told me. Nobody called. Nobody tried to contact me."

Mike Goretzka did get a call from a power company claims adjuster saying that he could be reimbursed for his repairs to the damaged property. But, he told the jury, "I wasn't concerned about the damages. I wanted an answer [about] why the line came down twice." A neighbor told him it had also fallen in 2003, though without causing damage, so that first incident went largely unnoticed. Then Specter asked Goretzka about the last time the line fell. Goretzka grimaced and inhaled deeply.

I was at my desk. It was 4:43 in the afternoon. I got a phone call. It was my neighbor, Ron Molnar...and he told me that I needed to get home right away. And I said, 'What happened, Ron?' You know, he says, 'You need to get home right away. There's been a terrible accident.' And I said, 'You've got to tell me. Is it the kids? Did something happen to the kids?' And he said, 'No, you just need to get home.' And I kept pushing him, and I said, 'You've got to tell me what happened.' And he said, 'Your wife's outside. She's been electrocuted.'

Goretzka dropped the phone, ran out to his pickup truck and sped home. The first thing he saw when he got close was a helicopter "and I knew then it was bad." Carrie was in an ambulance. He ran to the vehicle but "they wouldn't let me see her, and I said, 'You're not going to stop me!'"

So when the EMT let me into the side of the ambulance, she was on a stretcher, her shirt was peeled back, burnt off and...she just made a moaning, horrific moaning, groaning. It didn't even sound human.

Mike Goretzka, his face contorted like a tight fist, wiped his eyes with his fingers as he continued his testimony. His sister Carol and his mother wept silently as did others in the audience. He told how he went to his wife's side and tried to say something encouraging, even though he could see she was badly injured. "I told her, 'Don't give up on me. You've got to fight. You've got to fight for them two little girls," he remembered, openly crying now, snorting out the words. "You got to fight."

In an interview with Specter before the trial, the MedEvac helicopter technician remembered sensing that Goretzka comprehended the gravity of his wife's condition. He kissed Carrie and then asked the tech if she was going to die. "I told him, 'It's in God's hands now.'"

The helicopter didn't have room for him, so he went to see his daughters at his neighbor's house. As soon as he walked in the door, they jumped on him. "And they asked me if everything was going to be OK, and I said, 'I don't know.'"

At the hospital, Goretzka paced back and forth as he waited for the doctors to emerge and tell him about his wife. When they did, they told him that her situation was dire. They had had to amputate her arm because, he recalled them telling him, "it was down to the bone, had become mummified."

Carrie died three days later. His wife's pain was over. Mike Goretzka's had just begun.

"I was overwhelmed with grief," he testified.

He didn't know how to take care of his children. "I didn't know what to do. I didn't know how to comfort them. I didn't know how to comfort myself."

He felt terrible loss, and guilt for somehow not having protected Carrie. Over time, a long time, things got somewhat better. His family helped with the girls when Mike went to work. He buried himself in his job. He stopped going to bars after work. He spent more time with his children, as much as he could.

Goretzka recognized that he likely would never have another child, the son that he'd always wanted.

"Let's talk about you for a minute," Specter interjected. "What are you going to do for yourself, Mike? You're a young man." He was now 43.

"It's not about me right now."

"But you are a human, and you are alive, and you have a long life to live. So what are you going to do about yourself?"

"I don't have an answer," he replied, flushed with embarrassment. Mike Goretzka was a man who was uncomfortable talking about himself. "Right now it's my girls."

Specter noted it had been three and a half years since Carrie's death. He tried to lighten the mood just a little bit. "You're a fine-looking man, if I may say so. Have you had friends talk to you about meeting some of their friends?"

"Yeah, a lot of people ask me. I decline."

"Have you had a date?"

"No."

"Have you considered having a date?"

"No."

Several jurors were weeping now, blowing their noses and removing glasses to wipe their eyes. Specter was close to the end, but he wanted to know one more thing, he wanted to extract what Mike Goretzka envisioned for his future and his family's future. The lawyer knew from his experience that juries could handle sadness that victims brought to courtrooms, but that they also wanted to see some sign that things could get better.

"Do you have hope for the future?"

"I have hope for the girls."

"Tell us why."

"Because I made a promise, a promise I intend to fulfill."

"And what's that promise?"

"I made a promise to Carrie that I'll protect them, that I'll love them, and I won't let them fail. I won't let them fail."

The defense had no questions for the witness.

Chapter 102

Before the defense began its case, a number of matters had to be cleared up. One involved whether the jury would be permitted to see photos of Carrie's injuries. Levicoff renewed an earlier objection to showing the jury any photographs of Carrie at the hospital or at her autopsy. Specter took a contrary view. The photos were horrible, but he said it was necessary for the jurors to have them available if they wanted to see them, if they felt it necessary. Not only should the jurors be able to bear witness to the extent of Carrie's injuries, but the photos also provided what Specter felt was physical evidence that Carrie bore none of the burden of negligence: The defense had theorized that the victim used her left hand to contact the live wire, yet, as one photo showed, Carrie's left hand had remained relatively intact.

Specter's plan was not to show the photos in open court—and risk seeming too bracingly gruesome and perhaps alienating the jury—but to have several available in a sealed envelope at the time the testimony was finished and the jury went into deliberations. If some jurors wanted to look at the photos, they could. If they didn't want to look, they didn't have to. Levicoff didn't want the photos entered at all.

The judge compromised, allowing three photographs to be made available to the jurors. "I think they have, they being the jury, have a right to see what this poor soul endured," Della Vecchia stated, then looked at Levicoff and hastily added, "I'm not saying it was your fault, West Penn's fault, no judgment on that. But I think for damage purposes they have the right to see that."

Chapter 103

After Mike Goretzka's testimony, Judge Della Vecchia met with Specter alone in his chambers. He relayed a new offer from West Penn and their insurance carriers. It was $25 million. Specter gave the news to Baldwin and Guerrini. He also noted that the primary excess insurance carrier, AEGIS, had expressed a keen interest in using a settlement tactic that Specter rarely employed—the "high-low." It allowed the sides to set a maximum and a minimum they would pay in the event of a verdict. The arrangement reduced the risk for both sides. Specter initially opposed such an idea, telling his colleagues: "Every time I've entered into a high-low agreement, it's been a mistake."

In this case, the high-low had a benefit that was more than financial. It would get Specter—and, maybe more importantly, Mike Goretzka—a verdict. The case would not conclude with a whimper in the form of a settlement, and probably a confidential one that would allow West Penn Power to escape public and media scrutiny. Instead, the case would end with a bang, at least Specter hoped so. And, incidentally, a high-low provided a guarantee against what was now becoming more inconceivable: a verdict for the defense and nothing for the Goretzka family.

Specter didn't love the idea of a high-low, but the concept had its pluses: "It's protection against an irrational verdict, either too high or too low." But he didn't want a deal to be overly protective for the power company. Specter guessed that since West Penn Power was now offering $25 million, it would get back to him with a high-low of $15 million to $40 million, which he wouldn't be willing to accept. He was all right with a $15 million bottom, but he didn't like the idea of limiting West Penn Power's financial exposure to $40 million. It could go much higher, especially if there were punitive damages in the case. So Specter rejected any notion of a high-low arrangement in the Goretzka case.

It was personal history talking as much a calculation. In one previous case, he had agreed to a high-low with a $10 million high, only to win a $24 million verdict. In another, he accepted a $7.5 million limit on damages and won a $19 million verdict. And in yet another, he had agreed to a maximum $23 million, only to hear a jury deliver a verdict of $57 million.

"But you can't engage in seller's remorse," Specter maintained. The prior cases had taught him his lesson, and won him the confidence of his convictions. In many other cases since those three, he had rejected multi-million-dollar settlement offers only to obtain larger offers or larger verdicts later on. His intuition was generally correct in these matters, though, he knew from experience, not always.

Chapter 104

Court ended early for the day, and the judge summoned Levicoff and Specter to his chambers to try once again to settle the case. Settlements minimized risk for both sides and shortened arduous cases. For the plaintiffs, they also avoided lengthy appeals that could occur if they won verdicts. These trips by the lawyers to Judge Della Vecchia's chambers were becoming commonplace. After only a few minutes, Levicoff walked out, put on his coat, and gave a half smile and a wave good-bye to no one in particular as he made his exit. Specter remained with the judge.

Progress was being made toward a settlement. Specter was told that the total offer now stood at $40 million, or it could be. There was no official offer, but Della Vecchia had been given the clear impression from Levicoff that West Penn Power was willing to cough up an additional $10 million of its own money to make the case go away.

The finances worked like this: In the event of a large verdict, West Penn Power would be responsible for the first $5 million as a deductible. Its primary insurance company, AEGIS, would have to cover the next $35 million. Then an excess policy held with a secondary insurer, Energy Insurance Mutual (EIM), covered the next $75 million, or up to a total of $115 million. But for a settlement, the equation could differ. So far, according to what Specter had been told, AEGIS, which had a representative at the trial throughout, had only been willing to part with $20 million, or a total settlement of $25 million, counting the company's deductible. But now, Levicoff indicated that West Penn Power would consider kicking in $15 million more, raising the total to $40 million. Specter recalled Levicoff putting it to him directly, though without any concrete promise: "If the company put in $15 million, making the total $40 million, would you take it?" Specter said he would not.

It was a pretty hard number to turn down, but Specter was not willing to close such a deal. There was no reason, in his mind, why AEGIS shouldn't fork over its full $35 million coverage. Or why the secondary insurer, EIM, should not step in with a contribution even though its secondary policy didn't kick in until $40 million was reached and exceeded. After all, EIM could be on the hook for any verdict greater than $40 million.

Weeks earlier, Della Vecchia had told Specter in private that he felt the case was "worth" $40 million to $45 million. His view had not changed over the course of the trial, he added. The judge said he felt $40 million was reasonable. He sat back in his chair and grinned as he waited for Specter's response. When there was none, he looked at Specter and guessed what was on his mind. "You want 50, don't you?" the judge asked.

"Yeah," the lawyer replied, "you're right."

Later, when Specter mentioned the proposal to Mike Goretzka, his client raised an eyebrow. It was a lot of money, $40 million. But Specter and Goretzka had agreed before the trial started that their goal was $50 million.

"Let's keep going," Mike Goretzka told his attorney.

Chapter 105

Before the weekend, Specter sent Levicoff an email with a bunch of attachments, all of them newspaper articles about the Motiva case, which had produced a $36.4 million settlement from the Delaware refinery, which was believed to be the largest-ever settlement in the state for one injured worker. Motiva had similarities to the Goretzka case, namely that a single person suffered a singularly horrible death. Motiva brought a huge settlement and, Specter felt, Goretzka was heading in the same direction. He wanted it to keep going that way.

"Here are the articles, etc. on the $36.4 million Motiva settlement," Specter wrote in his email to Levicoff, sparing any embellishment. He added a note, though, that Delaware did not allow punitive damages in wrongful death cases. Pennsylvania did.

Chapter 106

On Saturday, December 1, Specter received an email from Levicoff.

"There was a conference call with both AEGIS and EIM yesterday. AEGIS is entrenched at $25 mil. EIM thinks that is a 'reasonable' offer. My client will make a decision Monday as to what it will do if the insurers do not move from the current posture."

Specter did not respond to Levicoff. He passed the offer on to Baldwin and Guerrini with just one word: "nota." Latin for "noted."

To Specter, the fact that West Penn Power was considering a move beyond its insurers' offer was a good sign, proof that the power company was willing to throw in more of its own money. An hour after getting Levicoff's note, he confided to several colleagues that he felt a settlement was very likely. He wrote: "There probably won't be a verdict."

Chapter 107

The first thing said by Michael Paul Thornburg, known affectionately in the West Hempfield neighborhood he served as Mike the Mailman, was an obvious untruth.

"Are you comfortable?" Avrum Levicoff asked the first witness called by the defense.

"Yes, sir."

Clearly, Thornburg, 58, was anything but comfortable. Out of uniform and wearing an olive-colored shirt with a jacket and tie, he looked nervous. Worse really, he looked scared. He seemed tense and his eyes were opened wide like those of a frightened animal. Compounding that image was the fact that Thornburg had a somewhat high, muffled voice, making him sound a bit like the muppet Kermit the Frog.

"I'm a letter carrier for the U.S. Postal Service," said Thornburg, noting he would soon celebrate his 27th anniversary there.

Although he had been close with the Goretzkas and felt terrible about Carrie's death—and undoubtedly would want to help the family —Thornburgh was called as a witness not by Specter but by the defense. There was good reason. Mike the Mailman injected doubt into the plaintiffs' theory of the incident, specifically that Carrie was unaware of the danger above when she walked into her side yard.

Levicoff wanted Thornburg on the stand to bring out one fact, a fact that was very important to the defense—that Thornburg had been working around the corner when he saw a "fireball" in the vicinity of the Goretzka house, then heard screams for help from JoAnn Goretzka. The crucial thing was the timing—fireball first, screams second. This, according to the defense theory, meant two things: that Carrie should have seen the eruption of fire and stayed away from the fallen power line, and that she had not. It made her appear at least partly responsible for her own injuries.

Using a large satellite photograph of the neighborhood and a laser pointer, Levicoff determined Thornburg's position at the time and established that he had had a "line of sight" to the Goretzka household. Then, he said, "Tell the jury what happened."

"I was either in my truck or just getting in my truck. I saw a huge ball of fire, [then] a big plume of smoke. And either at the same time or within seconds after that I heard someone yelling, 'Help! Please help!'"

The fireball and the screams happened "within seconds," Thornburg noted. Pressed about which came first, he answered, "My best recollection is fire and then the smoke and then the screams."

A critical matter. The order of events seemed to back the defense contention that the fire, seen from two blocks away by Thornburg near "the right front corner of the Goretzka household," should have been even more readily apparent to Carrie. And she should have avoided the area.

Specter sought to undo any possible damage to his case on cross-examination. At least, he wanted to cast some doubt on the order of events as recalled by Thornburg. The witness acknowledged that he was a "little nervous," and he started choking up as he remembered Carrie, whom he described to the jury as "utterly fantastic."

"Every time you saw the girl, she had a smile on her face, and she was a loving mother with those kids...Every time you saw them, they were out in the yard playing. The three of them were inseparable."

"Now," asked Specter, "would you agree as a general matter that a person's memory of what occurs is sharpest closest to the day and time those things occur?"

"Probably, yes, sir," came the reply.

Then he showed Thornburg a copy of the Pennsylvania State Police report and his statement made about an hour after the tragedy. The statement suggested that he heard the scream first and saw the fire second. But asked again which came first, he said, "In my best recollection, it was the fire first and then the screams."

Next, Specter pointed to page 18, line three of Thornburg's deposition testimony taken in September 2011, more than a year before trial. It read: "As soon as I got back in my truck, I heard someone screaming and yelling, 'Please help! Please come, help me!'...And...I saw a huge ball of fire and then a big plume of smoke just like that."

"So," Specter continued, "when you have recounted this for official purposes before today, the order of things was screaming and then ball of fire. But now it's fire and then screaming. Is that fair?"

"Yes, sir, it's fair...It happened so fast."

Chapter 108

Shanin Specter never lost his cool. Well, almost never.

During intense negotiations, pressure-packed cross-examinations, even while waiting for verdicts in colossal cases while juries deliberated, Specter remained calm while others fretted or wilted. But the Goretzka case began taking a toll even on this most unruffled of combatants.

Specter's meltdown came at the expense of Joe Starkey, the West Penn Power internal corporate lawyer who had largely been a bystander at the trial and who, midway through the proceedings, Specter had referred to with apparent affection. Speaking to the jury, he had pointed out Starkey among the audience members in the courtroom as "the good-looking gentleman with the moustache and the goatee." Specter had smiled at Starkey when he made the reference, and Starkey had smiled back. But that was then, and this was near the end of the trial, a time when fatigue and stress won out over fraternal civility and good will toward men.

It was a time when Joe Starkey decided, during a recess, to walk past the wooden railing separating the audience from the players and pull a chair up next to Specter at the plaintiffs' table. It also came just after Avrum Levicoff had pressed his motion for a directed verdict on the claim that Carrie had brought death upon herself. Specter didn't think twice about the unsuccessful motion, but Levicoff's words kept ringing in his client's ears: "The power line didn't basically come after her. She positioned herself close enough to it to come into contact with it." Mike Goretzka had been angry to the point of tears.

Perhaps Starkey felt that a settlement was near at hand and he could buddy up to Specter. He began to discuss something to do with the terms for remediation, for West Penn Power to inspect its lines. Specter was in no mood. He would not remember later what exactly sparked it, but suddenly the few remaining people in the courtroom—the jury had been excused— bore witness to an unusual outburst.

"Get out of here!" Specter shouted.

Joe Starkey refused to leave, insisting on speaking with Specter. But he was having no part of it.

"Get out of here!" he shouted again, louder this time. Baldwin looked up quizzically from her paperwork in the very rear of the courtroom. The eruption was very atypical for Specter, and awkward for the few lawyers and spectators remaining in the courtroom. "You're in my work area. Now get out of here!"

Starkey, red-faced, still wouldn't budge. A stalemate. Either that or Starkey was too shocked to move a muscle. Specter looked him in the eye, their faces inches apart. "You're really going to sit there when I asked you to leave?"

Starkey stared back, immovable. Specter did not blink either. Two men looked like they were about to come to blows in the middle of the courtroom. Finally, Specter turned his chair away and his back toward Starkey, who waited a few beats before getting up and walking away.

Chapter 109

James Beasley had been having a bad day in court. The way Shanin Specter's late mentor and boss had told the story, he had an expert witness on the stand who was "getting his ass kicked" on cross-examination. So rather than try to blunt the damage with objections or interruptions, Beasley took another tack. Positioned adjacent to the jury, he picked up one of the impeccably sharpened pencils from the neatly arranged row on his desk and proceeded to attempt to balance it on its pointed end. An impossible feat, to be sure. He would hold the pencil vertically and steady and then let go, watching the wooden utensil fall each and every time. A couple of the jurors watched Beasley. Then a few more. Did he see one juror nudge another to look over? Most of the jurors soon were diverting their eyes from the witness and watching Beasley and his ridiculous balancing act. But the legendary courtroom master, who had won Philadelphia's first million-dollar verdict and many more thereafter, had a purpose other than redirecting the jury's concentration. He was sending a message: "This testimony is unimportant." After he won the case, Beasley spoke with members of the jury.

"What did you think of my expert?" he asked.

"We didn't think he did very well," one juror replied. "But we didn't think it mattered because you weren't even paying attention."

"I don't know if the story was true or false," Specter would say many years later. But he remembered it. Which was why he did something more radical than try to balance a pencil on its point when the defense presented the transcribed testimony—actually a deposition for purposes of trial—of expert Richard Nigel Hampton. Specter left the courtroom.

"I left because I wanted the jury to know that it wasn't important."

It probably didn't help the defense much that Levicoff and the judge also walked out after a little while. According to one account, Levicoff was upset at a technical snafu that had prevented the witness from testifying live via a satellite hook-up. The reading of prior testimony was, by comparison, a pretty bland affair.

Nevertheless, the defense gave it the old college try with Liz Deemer asking the questions and another attorney, John K. Gisleson, reciting from a transcript the answers that Hampton had given in prior testimony. The whole thing had the feel of a high school play. And not a good one. If Deemer's questioning was monotonal, Gisleson, a handsome young lawyer with a booming voice, offered a relatively melodramatic rendition, his sentences rising and falling in a somewhat over-the-top fashion. Like Al Pacino doing King Lear. The overall performance took on a tone that was at once hypnotically dull and oddly comical.

Two jurors smirked. Another two, recognizing in short order that the man on the stand was not the real thing, looked off into space. A few others looked down with one, after a time, appearing to have fallen asleep.

Meanwhile, the words of the expert Richard Hampton, of the Georgia Tech department known as NEETRAC, the National Electric Energy Testing, Research and Application Center, echoed off the walls the opinion that brushing the lines before installation versus not brushing them made little difference, that it didn't seem to have a practical effect one way or the other. In fact, the man with a Ph.D. in physics said he had conducted a meticulous test study in which lines that were brushed actually worsened their performance slightly. But later, during questioning by Kila Baldwin in the same transcript testimony, Hampton had acknowledged that his study had used only six automatic splices of the type above the Goretzka property (and a second study used none) and that such a small sample didn't really allow for any clear conclusions to be formed on brushing versus non-brushing. Hampton also agreed that the instructions on Hubbell's automatic splices specified that brushing be performed before installation. And, despite his opinion that brushing did not have a practically significant effect, it was still a good idea to do it before installation.

The differing statements presented to the members of the jury seemed to cancel one another out. That is, if any of them were still listening.

Chapter 110

Finding an expert with a résumé as long as Campbell Laird's was probably impossible, but Levicoff seemed to have found one almost as impressive in Dr. Catherine Ford Corrigan. She had attended three of the nation's most prestigious schools—the University of Pennsylvania for her undergraduate degree in bioengineering, the Massachusetts Institute of Technology for her master's in mechanical engineering and a joint MIT-Harvard Medical School program for her 1996 doctoral degree in medical engineering and medical physics. She had lectured at Princeton University, had won fellowships and awards and been published in dozens of periodicals. After finishing school, Corrigan had gone to work for the Philadelphia engineering and scientific consulting firm Exponent, where she now was a group vice president and a principal of the company. Dr. Corrigan had been with the firm for 16 years and addressed issues involving the biomechanics of human injury or, as she answered Levicoff's introductory questions, "trying to understand the movements and the forces that created the injury."

In this case, Carrie's injury. Corrigan told the jury that she had worked on hundreds of biomechanical projects over the years. An attractive woman who wore her dark, straight hair to her shoulders and a black suit over a crisp white shirt, Catherine Corrigan looked sharp, and she was sharp. She was well-educated and articulate. By her own estimate, she had worked on about 200 lawsuits and was no stranger to a courtroom. She sat straight in the witness chair and smiled affably.

Specter started his questioning about Corrigan's qualifications by reading the dictionary definition of her company's name, Exponent: "one that speaks for, represents, or advocates." Then he asked his first question: "Are you an advocate?"

"No."

On questioning, Specter established that Exponent was billing at the rate of $600 per hour for Corrigan's time, even more than Laird's hourly remuneration. Corrigan said that roughly three-fourths of her time was spent on litigation matters and "in excess of 95 percent" of that was working for defendants.

"Well," Specter continued, "100 percent would be in excess of 95 percent. Would it be as high as 100 percent?"

"No," Corrigan answered pleasantly. If Specter thought he could easily rattle this witness, he was mistaken.

"There's the occasional plaintiff's case?"

"Do I have an occasional plaintiff's case? Yes."

"You know my firm, right? Kline & Specter?"

"I do."

"Have you worked for us in all the years we've had a law firm? You've been right up the street from us."

Corrigan's answer provoked a smile from both her and Specter.

"You've never called."

Sharp.

Chapter 111

Captain Lionel Mandrake needs to make an urgent call to the President of the United States. Rogue Air Force antagonist Brigadier General Jack D. Ripper has ordered a nuclear air attack on the Soviet Union and the president, with the bombers just hours from their target, represents the last chance of halting the attack and an apocalypse. Mandrake, played in the movie *Dr. Strangelove* by Peter Sellers, steps into a phone booth and starts to make the call. But he's 20 cents short of the necessary toll charge. So he orders his armed escort, Colonel "Bat" Guano (Keenan Wynn) to shoot a nearby Coca-Cola machine to appropriate the coinage necessary to try to save the world. Guano hesitates before finally agreeing to shoot the machine, but not until he issues a warning to Mandrake: "OK, I'm going to get your money for you. But if you don't get the President of the United States on the phone, do you know what's going to happen to you?

"What?" asks Mandrake.

"You're going to have to answer to the Coca-Cola Company."

The movie scene was one of Shanin Specter's favorites, and he repeated it several times outside the courtroom. He saw a parallel in the scene with the Goretzka settlement negotiations: Colonel Guano was almost as concerned with the ire of the Coca-Cola Company as he was over the prospect of a nuclear holocaust. To Specter, executives at West Penn Power seemed more concerned with the company's public image than with public safety.

Throughout the negotiations, the utility had demanded that any settlement be strictly confidential. In other words, it was willing to write a check to end the lawsuit, but if it did pay millions, the company certainly didn't want the public to know. At one point, it even asked that a $1 million penalty be assessed if a settlement amount was leaked to the news media. Specter planned to fight any such confidentiality clause.

He knew that West Penn wanted to settle, in part, to avoid publicity. On top of significant pretrial publicity, *The Pittsburgh Tribune-Review* had already produced daily local coverage of the trial. But a story about a big verdict against the company on the Pittsburgh TV stations or, worse, in *The Wall Street Journal*, could end in the rolling of heads, such as those of certain executives at West Penn Power. Publicity about big verdicts or settlements also can tend to have a ripple effect, with the news spawning more lawsuits.

But Specter wanted the publicity. And so did his client.

Chapter 112

As the trial progressed, the prospect of a $40 million settlement played on Specter's mind. Just as Levicoff had presumably hoped it would. Turning down so much money—as Specter had indicated he would—was taking a big gamble. There were very few attorneys, if any, who would say no to such a sum. You could get burned.

And Specter had been burned in the past. In two cases, he remembered vividly that he had taken the chance of rejecting a settlement offer, and lost. In one, he had refused to accept $2.5 million to end a case for a woman who had suffered brain damage because of a mishap at a Harrisburg hospital. Specter, whose experts calculated that it would cost $4 million to care for the patient at a private facility for the rest of her life, had held out for more money. The hospital refused and the case went to a jury. When the jury returned with a verdict, Specter was bowled over. The defense won. His client would get nothing.

"I was devastated by the verdict. I thought about it day and night for a week," he recalled, saying that only long afterward did he come to believe he had done the right thing, even though the result was wrong. Had he taken $2.5 million, his client would have only been able to get several years of expensive residential care specialized for behaviorally brain-injured people before the money ran out, and then she would have been moved to a nursing home, which was where she remained after the trial. (Specter saw the institution and was comforted that it at least was clean and well-run and that the caregivers seemed empathetic.)

The other case involved a baby boy born with cerebral palsy and the Erie nursing staff responsible for failing to adequately monitor the child's fetal heart rate when complications arose during a breech birth. As the trial was going well for Specter and was getting close to jury deliberations, the hospital offered $15 million to settle.

"I felt that was fair, but that the jury was likely to do better," he recalled.

Instead he agreed to a high-low of $15 million low and $30 million high. The jury handed down a verdict that was worth about $7.5 million, half of the settlement offer of $15 million. Worse, the high-low agreement also prohibited any appeal of the verdict. And Specter felt certain that he would have won an appeal because the jury had found liability on the part of the hospital, but awarded not a penny for pain and suffering and loss of the pleasures of life. He had seen the effects of cerebral palsy in the past, and he knew there had been and would continue to be much pain and suffering for his client's lifetime. He felt bad for his client and the little boy's parents and frustrated by the deal he had cut. Since Specter had signed the settlement agreement, he had lost the option to appeal. The case was over. Done.

"I outsmarted myself," he conceded.

Chapter 113

Catherine Corrigan testified for the defense that she had studied medical records in the case, read deposition testimony, analyzed photographs and even visited the Goretzka property. She had filed a 23-page report on the case and her findings. All the information, she said, allowed her to pinpoint Carrie's location just prior to her being injured.

Corrigan's conclusion and reasoning didn't seem to require scientific degrees from Ivy League institutions. Her "biomechanical reconstruction" seemed simple enough. Using a laser pointer, she flashed its red light on a place in the grass on the side of the house and toward the front of the Goretzka property near a small tree. Also in the photograph were Carrie's shoes, the blue-green rubber Crocs. "So in my opinion," Corrigan testified, "the location of the shoes proximates her position." Carrie had been where her shoes were.

Perhaps the most impressive part of the testimony came in the form of an animation snapshot that she constructed based on the evidence, including the position of Carrie's shoes and burn marks in the trees. The animation spoke a thousand words without Corrigan having to say much at all. It showed a cartoon of a woman standing on the grass just a step or two from a wire hanging from a small tree. The wire hung right in front of the woman's eyes at a distance from which she could reach out and touch it. And the animation suggested as much—that Carrie was just about to either walk into the wire or reach out for it. There was no follow-up animation, no video with moving images, and Corrigan did not give an opinion on Carrie's next action. But the suggestion was as clear as the skies on that day: Carrie had, voluntarily and on her own, approached the deadly live wire. She had courted disaster.

Specter bristled silently as he heard the testimony and saw the animation presented to the jury. It purported, in one still animation, to show what had happened and how. Yet he felt that was not possible. There had only been one person who could say for sure what had happened, and she was dead.

Specter's cross-examination:

Q: The reason that you're here is to support West Penn Power in their claim that Carrie Goretzka is to blame for her own death. Correct?

A: No. That is not correct.

Q: You're here arguing, or contending, excuse me. You're here to expound on the proposition that Carrie Goretzka was in a position to see this line and she should have avoided it. Correct?

A: I've not offered either of those opinions.

Q: Well, I know you haven't offered the opinion, but just looking at that photograph or that...animation that you showed a few moments ago with her just appearing to walk into a power line, that would be the natural conclusion anybody would draw if they believed that to have been the case. Correct?

A: No, I don't believe that is correct.

Q: Well, do you think Carrie Goretzka was at fault?

A: I have no opinion in that regard.

Specter sought to debunk the animation. He questioned even Corrigan's simplest calculation—that where Carrie had stood could be determined by the position of her shoes. Yes, the shoes had been found near the small tree, but one had been facing one way and one the other way. He tried to put his own feet in the same position as the shoes. It looked like he was playing the game Twister. "You certainly don't contend, do you, that... and I can't even get myself in that position. I'm not flexible enough," said a struggling Specter who, as a trim and avid squash player, was pretty flexible.

"Neither could I," replied Corrigan, conceding that Carrie's feet could not have been positioned the way the shoes were found.

"And," Specter continued, "actually, do you even know that the shoes pointed in opposite directions are the way they were pointed when the incident occurred?"

"I do not."

The lawyer went on to note that at some point after Carrie was taken away to the hospital, the shoes had also been flipped over.

Q: And since the shoes were moved presumably after she was injured in order for them to have gone from right-side-down to right-side-up or the other way around, they also may have been moved in terms of their location. We just don't know that. Is that fair?

A: Well, I think there's a lot we don't know about the shoes.

Q: Can you agree with what I just said?

A: Yes, we do not know exactly where the shoes are at the moment of injury.

Catherine Corrigan conceded that there was no way to tell precisely where the shoes were when the incident occurred and that her diagrams were "intended to depict generally the location where I believe she's standing" consistent with other data such as her height and the burn marks in the small tree.

Was it possible, also consistent with the known data, Specter wanted to know next, that the incident could have occurred as he had theorized: the power line fell on top of the telephone lines, stayed there long enough to damage the phone lines and for Carrie not to see it, then toppled down on top of Carrie and the small tree?

Levicoff objected immediately. Corrigan had done no such analysis, he protested.

Now Specter objected, saying Levicoff was coaching the witness.

"Now it's time for the judge to speak, OK?" Della Vecchia broke in. "I believe the question was properly asked whether, to short circuit, plaintiff's theory of liability here is in any way contrary to what you're saying, and she says it isn't. All she did was locate the person on the ground. And that does not dispute your theory as to how it happened…and I think the jury understands she located the person on the ground, she did not locate the wires up above."

But Specter wanted the witness to say the words, to acknowledge that his theory of the incident could be correct. "I'm just looking for her to agree with that," he stated.

"I think she did," said Della Vecchia.

"If she did, that's good enough for me. Judge, that's good enough for me."

The animation that had been put on the large screen and the smaller monitors throughout the courtroom still bothered Specter. It showed Carrie about to walk into the downed wire, even if Corrigan insisted the still animation projected no movement. The suggestion remained, and strongly.

Even if Dr. Corrigan was correct about where Carrie had stood and where the power line had rested in the small tree at a height of roughly five feet, there remained one critical factor neither Corrigan nor anyone else could know: When? When did these things happen? There was no proof of the sequence of events. Carrie was standing in that spot at some point, and the line did come down and hit the small tree at some point. But there was no way to prove that she had walked into the line or that it had fallen on top of her. Specter felt certain that Carrie, or any human being, would not walk into or try to grab a live wire right in front of her. But the animation showed the wire down in the tree, just a few feet from Carrie, before she was electrocuted. Specter felt he needed to refute the implication. He had decided the night before—if the defense attorney and the judge allowed it—that he would try something novel to discredit Corrigan's animation, to dispel the idea that the wire had been downed, right in front of Carrie's eyes, before the fatal contact.

Q: And this power line as you show it here, it's directly at eye level, correct?
A: In the vicinity of where the shoes are and the burn mark in the tree, it's at that level, in terms of the smaller tree.
Q: It's right in front of her face, correct?
A: It is essentially at eye level at this location.
Q: You're a scientist of sorts, correct?
A: Yes.
Q: I want you to help me out with a little bit of an experiment, if you don't mind.
A: OK.
Q: Trust me, nothing bad is going to happen to you, but I want you to close your eyes for a second. Do you mind?
A: No.
Q: Tell me the color of the ceiling right above you.
A: Don't know.

Q: No idea, correct? Open your eyes please. Now, what's the color of my tie?

A: Well, it appears red.

Q: How about my shirt?

A: Looks white.

Q: And my suit?

A: Dark blue.

Q: OK. And you tend to notice things that are directly in front of you, correct?

A: Oh boy, we're getting way out of my area.

Q: I'm talking about you, not anybody else. You.

A: I tend to notice whatever my attention is directed to, I imagine.

Levicoff had finally heard enough and rose to object. The judge sustained his objection. Specter moved on, but not really. He pressed his point a bit further.

Q: Did you analyze as part of your work whether there was something about Mrs. Goretzka that would have rendered her incapable of being able to recognize a power line right in front of her face, if one was there?

A: No.

Chapter 114

The telltale is a metal box extending 17 inches upward from the base of the front wall of a squash court. A red line is painted at the top of the box indicating where the ball must be hit. Above the line is in, below it is out. When the small rubber ball hits the telltale, or "tin," it makes a loud thunking noise and the point is over. The telltale has undoubtedly prevented many disputes over a shot being in or out over the 200-year history of the game invented at London's Harrow School.

The telltale also has the effect of keeping rallies going for quite some time since the ball must be hit high enough so that a speedy contestant can reach even the most well-hit shot most of the time. The result is that it's difficult to win a point with a single shot. Thus squash becomes more of a tactical game—a "thinking man's game"—with a variety of lobs placed to the back of the court followed by "drops" hit softly near the telltale at the front. "Rails" are hit hard or high along a side wall, and "boasts" carom off a side wall before the ball hits at an angle off the front. The back-and-forth activity can make for rallies that are long and almost (keyword: almost) boring. The best players in the world have points that can last 30 or 40 or more shots, often with the ball going back and forth until one player makes a mistake. Squash makes for a great workout. An article in Forbes magazine in 2013 rated it the "No. 1 healthiest sport."

Squash was Shanin Specter's sport of choice as well as his father's. Like Arlen, he played most days. In 2005, the younger Specter was a member of a U.S. team of players aged 45 to 49 that won a gold medal at the 17th Maccabiah Games played in Israel. In 1982, Specter had met his wife, the former Tracey Pearl, on the squash courts at the University of Pennsylvania. In 2012, he and Tom Kline donated funding for squash courts at Drexel University. They were named the Kline & Specter Squash Center, and were the site of the annual U.S. Open featuring the world's top-ranked players.

Senator Specter would half-joke: "I used to say that squash was the most important thing I did each day. Now I say it is the only important thing I do each day." In his book *Never Give In*, about his travails with cancer, he likened his squash games to trips to the "health bank," with each counting as a deposit. He concluded, "Squash may well have been a lifesaver during my many medical ordeals."

Being on trial was no excuse for Shanin Specter not to play squash. Indeed, it provided more of a reason. Strenuous exercise helped relieve pressure. For Specter, it helped his body catch up to his racing mind. Even though he felt the Goretzka trial was going well, there was still pressure. Squash reduced the stress and made sleep come easier. Specter got in some games whenever and wherever he could find one after the trial recessed for the day. He thought ahead about his next match and suitable opponents. A typical email to Grimmie: "Please get me a game for Monday in Pittsburgh at the DC [Duquesne Club] if we don't settle Goretzka today [Friday, November 30]. That fellow Dave is a good match for me."

Specter played one day during the Goretzka trial with a judge whose office was on the same floor as the trial and whom he'd heard was a good player. (He beat the judge.) One night, he played with a young woman who had been a college player and was the wife of a Pittsburgh Penguins hockey player. (He beat her.) He played against the recent winner of a tournament at a local club near the courtroom. (He beat him.) One day, Grimmie arranged a match with a professional at a local club. (He lost.)

Specter would email, even occasionally in the courtroom during breaks in the Goretzka trial, to arrange games. He would move meetings or dinner to suit his squash schedule. He would even skip out early on some meetings with witnesses or experts and have Guerrini or Baldwin cover for him so he would not be late for squash. During one prep session with an important witness, Specter announced that he would have to leave promptly at 5:15 p.m. for an important engagement. His colleagues discovered later that Specter had a squash game. And that he wasn't fibbing. To him, a squash game was an important engagement.

Squash also provided a lesson beyond the physical, and perhaps for the Goretzka trial as well. As his father once said, the game is "conducive to unlikely comebacks." In *Never Give In*, the senator wrote that he had witnessed many matches in which one player seemed to be trailing hopelessly "only to catch up through tenacity and ultimately win the match." Such perseverance extended to everything. Even trials. As Arlen Specter noted: "Squash is a great lesson for life: You're never too far behind to win, and you're never too far ahead to lose."

Chapter 115

Joseph Turek was one of the defense team's big guns, probably its biggest. He was a materials expert the defense would use to try to blunt the testimony of the esteemed Campbell Laird. But while Turek might have been lacking in the credentials department—he had one degree, a bachelor's, and he had never been published—he did have one thing in his favor that Laird did not. He was a local product. Turek had attended the University of Pittsburgh. He had worked at several companies in the region. Folks from Pittsburgh took a provincial outlook on things. They loved their city, their Steelers and their own kind. And Turek, who went by Joe, was one of them. Specter was very conscious of this fact and that there was general disdain for Philadelphians in the rest of the state. He avoided unnecessary mention of his being from Philadelphia when he tried cases out of town.

Turek wore a dark suit to court this Monday morning, but he did not look like the lawyers or the insurance men who crowded the courtroom. His dark-gray hair was long and parted in the middle. He had a thin moustache and a "soul patch" below his bottom lip. (Specter once noticed a younger partner at his firm sporting such a growth and told him, unceremoniously, to shave it off.) Turek wore glasses whose temples were attached behind his head by a cord, but the cord was too long and drooped down on either side of his head and down to his shoulders like the ears of a basset hound. When Joe Turek smiled, which he would have little occasion to do during his two days on the witness stand, wide gaps appeared in his lower teeth.

Turek told Levicoff on direct examination of his qualifications as an expert with a degree in materials science and metallurgical engineering. He had worked 15 years at the Bettis Atomic Power Laboratory, a federal government-owned research and development facility outside of Pittsburgh, where he was a staff engineer and had been assigned in his later years there to the metallurgical lab. He also worked for a second testing laboratory, Matco Services, doing failure analysis. He told Levicoff that he was a member of the American Society of Materials and the Microscopy Society of

America, and had been associated with the National Association of Corrosion Engineers (NACE), but that he had let that last membership lapse.

Levicoff then asked Turek about any major projects he had worked on. His response was that he had participated in a legal case involving a crankshaft failure in a small airplane. The case ended with the manufacturer of the airplane engines having to pay a $92 million settlement. Turek's answer was astonishing, at least to Specter, who was surprised that Levicoff would have his witness speak about that case, much less make mention of the settlement. Specter was happy for the jury in this case to get wind of such a large settlement made against a relatively small company. Would it plant a subliminal suggestion with the jury on what to award in the Goretzka case?

Specter, who had turned 55 over the weekend, rose for his cross-examination on Turek's qualifications as an expert. The plaintiffs' counsel didn't plan to attack the owner of Joseph Turek Consulting, although he did want to take him down a notch or two and certainly to a position somewhat lower than the high perch occupied by Campbell Laird.

"Are you a professional engineer?" he asked.

"No, sir."

"Are you a mechanical engineer?"

"No, sir."

Specter noted that Turek's résumé cited his work for the defense on the airplane engine case, a defense loss that the lawyer didn't mind repeating for the jury. Turek had testified only moments earlier when questioned by Levicoff that there had been a settlement in the case. But Specter noticed that Turek's résumé had termed it a "judgment," implying a verdict. A verdict was far worse than a settlement agreed to by the two sides. So which was it, a verdict or a settlement? Specter wanted to know.

"It was a jury verdict," said the witness.

Specter ran a finger down Turek's résumé and next asked about his membership in the American Society of Materials. He knew there was a fine line between tough questioning and ridicule, the latter being frowned upon by most juries. But he risked walking the line with Turek.

"Is that professional society membership something where you have to be invited by your colleagues to join based upon a demonstrated excellence in the field, or is it something where you filled out a postcard or application form and you're in?"

"There are no requirements for acceptance," the witness replied.

"The same thing true about the Microscopy Society of America?"

"That's correct."

Turek told Specter that was not the case with the third organization. NACE required a member to pass proficiency tests. But he had let that membership lapse. "Actually," he told Specter, "the Microscopy Society lapsed as well...."

Turek said it as an aside, but Specter didn't let it go. He noted that all three groups were listed on the witness' résumé and that someone just reading the document wouldn't know that Turek was no longer a member "because you list yourself as a member of these two organizations on the information you provided. Correct?"

"That's correct."

Specter asked if Turek had ever been invited to be a fellow of one of the many professional organizations of which Laird was a member?

"No, sir."

Chapter 116

Joe Turek claimed to have found proof of something everyone else had missed, namely, wire brushing and, by extension, evidence that West Penn Power's linemen may not have been at fault.

Turek had worked on the Goretzka case for more than a year, he told Avrum Levicoff under direct examination. He had performed electrical testing, resistance testing, tension testing, unseating testing, you-name-it testing. He spent hours explaining technical details to the jury—the make-up and hardness of the composite power lines, the inner workings of a splice, the depth and angle of penetration their teeth made into the aluminum wire to maintain a solid grip, the melting points of various metals. He used charts, videos and microscope photography to support various assertions. He disputed the opinions of plaintiff experts Campbell Laird and John Dagenhart that only a small force was exerted by the teeth into a line when it was installed by a lineman, noting the substantial "sag and weight" of the line itself. Joe Turek would be on the stand—and off it, stepping down to work with various exhibits—for two days, more than any other witness.

His most critical testimony was that he had seen, with a microscope, what he said were brush marks on the power line. Under 40X magnification, the scratch marks were apparent on the unfailed side of the splice where the line had broken. Turek flashed a black-and-white photo on the screen with arrows pointing to the scratches. The marks were faint, but they were there. His conclusion: "I believe the evidence is indisputable that it was brushed clean on the unfailed side of the splice."

Levicoff also had his witness inspect the burned, or failed, end of the power line. It was badly damaged and in pieces, but Turek said he saw similar, albeit fainter, scratch marks. A black-and-white magnified photo was put up on the large screen in the courtroom. It took a bit of eye straining, and maybe a tad of imagination, for others in the courtroom to see what Turek saw. Nevertheless, the theory was that if one end of the line had been brushed prior to installation in the splice, so must the other. Why would Jeffrey Falo or Thomas Jones have brushed one side and not the other?

"I believe," Turek testified, "that there may have been brushing local to where the grips were because I saw some evidence of that near that other sample, the intact sample...."

The witness also noted evidence of heavy corrosion on a part of the wire inside the splice, corrosion that could have caused "arcing," which he explained as a plasma that forms in the air and conducts electricity. This, in turn, could have caused the wire to burn up: "There is no way that this corrosion could have occurred from the lack of just brushing the surface of these conductors." Turek went on to explain how moisture can seep into a splice and cause corrosion of a wire, whether brushed or not.

Chapter 117

Evidence that the jury was engaged in the case became clear when Joe Turek measured a piece of wire while testifying. The length, he told the jury, was two and one-sixteenth inches.

"Can you give me that in decimals?" Levicoff asked.

"I don't know that off the top of my head."

At which point Specter chimed in: "Point 07."

In a true rare instance during a trial, one juror—Juror number 5, the scientist whom Specter had hoped would lead the cause for his client—spoke out loud. He supplied an answer, and the right one: "Point 0625."

"Point 0625," Specter repeated, smiling, and then he said it more loudly for the record. "I have been corrected."

Chapter 118

Joe Turek also claimed to have made an astonishing discovery in the case. He had found the true culprit behind the fallen power line, a villain with a long and proven history of causing havoc throughout the land—Mother Nature.

Through his various microscopes, Turek noticed that on the piece of power line that had been inside the failed splice there were marks between those made by the splice teeth. This meant, he maintained, that the teeth had moved, and done so several times, and that they had become "seated and unseated." The phenomenon was termed "chatter." The teeth had chattered along the line, hopping up and down ever so slightly into different spots. And, he theorized, this chatter on the line was likely caused by the wind. He gave it an elaborate name: "Aeolian dynamics." Turek put all this in his report prepared for the West Penn Power's legal defense.

But a curious thing happened on the way to the Goretzka trial. The defense team decided not to bring up the theory of Aeolian dynamics, a theory of wind vibrations that might exonerate West Penn from liability. Levicoff had decided not to mention it to the jury. Specter felt he knew the reason—because, as he put it, the theory was "preposterous." First off, as he had told Kila Baldwin the night before Turek took the stand: "Do you know what Aeolian dynamics is? It's wind. That's it…wind! It's just a fancy word for wind." In fact, according to the dictionary, the word Aeolian means, "of or relating to the wind," taken from Aeolus, the Greek god of wind.

Specter became so incensed over Joe Turek's Aeolian dynamics theory that he decided if the defense wasn't going to bring it up at trial, he would. He felt the whole thing was so ridiculous that the jury would think so too, and it would undermine Turek's credibility as a witness. However, a few sentences after Specter brought up the topic during his cross-examination of Turek, Levicoff rose with an objection.

"I specifically didn't go into these matters regarding Aeolian vibration or any of the other forces that may have caused this," he told Judge Della Vecchia in a sidebar. If Levicoff hadn't brought up the subject in his direct

examination, it was off limits to Specter in cross-examination. "I specifically stayed away from it with this witness. So it's beyond the scope."

Although Levicoff had not asked his witness about the wind specifically, Turek had told the jury about vibrations and "chatter" marks on the
line, saying, "I believe this conductor movement was the primary event or
the primary cause leading to the failure of the splice." The judge overruled
Levicoff's objection.

"So as I was saying," Specter continued, "you told the jury a few minutes ago that this line fell because of seating and unseating, and you talked
in your report about Aeolian wind vibrations. Do you recollect that, sir?"

"Yes, sir."

"Basically, as I read your report, you were saying [it] was vibrations on
the conductor caused by the wind [that] caused this seating and unseating
that you described?"

"Yes. Effects of the wind, the nearest we can tell. Yes, sir."

"Effects of the wind," Specter repeated the phrase. He pressed his index
finger to his lips and looked heavenward. "So let's start off with this: West
Hempfield, Pennsylvania, West Hempfield Drive. Is there some sort of
wind tunnel going on out there on the Goretzkas' yard, some special meteorological circumstances there, sir?"

"Wind is a hard thing to pin down as far as what is going on unless you
have instrumentation available on site," replied Turek, appearing now like
a mouse cornered by a hungry cat. "But wind speeds as low as 15 miles an
hour are known to cause a number of phenomena on distribution lines."

"Please try to focus on my question. I'm asking about whether there is
something meteorologically unusual about the Goretzkas' side yard...."

"Not meteorological that I'm aware of."

Specter noted that Turek had consulted weather station records for the
region and asked, "That didn't support the idea that there was any sort of
freakish meteorological phenomenon occurring on West Hempfield Drive,
correct?"

"That's correct. We found nothing that was out of the ordinary, as it
were."

In reviewing West Penn Power's records about splices or in reviewing
data about "hundreds of millions...maybe billions" of splices installed over
the last 20 years, Specter asked, "You're the only person who's come up

with this idea that the splicing failed for these Aeolian wind vibrations. Right?"

"I don't believe I would be the only guy to interpret this evidence in the fashion that I have," Turek replied.

"That's not my question." Specter wouldn't let it go. "You have not seen in the literature a report about a splice on a distribution line failing for the type of reason that you just said. Correct?"

"Not in this exact manner, no."

Chapter 119

Joe Turek testified that he had seen evidence of what he believed was wire brushing on the line that fell. But even if he had not, it didn't matter. You didn't have to use a wire brush to sufficiently clean a line. A knife or the back edge of a pair of pliers would do the trick just as well. Even if you didn't clean the power line at all before installing it into a splice, that was OK. The teeth inside the jaws of the splice would bite deeply enough to hold the line, even through any possible corrosion. This was Turek's contention.

He had run the tests. He had taken new power lines and used a "salt fog" to create corrosion. Then he had used a wire brush, the back of a razor and a knife to clean the artificially weathered wire. Both removed the oxidation just fine, he testified. "We concluded that as long as something was harder than the conductor, it would be effective in removing the oxide...."

Levicoff asked whether there were many materials harder than aluminum.

"There are quite a few, yes," Turek responded. "A rock. There are many materials that are much harder than the aluminum."

Perhaps the grandest pronouncement made by Joe Turek was that the "alleged failure to brush," as Levicoff put it in his question, was not a "causal factor" in the failing of the power line. "I don't believe that surface preparation has any effect on the performance of these splices," he told Levicoff and the jury.

Turek explained that the weathering oxides were so thin that the steel teeth of the splice would easily bite through any corrosion and penetrate the aluminum strands deeply enough to hold the line. Whether the line was cleaned or not cleaned, he said, was "irrelevant."

Specter rose to cross-examine the witness. Among other things, he wanted to try to show bias on the part of this expert. So he asked why Turek had bothered using a salt fog—for 885 hours—on new wires to try to approximate the condition of the 47-year-old line that had fallen at the Goretzka property. Why hadn't he just used the actual wire? It had been in Turek's possession for some eight months, and there had been about 150 feet of it available.

"You could have tested that, right?"

Turek gave a straightforward answer: "It requires approval from opposite side counsel, which is a pain."

"Ah, yes," Specter followed. "Let's talk about that for a minute. It requires notice to your opponent, right?"

"Because they're destructive tests, right."

"Right, and not only are they destructive, but your opponent gets to know what the test results were…and the results would be there for everybody to see, correct?"

"That is correct."

"Whereas, if you do your own experiments with something that is not the subject of physical evidence, you can decide what you want to do. You can make your own protocol. You don't have to advise your opponent. And you have quite a bit more freedom. Is that fair?"

"Fair to say, yes, sir."

At one point in his cross-examination, Specter wanted to look at several exhibits, so he asked the judge for approval to allow Turek to step down from the witness stand.

"As long as you're not going to hurt him," the judge joked.

Specter didn't crack a smile, neither did Turek. (Earlier, Specter had noted that two other experts from Turek's firm had not testified for the defense, but had designated him to appear in court. "Unfortunately, yes," Turek had replied.)

Next, Specter wanted to know about the other two splices that had been on the Goretzka line, the two that had not failed. If the scratch marks Turek had found on the intact end of the failed splice were evidence that either Thomas Jones or Jeffrey Falo had used a wire brush, those two other splices seemed to be evidence they did not. Or at least that one of them wasn't in the habit of using one.

"Did Mr. Jones and/or Falo wire-brush the conductor on those four ends before placing them into those two splices?" Specter asked Turek.

"I believe the evidence shows that they were likely scraped, likely with the back of a knife."

"And that would be a violation of West Penn policy. Correct?"

"I believe that's true. Yes, sir."

Specter wanted to tackle Joe Turek's assertion that the whole issue of wire brushing was "irrelevant." He asked the witness if he had been apprised of Chris Havlik's work with splices and the fact that the employee of Hubbell—the manufacturer of the device—had evaluated 250 splice failures over nine years, including 20 "burndowns" of aluminum power line splices that he attributed to improper cleaning. Turek said he had not known that. Nor had he seen the email introduced at the trial in which Haven Bearley, the head of West Penn Power's standards department, told Jill D'Angelo that the majority of the company's splice failures had been "attributed to poor conductor preparation and improper splice installation."

"Is this the kind of document you would have wanted to have seen before coming here today?"

"Yes," Turek answered, "You can never have too much information."

Specter also asked if Turek had seen the film prepared by Hubbell that stressed the importance of wire brushing for proper installation. Turek replied that he had not when he prepared his report, but he had since been shown the film on the weekend prior to this testimony in court.

Now Specter noted Turek's opinion that brushing wasn't necessary and he wise-cracked: "Do you plan to send a copy of your study to Hubbell?"

Levicoff objected and Specter backed off.

Instead, he asked if Turek knew that Hubbell had done its own testing. This he did know. How about that its packing for its splices still bore printed instructions for linemen to use a wire brush to prepare the line? Yes, he knew that also. And that the standards manual also instructed that power lines be cleaned with a wire brush and followed that with a warning: "Clean conductor with wire brush…Unclean conductor will set up overheating and eventual failure of the splice." Specter asked, "You're aware of that, correct?"

"Yes."

"So it would be just as safe if we were to erase the first sentence, correct? Just as safe, according to you?"

"I don't believe I ever stated that not cleaning is good practice."

"I'm confused," Specter claimed, though no one in the courtroom believed that. "I thought you told us that it doesn't matter whether you clean it or not? Correct? Performance is the same?"

"I've indicated that test data supports that, yes, sir."

"I want to know what you think. I'm not asking about some test that you ran. I'm asking you what you think. Are you saying that it doesn't matter whether you clean the conductor? Yes or no?"

"I believe cleaning is prudent. I've never recommended not to clean."

"OK, so cleaning is better than not cleaning, right?"

"It may be slightly better, best on test data."

"Does that mean, respectfully, sir," Specter followed, though not a person in the courtroom believed he was being all that respectful, "does that mean that you don't believe your own test data?"

"I know that aluminum oxides are insulators, and from a first approximation, it is prudent to remove them."

It went on like that for some time. To brush or not to brush, that was the question. Turek was getting tangled up. He tried to explain his position this way: "It's like waxing or not waxing a car. It doesn't matter. It's going to have no effect on a wreck. It just looks better."

"We're not talking about looking better," Specter countered. "We're talking about being safer, right?"

"Correct."

"We're talking about seatbelt versus no seatbelt, if you want to take it to the car analogy. OK? Fair enough?"

Turek finally conceded the point. "OK," he said.

Chapter 120

With the last witness having testified, both sides asked for a ruling by the judge on what Dominic Guerrini termed "can't-hurt-to-try motions," technically known as requests for a directed verdict. Judges almost always ruled against such motions, which sought to have them take a case out of the jury's hands and decide the matter themselves from the bench. Evidence had to be awfully lopsided for a judge to do so. But it couldn't hurt to try, or so the two sides believed.

Both lawyers, knowing the odds against prevailing on motions for a directed verdict, kept it short. They addressed Judge Della Vecchia outside the presence of the jury. Levicoff went first.

Our position is the evidence makes it indisputable that the plaintiff voluntarily, under no particular compulsion, left her house, a position of complete safety, aware that a power line was down in the yard, aware that the power line was energized, walked outside, made a left-hand turn and positioned herself, according to undisputed evidence, directly under where the power line was and put herself in the position to be contacted by. The power, basically, didn't come after her. She positioned herself close enough to it to come in contact with it...The fact is, her conduct was voluntary, and it was undertaken under circumstances in which there was a known and observable danger of great magnitude. The undisputed evidence is that she was safe, walked to a position of grave danger and was injured.

Levicoff said that such a voluntary action by Carrie Goretzka "negates any duty of care owed by the defendant." Della Vecchia made no comment. "Mr. Specter?" he inquired.

Specter, perhaps sensing the judge would not, after weeks of testimony, prevent the jury from completing its task, kept his response unusually brief: "Not only is there not incontrovertible evidence of the plaintiff's negligence, there is no evidence of the plaintiffs' negligence. And so we oppose the motion."

For his part, Specter said the plaintiffs merited a directed verdict from the judge because of the fact that the power line fell on a clear and sunny day. There was no way possible, he argued, that "a reasonable jury could find that West Penn Power was not negligent. Unless there had been an error in the installation or maintenance of the power line, it would not have fallen. He added that there was not "a scintilla of evidence" that Carrie was contributory, though "Frankly, for tactical reason, I would rather have Mr. Levicoff argue she was negligent. I think that's going to mean something to the jury."

Judge Della Vecchia denied both motions.

The proceeding was not without some result. Mike Goretzka had listened to both arguments, and Levicoff placing the blame on his deceased wife infuriated him yet again. Hearing the charges directed at Carrie stiffened his resolve to avoid a settlement unless his attorney strongly advised he accept it. More than ever, Mike wanted to hear the jury announce a verdict.

Chapter 121

On Monday, with the weekend to think it over, West Penn Power formally upped its offer from $25 million to $40 million. It was a very large jump. Specter responded with his usual refusal, relaying that he still was insisting on $50 million. He was sitting in the jury assembling room with Levicoff and Joe Starkey, the in-house West Penn Power attorney at whom Specter had erupted earlier in the trial. Things had simmered down to the point where they could at least talk to each other.

"You know," Starkey said, "some people on our side think you don't want to settle this case."

He wasn't merely commenting on Specter's stubbornness. He was probing and goading Specter. West Penn Power had been willing to move its negotiating stance several times now. Why wouldn't Specter? Starkey wanted, and apparently expected, Specter to deny that he did not want a settlement. As was becoming typical, Specter did not respond with the expected.

"You're right. I don't want to settle." He uttered the comment and let it hang in the still air for a few beats before continuing, before giving Starkey a little breathing room. "But I have a responsibility to my client. If the money is right and the remedial steps are right, then I'm willing to recommend that we settle the case."

Chapter 122

Success breeds success.

The word around courthouses in Pennsylvania was that when Shanin Specter or Tom Kline walked into a room, "the price went up." That is, the price to settle a case. Both were hard-nosed negotiators.

Years earlier, Specter had taken a call during a trial in which the top lawyer for a major American automaker told him, with some bravado, that its board had just approved an extremely generous offer to settle his lawsuit against it.

"And?" Specter asked.

The amount was $25 million.

"Rejected."

There was a pained pause on the other side of the line. If it was possible to communicate disbelief without saying a word, the corporate lawyer did just that. The next words came with a slight stutter.

"B-but Shanin, this is the most we have ever offered—by far—for a single injury."

"OK?" said Specter, as in "So what?"

He reminded the lawyer in Michigan about some of his past cases, including the $153 million verdict against Ford, and the inherent bad publicity that came with such a verdict. He mentioned the fact that the case was being tried on his home turf of Philadelphia, a place where juries were sometimes known to award huge verdicts to sympathetic plaintiffs. In this case, the plaintiff was a little girl. During trial, when the offer improved to $30 million, Specter accepted.

It wasn't only Specter's negotiating skills that resulted in bigger settlements. It was also his reputation, his willingness to say no and to mean it. He was, his opponents knew, a wealthy man thanks to his previous victories in court and at the negotiating table. He didn't need the money. (His partner, Tom Kline, would later donate $50 million, money earned from 30 years of courtroom victories, to the Drexel School of Law, now the Thomas R. Kline School of Law at Drexel University.)

Specter's personal wealth actually helped his clients. He had no interest in "picking the low-hanging fruit." Everybody knew he didn't need to grab the first or second or even the third offer of a settlement, so he could keep the lights turned on. And everybody knowing that only enhanced his reputation and drove up "the price." To quote a fictional Philadelphian, Rocky Balboa, "They don't remember you, they remember the rep...."

One afternoon during a recess in the Goretzka trial, one of the defense attorneys asked Kila Baldwin a simple question. "What kind of plane does Mr. Specter own?" Word had gotten around that Shanin occasionally flew in private aircraft from Philadelphia to Pittsburgh and back home again. Baldwin's answer was a mistake—it was the truth. She answered that Specter didn't own a plane, he merely chartered one. The correct answer, someone on the plaintiff's side quipped, would have been: "Which plane?"

Overhearing the conversation, Specter told Baldwin that the next time she was asked, she should say simply that the topic was not one the firm discussed. No comment. He refused to lie, but if folks involved in the trial wanted to believe he owned a fleet of Lear jets, so be it.

Chapter 123

Upon receiving an actual offer of $40 million to settle the case, Specter huddled with his client. But Mike Goretzka wanted something more than money. He wanted revenge. He wanted to hear the jury say out loud and in public that the power company was guilty. Even though the jury would not use that word, a verdict would mean the same thing to Mike.

"What do you think the jury will do if [the case] gets to them?" he asked Specter.

"They're going to get crushed by the jury," Specter replied, even though he wasn't as certain as his words. He had a gut feeling, and a strong one.

Specter speculated that the jury would return with compensatory damages of perhaps less than $40 million, but, he added, "When you add in punitives, I think it will be more than $40 million. That's it."

He threw in the clincher, the one statement that probably helped Mike Goretzka make his decision: "An award of punitive damages is the same standard as for homicide. It's as close as you're going to get to criminal charges."

Specter also speculated that the power company would increase its settlement offer, but that it would stretch things out as long as possible. "I think they're still going to go up to $50 million, maybe during jury deliberations," he added.

Mike Goretzka was silent for a few seconds. "You know, as this continues to go on, I get madder and madder," he finally said. "I'd like to see a verdict and see them get crushed. Let's let the public know. Let's vindicate Carrie. Let's let the jury find that West Penn was wrong and crush them for it."

Chapter 124

Specter and West Penn Power finally pounded out an agreement for remedial measures. As part of any settlement deal, the Goretzkas wanted not only a monetary payment, but also to ensure that the utility would work to make its lines safer. Its officials had said initially that they would inspect and fix lines as part of a deal, but their proposal would take six years to complete. Specter and Mike Goretzka had balked at the notion. How many bad splices could burn up and cause energized lines to fall over six years? How many more people could get hurt or killed over that time? Six years was no good.

Specter had insisted that West Penn Power inspect all of its lines—and he wanted infrared technology to be used—within one year. The power company had responded that that was impossible. The two sides wrangled in vain. Then the Public Utility Commission, which regulates the electric industry, was brought in for its perspective. The commission agreed with Specter that six years was too much time. The PUC suggested cutting the time in half. Three years to inspect and repair any bum splices.

Specter agreed, and so did West Penn. On the morning of December 5, the penultimate day of trial, an agreement was reached on remedial measures, subject to the case being settled on all other issues, namely, a sum of money and confidentiality. Under the terms, West Penn Power would conduct regular "refresher training" courses for its linemen on the techniques for "properly preparing conductors for automatic splice installation." A second clause mandated a program of inspection of all lines containing splices—including primary and secondary lines—to be completed within three years and a second round to be completed within five years unless the PUC deemed such a reinspection unnecessary. Infrared technology would be used. One other facet of the deal was that West Penn Power would report back to Specter's office as to its compliance on a yearly basis.

Specter apprised Mike Goretzka of the terms. His client was satisfied.

Chapter 125

At this point, it appeared only logical that a financial settlement would be reached. The sides were too close for a deal not to be finalized. Surely the gap could be bridged.

After coming off his initial figure of $68.1 million, Specter held firm at $50 million. He had never realistically expected to get $68.1 million; it was only an opening gambit, but one he had set high enough to let West Penn Power know he was serious and that it would take serious money to get the case settled. Nothing in his comments or demeanor thus far indicated that he would budge from $50 million. He had been a staunch negotiator to this point. He had stood his ground and watched West Penn cede its turf since the beginning, from an initial $10 million offer to $20 million, then to $25 million and, most recently, $40 million. The utility had moved not in baby steps but in large leaps. Surely, Specter could now see his way to reasonably make a small move in their direction. Would a $50 million settlement make an appreciable difference to Mike Goretzka's future lifestyle compared to $40 million, or something in between? Would it mean much to Specter's burgeoning firm, which during the trial had hired its 35th attorney?

At this point, at a time when President Obama and House Republicans were negotiating a way to avoid the nation falling over a "fiscal cliff," couldn't Specter see his way to compromise to avoid the uncertainty of a jury verdict? It seemed crazy not to.

Chapter 126

With the weekend approaching and the defense having just one witness left in its case, a settlement seemed imminent. "I think they're going to come up with the money," Specter told his colleagues, meaning the $50 million. He noted that Levicoff had spoken with West Penn Power's secondary insurer and that "they were interested in concluding the matter."

He felt confident enough that he had packed a tuxedo and directions to Washington, D.C., which he noted was 240 miles away. Specter had been invited to a party at the White House that began at 6 p.m. on Tuesday, a date he could make only if the case settled. He posed a question to Dominic Guerrini: "What's the chance now that the case won't settle—one percent?"

Guerrini agreed, but he had a question: What if it didn't? "Well," quipped Specter, "I always wanted to do a closing speech in a tuxedo."

The only possible hang-up to a settlement, Specter estimated, would be his stipulation that a deal be nonconfidential. "They are determined not to have a verdict because they want to sweep it all under the rug," he said angrily, "but I'm going to say no. I'm going to say I'm not going to do it."

A mischievous smile came to his face as he envisioned how a negotiation planned for the next day might go. "Levicoff's going to have a heart attack when I tell him 'no.' And the judge is going to get really mad at me. And then we're going to see the whites of everyone's eyes."

Guerrini told Specter he couldn't see any way that West Penn Power would not insist on confidentiality. After all, if they were willing to go to this length to avoid the publicity of a potentially large verdict, why would they agree to bare their surrender to the public? "It would be the same as a verdict," he said.

"No, you're wrong, and I'll tell you why. If they agree to a settlement being nonconfidential, I'm going to put out a press release and I'm going to commend the company for taking remedial steps and I'm going to go to the PUC and withdraw my complaint." Besides, he wouldn't give his opponent a choice. He would draw a line in the sand.

"We're going to see who's going to blink first."

Chapter 127

A person blinks an average of roughly 15,000 times a day. Was it too much to expect Specter to last the entire case without doing so once?

Even though it was late in the proceedings and the power company and its insurance carriers seemed worried, Specter's confidence that he could avoid a confidentiality clause as part of a settlement had been misplaced. He was more determined than ever to get $50 million in a settlement together with West Penn Power's promise to inspect and make necessary repairs to all of its power lines. Plus, no confidentiality. He had been adamant throughout the mediation process on that last point.

On the eve of what he thought would be the trial's last day and the finalizing of a $50 million settlement, Specter drew back slightly from his demand. West Penn Power still wanted to keep any deal out of public view. "I don't think we'll be able to announce it to the news media, but we'll be able to use it on our website," he speculated, adding that other publicity about the case at a future date would probably be allowed as well.

The following morning, after further negotiations in the judge's chambers, the $50 million offer Specter had sought was finally presented along with the deal for full remediation, including retraining and power line inspections. There was just one condition: total and unequivocal confidentiality.

Was Specter willing to give up his fight against confidentiality at the risk of $50 million and a comprehensive inspection and repair project for all of West Penn Power's lines? Had he bargained this far to let confidentiality hold up the entire works? He had to admit to himself that the answer was no.

Specter didn't love the idea. He wanted the power company to suffer the spotlight of public embarrassment. He and Mike Goretzka wanted what amounted to an admission of guilt displayed in newspaper headlines and on the TV news. But this time, with such a large amount of money on the table, an amount he felt would not only punish West Penn Power, but also assure the financial well-being of his client and his family for generations—plus inspections and better training that could protect millions of others—Specter was forced to abandon his final condition. This last offer by the power company was, as they say, one he couldn't refuse.

Specter emailed Tom Kline to tell him the case had likely ended just before the closing speeches were to have taken place. At 5:02 p.m. on that Tuesday, he wrote: "Evidence concluded. Closing is possible although unlikely to occur. We've agreed to settlement amount (50mm) and confidentiality on the amount of the settlement."

Chapter 128

"Kina Hora."

Specter smiled as he said the words. On the eve of what he expected would be a $50 million settlement in the Goretzka case, someone on his staff asked about preparing a news release.

"Kina Hora," Specter said again, this time wincing.

Did he want to alert the news media?

"Kina Hora!" Specter repeated, louder now, holding up his hand as though the mere suggestion caused him pain. He waited for someone to ask him to explain what he was talking about. Or even what language he was using. When no one did, he volunteered.

Basically, Kina Hora was Yiddish for jinx. It was bad luck to talk about such things as announcing a $50 million settlement before the deal was officially done. Variously spelled and defined, Kina Hora was an expression used to ward off the Evil Eye, which was, according to one definition, "the bad luck that targets you just because something good has happened, the engine block that cracks two days after the warranty expires." Kina Hora was a sort of slang or shortened version of the more technically correct *Bli Ayin Hara* in Hebrew or *Kein Ayin Hora* in Yiddish. But each was uttered, often rapidly, to prevent something good from turning into something bad—to avoid "jinxing it."

The $50 million deal was about to happen. It was so close that Specter could see it, could feel *Goretzka v. West Penn Power* finally coming to a close. But he wasn't spending the money quite yet, and he didn't want to speak of the impending settlement as a fait accompli.

Kina Hora.

Chapter 129

Less than an hour after Specter's email to Tom Kline, he heard back from Levicoff. There were still some things to work out.

From: Avrum Levicoff
Sent: Tuesday, December 04, 2012 05:52 PM
To: Specter, Shanin

We are not going to be able to achieve settlement until the insurers approve the amounts, which has not occurred. I am told they need 24 hours after we set out the terms in writing. Even if we got the writing prepared tonight, I do not see how we have time to get the approval of the amount by tomorrow. If you have any ideas, please let me know.

Twelve minutes later, at 6:04 p.m., Specter responded with a four-word idea: "Company guarantees the settlement." Levicoff responded with four words of his own: "I will propose it." But Specter didn't believe West Penn Power would agree to such a thing, going it largely alone without an official sign-off by the insurance companies. He forwarded Levicoff's email and lamented the situation to his colleagues with the added note that they needed to continue to prepare for the battle in court. They could not put down their arms, not yet.

From: Specter, Shanin
To: Baldwin, Kila B.; Guerrini, Dominic
Date: Tuesday, December 04, 2012 6:35:55 PM

It's always one step forward and two steps back with these folks, per the below. Not relatedly, please tell me what occurred in the past two days that I should discuss in my closing.

Chapter 130

The concept of punitive damages has been around for thousands of years. The intent is twofold—to punish a defendant found to have acted so badly that mere compensation to an injured party is not enough and, secondly, to deter others from ever acting in the same manner in the future.

Punitive damages are considered in only the most egregious of cases and remain a relative rarity in American jurisprudence. According to one account citing studies by law professors and the U.S. Department of Justice, punitive damages are awarded in only one of every 50 civil cases that make it to trial.

For "punitives" to be handed down in Pennsylvania, a defendant must be found to have acted "recklessly" or "outrageously." Mere negligence is not enough. Usually, the harmful action has to have been intentional, malicious or, as Specter was claiming in the Goretzka case, there was "reckless disregard" for another person's well-being. Some jurisdictions considered it acting in a "quasi-criminal" fashion. Judges had to decide whether to even allow a jury to consider punitive damages, and usually they did not.

In his legal career of almost 30 years, Specter had sought punitive damages in about a dozen cases. In only three had a judge allowed a jury to weigh the question. In one, involving a drunk driver who struck and injured a pedestrian, the jury voted against punitive damages. In another, Specter won punitive damages for a college student who suffered severe brain damage when hospital staffers delayed in responding to a clogged airway, then altered medical records in an attempt to cover up their negligence. But that jury awarded just $15,000 in punitive damages, evidently feeling its prior $20 million compensatory award was plenty.

Even when a punitive award is large, which, despite popular belief, is uncommon, many are later chopped down or thrown out by the appellate courts. Specter's third case involving punitive conduct occurred in 1998 in *White v. Ford*, a case in which a child was killed when he was run over by a truck with a defective parking brake. Ford had failed to warn drivers of the dangers of the brake system in a recall notice. The jury awarded $150.9 million in punitive damages following an award of $2.3 million in compensatory damages. But the federal trial judge, David Hagen, reduced the punitive award to $69.2 million on the grounds of "proportionality"— that the award was too large compared to the compensatory verdict. Several years later, an appeals court panel, voting 2-1, upheld punitive damages generally but threw out the amount, saying it was based on erroneous jury instruction and went beyond the "territorial limitation" of the possible harm caused only to people in Nevada.

So the punitive award was vacated and a second trial ordered on the amount of punitive damages. Specter tried the case again and a second jury in 2004 awarded $52 million, an amount an appellate court also later struck down. Before he could begin a third trial, his clients, the deceased child's parents, worn down by years of legal battle, agreed to a confidential settlement. So Specter knew firsthand that getting and keeping a substantial punitive damages award was against the odds. Still, he felt the Goretzka case merited a punitive judgment.

His first hurdle was Judge Michael Della Vecchia. In his 11 years on the bench, Della Vecchia had never allowed a jury to even consider punitive damages. Not once. Even in his prior 30 years as a lawyer, he would later tell the attorneys in the Goretzka case, he had never been involved in a case in which punitive damages had been found to be warranted.

Chapter 131

Judge Della Vecchia had put off considering whether to allow the jury to decide punitive damages until after he had heard all the evidence in the case. Now that he had, he wanted to hear what the lawyers had to say one last time. If he allowed punitive damages, it potentially placed a new limit on a verdict—not quite the sky, but close. However, the jury would have to meet the rigid threshold of finding that West Penn Power had acted "recklessly," "outrageously" or with "reckless disregard" of others' well-being.

After the jury had been escorted out of the courtroom, Levicoff went first. There is a "very high bar" for putting punitive damages before a jury, he told the judge. He noted that the burden of proof is on the plaintiffs to make a case for such exceptional damages, not on the defense to disprove it acted recklessly. Additionally, the plaintiffs had to produce evidence that West Penn Power had a "subjective appreciation of the risk of harm" and then "failed to act in conscious disregard of that risk." In other words, the company had to have known that someone could be hurt or killed and basically said "what the heck" and did nothing to prevent it. What's more, West Penn Power had to have known that a particular person was at risk, not simply the public at large. Levicoff argued that Specter had not made such a case. At best, he said, the evidence showed negligence.

"Is it gross negligence?" the judge asked.

Levicoff refused to concede that point but, he said, even if it was gross negligence, "that's not enough" to make a case for punitive damages. He argued that no evidence had been presented during the trial that anyone at West Penn Power had a "conscious appreciation" that their conduct would harm Carrie or members of her family.

Just the opposite, debated Specter. The utility had "subjective personal knowledge through their employees of the risk and of the meaning of what they were doing." He began to read off a litany of complicit company players. First, he said, the lineman knew of the potential risk of an improperly installed power line, as did corporate safety manager Frank Gogol. As for the company knowing that the risk potential affected one particular customer, West Penn Power was fully aware of the prior episode in which the very same line fell on the Goretzka property, and he had seen Mike Goretzka's messages voicing his concern. Specter cited his experts' testimony that the power company's behavior had been reckless. The most damaging testimony, he maintained, came from Jill D'Angelo, the lineman supervisor and company manager, who testified that long before Carrie was killed, she was aware of multiple incidents that failure to properly clean a wire could cause a splice failure. She knew that the company "standard on splice installations needed to be strengthened and the dangers of not doing so communicated to the company's linemen...." And she knew that was not done.

Della Vecchia put up a hand. He had heard enough from Specter. "I don't really want a recap of everybody's testimony," he said. To the judge, the case was pretty simple. It boiled down to two things.

One: "This line falls on a bright, sunny day. There is no storm. There are no falling trees."

Two: "Mr. Goretzka in 2004 emails the power company and says, 'I'm concerned about my family's safety and well-being as a result of [the previous fall of the] line.' That alone is enough to cause some concern and give them a personal knowledge, if you will, about the situation."

Della Vecchia also suggested that the utility didn't show adequate concern over the falling line, and it did not take remedial steps. It never questioned Thomas Jones or Jeffrey Falo about the 2004 failure. No meetings were held about the fallen line. Veteran linemen were not retrained afterward.

"I think enough is raised. They were on notice since at least 2004 of a truly dangerous condition and saw fit not to act," the judge pointed out, adding about a punitive a damages award, "At this point there is enough in the record to allow the jury to consider it."

Then he cast his eye to the back row of the courtroom and the lone reporter there that day, Paul Peirce of *The Pittsburgh Tribune Review*, who had been filing daily dispatches on the trial. The judge wanted to make sure he got the story right. "Now, Mr. Peirce back there from the media, I'm not ruling that there are punitive damages. It's merely whether there is sufficient evidence in the record for the jury to consider it and conclude it, if they wish to or they wish not to."

Chapter 132

On Wednesday morning, before Avrum Levicoff was to give his closing speech to the jury, Specter finally got the deal he was waiting for—in writing. Two full typed pages with several sentences on the third page spelled out the deal.

Specter didn't love every aspect of the agreement, particularly the confidentiality agreement, which included a $1 million "fine" for a violation and a clause that said if asked about the deal, "the parties will reply only that these matters have been 'confidentially resolved.'" Yet he liked the fact that West Penn Power would implement a full program of inspections and remediation. And, he had to admit, the first clause of the settlement had a way of assuaging any other concerns he or his client might have. It read: "The payment of Fifty Million Dollars will be made to Plaintiffs and their lawyer by or on behalf of the defendant by December 19, 2012."

"Fifty Million Dollars."

Whatever else that amount invoked, it surely represented victory—and that West Penn and its insurers had surrendered. They had given up the fight. They had moved from $10 million all the way to $50 million, Specter's stated sum early on in the trial for settling the case. He hadn't budged, his troops had held the line and coerced this large corporate entity to wave the white flag. No verdict would be read aloud in court, no public punishment or admonition of the utility, no publicity of its capitulation. Yet West Penn Power would be forced to change its ways and mend its mistakes. And $50 million was a heavy punishment.

With Mike Goretzka's knowledge and approval, Specter took the top off a Bic "Round Stic" pen and wrote on the paper before him. "Approved: Shanin Specter, For: Plaintiff" and signed his name.

He slid the paper over to Levicoff, who affixed the date and time—"12/5/12 noon"—and printed and signed his name as well. The case was over. Or so Specter thought.

He sent another email, this time to his entire law firm.

To: All K&S Employees
Subject: Goretzka
Date: Wednesday, December 05, 2012 11:43:09 AM

This case is close to settlement. The remaining issue prior to approval by the excess carrier of the settlement amount is their demand concerning confidentiality. I have agreed that disclosure by our clients or our firm (which means any firm employee) of the settlement amount is subject to fine and that 1mm is presumed reasonable. Therefore, obviously, no disclosure shall be made of the proposed or eventual settlement amount.

A few minutes later, the first employee of the 110 employees of Kline & Specter, a legal assistant, sent a response: "Congrats to you and your trial team!"

To which Specter immediately responded: "Hasn't happened yet." Kina Hora.

Chapter 133

The $50 million deal had one stipulation. Contained in the next-to-last paragraph under the heading "Conditions," it read: "The parties acknowledge that this term sheet is subject to and conditioned upon the defendant's ability to finalize an agreement with its insurers to fund the settlement amount referenced above. Defendant shall be permitted 24 hours...to finalize an agreement with its insurers."

Twenty-four hours.

West Penn Power was willing to pay $20 million out of its own pocket, going a great length to avoid a verdict. Levicoff had said so himself, much to Specter's surprise, when meeting with the judge in his chambers. "We can't afford to have a verdict in this case," he had said before the plaintiffs' lawyers and West Penn Power's insurers. The utility wanted desperately to avoid the publicity of a possible large verdict along with the additional lawsuits and legal fees that could come with it.

Specter didn't know if West Penn Power had both insurance companies solidly on board with the settlement. He did not know whether the 24-hour waiting period posed a problem or if it was a mere formality. He assumed the latter.

Chapter 134

On August 6, 1890, William Kemmler, known as "Philadelphia Billie," was dressed in a suit, white shirt and tie. He was seated in the invention of Harold P. Brown and Arthur Kennelly, both employees of Thomas Edison. Their invention was the electric chair, and Kemmler was to be its first occupant. A habitual drunk who had moved from Philadelphia to Buffalo, he had murdered his common-law wife with a hatchet. His lawyers had lost an appeal to the U.S. Supreme Court on the argument that the electric chair represented "cruel and unusual punishment." Not coincidentally, one of the active backers of his appeal was George Westinghouse, still fighting Edison's campaign to prove the dangers of alternating current. However, throwing even more financial support into fighting the appeal was J.P. Morgan, Edison's chief financial backer. The appeal lost.

An electrode was placed against Kemmler's shaved head and another through a hole in his clothing. "Take it easy and do it properly, I'm in no hurry," Kemmler said through a cover over his face, displaying a sense of humor to the end.

Kemmler was struck with 1,000 volts, a surge prison officials had believed would be enough to produce cardiac arrest and death. Indeed, they had successfully tested the same voltage a day earlier on a horse. After 17 seconds, the power was shut off and Kemmler was declared dead. But then several witness thought they saw him breathing. Seconds later, the attending physicians realized he was still alive. One of the doctors hollered: "Have the current turned on again, quick—no delay!" The second time, Kemmler was hit with 2,000 volts. A report the next day in *The New York Times* carried the headline: "Killed by Shocks—Electrocution of Kemmler at Auburn Prison—The First Bolt a Failure—Horrible and Sickening Convulsion and Respiration Ensued." The newspaper article went on to describe a smell of burning flesh that was "unbearable," with nauseated witnesses fleeing for the exits.

In all, the execution of William Kemmler took eight minutes. Yet the gruesome spectacle did nothing to stop further use of the electric chair. For many years, electrocution was the most common means imposing the death penalty in the United States. Lethal injection, considered more humane, was first used in a Texas prison in 1982, and it in turn became the most common form of execution.

Chapter 135

Since the settlement deal was not yet official, Avrum Levicoff proceeded with his closing speech. He rose slowly from the defense table to stand before the jury one last time. Levicoff wore a black double-breasted suit with a white shirt and black-and-white tie. He looked sharp but serious. On several occasions during his summation, delivered 20 days after his opening, Levicoff would open his jacket and pull his pants up. Perhaps, like Specter, he had lost weight over the course of the trial.

"Members of the jury, it's been a long trial. It's been a long trial," Levicoff began his closing speech, his voice low and deliberate. He looked worn out, even sad. He started the way many attorneys do, by thanking the jury for its service. He spent a good deal of time doing so and spared no platitudes.

"In this particular case, with what we've all been through for the past three-plus weeks, just to thank you for your service just really, really doesn't say nearly enough. The service that you've provided in this particular case is remarkable. It is remarkable. I just don't have enough words to convey the degree of appreciation that I would like to express on behalf of myself and on behalf of my client, West Penn Power Company, or the court or the Goretzka family or the plaintiffs' team of lawyers. Your service in this case has been remarkable. When you stop and think about it, for you folks to have taken three-plus weeks out of your daily routine, come in here day after day, and you have no stake in the outcome, no interest in the outcome and your function in being here is simply to help these parties resolve their differences is, well, it goes beyond any eloquence that I'm capable of delivering."

When it was his turn to address the jury, Specter would take a different approach, one that even some veteran trial observers would say they had never heard before. He would tell the jurors that if they found that sitting in the courtroom all this time and missing their regular routines was a deprivation, well, essentially, too bad. It was their duty.

"Chief Justice Earl Warren said that aside from putting on the uniform of your country in time of war, the most important thing you can do as a citizen is serve on a jury. He said it was more important than voting and more important than paying your taxes...And while I join Mr. Levicoff in thanking you, I don't necessarily completely share his view concerning hardship."

Specter said he realized the trial had been a disruption of the jurors' daily lives, "but all of us have important things to do in our lives. Sometimes the important things we have to do in our lives, they're not of our choice." He mentioned, for example, caring for an elderly parent or a child with special needs.

"Or because you're a citizen of Allegheny County and you take a jury summons seriously, you're asked to resolve a remarkably and enormously important issue. Not just for the Goretzka family and for West Penn Power, but for the community. And respectfully, I think it's an honor," he said, waiting a moment to look at the jurors one by one before repeating the line, "I think it's an honor."

Chapter 136

"I'm up here first," Avrum Levicoff said early in his closing speech, which he told the judge he expected would last about an hour. "We get one chance and one chance only. So in effect, members of the jury, this is the last time you're going to hear from me in this case."

The veteran defense attorney explained how he would get a closing speech and then Shanin Specter would get his, with no rebuttals. The practice was different in different county jurisdictions, but this was how it was done in Allegheny County. Levicoff did not say the system was unfair, but he did imply that he had the tougher job. He had to lay out the entire case and West Penn Power's side of things. "And I may forget some things because I'm prone to do that," he added, telling the jury he did not work from a "prepared script." (This was something that attorneys debated among themselves—whether or not to work from a written text for their closing speeches. Many felt, as did politicians and political candidates, that the use of prepared scripts or even notes undercut the influence or passion of their words. It made the speeches seem, in their minds, more stiff and less from the heart. Specter did not feel this way. He prepared his speeches over and over, in his mind and on paper. He didn't care about seeming impromptu or spontaneous. He had important topics and facts to cover, and he didn't want to forget a single one. His partner, Tom Kline, felt the same way, entering this phase of a trial with a thick tablet of pages, each with separate thoughts written in large, black magic-marker letters. The device did not sap his speeches of emotion. Jurors often wiped their eyes or even openly sobbed as Kline, a thespian at heart, flipped his pages.) Levicoff told the jury that he was also at a disadvantage because he had to try to anticipate what Specter might say, then try to refute it. He asked for assistance.

"If an argument is advanced by the plaintiffs' side of the case that I do not get to answer, think of it. Ask yourself, 'Based on the evidence that has been presented, what might Levicoff have said about that...?' I'm not asking you to take my side in it. All I'm asking you to do is realize I don't get a chance to answer. I need your help."

The defense attorney had an important caveat for the jurors—do not base your decisions on sympathy. The panel was the arbiter of fact, nothing more. No matter what they might feel for the harm that came to Carrie, no matter their feelings for the family she left behind, Levicoff told them, "You have to be very careful not to be so overwhelmed with the harm and injury that you take your focus off the evidence ...You may be moved or an attempt may be made to move you with passion, and that could be a distraction, and you need to focus on the evidence." He asked the men and women now staring at him to exercise a "cool, dispassionate, rational focus."

"When I'm done speaking and the plaintiffs' attorney addresses you, I suspect you will hear a very impassioned address," he continued, cautioning the jury about Specter's possible next move, but stopping just short of an accusation. "I suspect that you will hear some things perhaps designed to take your focus off the evidence to some degree. I don't know that. We'll have to wait and see. But it could happen."

Then Levicoff plunged into the evidence, a lengthy and detailed recital of points in which he tried to pick off the plaintiffs' case and its witnesses.

One, the argument that West Penn Power had used a fuse on the power line outside the Goretzkas' house that was too large, was irrelevant at best and fallacious at worst, he held. The plaintiffs' own expert witness, John Dagenhart, had admitted as much from the witness stand, noting under cross-examination that the difference between the fuse used and a smaller one would have been to cut off the power a mere fraction of a second sooner. Not enough to make a difference.

Two, Carrie had, regrettably, put herself in harm's way. "They became aware of a problem, according to the testimony of JoAnn. They knew the power went out. JoAnn further testified that they looked at the back windows, as I recall her testimony, and they saw trees on fire. So they recognized that the line had not only come down, but it had come down energized." Levicoff didn't say it, but the logical thing, the smart thing, would have been for them to have stayed inside the house.

As several jurors jotted notes on pads given them by the court, Levicoff put up several exhibits to show Carrie's path. "We know that at or about this time she went outside, and we know—and there can't be any dispute about it—that she then walked over to an area in the side yard." He then pointed to his expert Catherine Corrigan's diagram that "shows the relative location in which she thinks Carrie Goretzka positioned herself, which puts her almost directly under this item, which is the A-phase conductor," the power line that killed her.

Levicoff took a breath. "Now, you probably are going to hear an attack on my client from the plaintiffs' attorney—'Well, Mr. Levicoff is blaming her.' Members of the jury, I want to be very clear on this. I'm not blaming anybody. What I'm suggesting to you is that you need to determine why that occurred in order to render a verdict in this case. You just need to determine why that occurred."

Three, the plaintiffs' theory of how the incident happened was off-kilter. If, as their experts had said, the downed wire had hung up for a time on the cable wire beneath it, wouldn't Carrie have seen it burning there? Wouldn't she "logically" have looked up rather than down? Levicoff asked. "Wouldn't you think that if you know there is a downed power line...that the first thing you might do is look up to see whether you can see it or not?"

Other evidence also did not make common sense, he asserted. Such as the cable wire not being damaged where the plaintiffs said the power line had landed on it. And if it had, it would have arced and sparked, "And yet somehow it stays up there and Mrs. Goretzka doesn't see it." Levicoff noted that the mailman had seen a "fireball" up in the air about the same time JoAnn started screaming for help. "And members of the jury, I simply ask you to take your common sense and apply it to this question: Is it realistic to believe that even if she didn't look up to begin with, that Mrs. Goretzka would make the turn toward the side yard and not notice that going on 18 feet above her head and position herself right under it?"

Four, the testimony of the plaintiffs' experts was not credible, Levicoff maintained. He held up the top expert, Campbell Laird, to near-ridicule. He described the professor as someone who had testified 200 times in cases and "had more trial experience than I do, and that's a lot." He noted Laird had worked on 10 cases with Specter and mockingly dubbed them "a dynamic duo."

And yet Laird, as scholarly as he was and despite having written a 60-page report on the case, had failed to recognize wire brushing on the downed power line. "He writes a report. The report says five times [that] none of the conductors in any of the splices was wire-brushed." But, he noted, that during the trial—and not sooner—Laird acknowledged evidence of wire brushing. The defense attorney reminded the jury of Laird's answer as to why he hadn't spotted that evidence earlier. "Do you remember the answer? 'Missed it.'"

That spoke to competence. Now Levicoff attacked the witness' credibility, noting that Laird acknowledged seeing the evidence of wire brushing (after seeing another report prepared for trial by the defense) before he submitted his report, yet the report made no mention of it. Levicoff turned to the jury and posed a question: "Can you trust much of anything that witness has to say?"

He similarly attacked Chris Havlik of Hubbell for missing evidence of wire brushing because "this expert, top three in the world, never bothers to look at it under so much as a magnifying glass. Not a 25-cent magnifying glass to see really whether it was wire-brushed or not." Again, a lack of competence.

"Next is Mr. Dagenhart." Levicoff held particular disdain for this plaintiffs' expert witness, who had written in his report that he did see evidence of wire brushing only to change his opinion for trial. John Dagenhart had testified that his view was "evolving," that "I'm leaning toward that not being wire brushing at this point." Levicoff read the testimony aloud so the jury could hear it again. Then, his voice tinged with sarcasm, the attorney commented, "His views are *evolving*. We've been litigating this case for years. We're at trial. He's written two reports—clearly wire-brushed. I make an issue of the evidentiary value, and all of a sudden his views are *evolving*…Can you trust anything that witness has to say about anything?"

Finally, there were the defense witnesses, some of whom Levicoff noted had been picked apart by a crafty Specter. But although lacking the experience and savvy of Havlik or Laird, the defense witnesses had been forthright, he contended.

Joe Turek, although not a world-renowned metallurgist like Campbell Laird, had nonetheless given the jury the straight poop. Levicoff reminded the jury that Laird had not seen evidence of wire brushing, but then said he did, while Turek spotted it from the beginning. "There is no question that Dr. Laird stands head and shoulders above everyone in intelligence… degrees, publications…Joe Turek, different story. Never published anything. Not an engineer. But is there any doubt in your mind about the care he took examining the physical evidence?" Turek didn't "miss a thing," as Laird had, and his opinion had not "evolved" as did Dagenhart's. He was a careful, local guy who could be trusted.

Jill D'Angelo, the West Penn Power standards manager, had been "no match" for Specter, who at one point had her "virtually in tears," Levicoff recalled. And while Specter had been critical of D'Angelo's failure to do more to safeguard customers like the Goretzkas, the defense attorney pointed to her sincere efforts to make things better. She had issued a newsletter about installing splices. And "this individual, who was alleged to be callous and indifferent," also wrote an article for the newsletter reminding employees about the importance of proper installation practices. She published a standard in the company manual noting that failure to clean a power line could produce overheating and "eventual failure of the splice." Levicoff added, "Does this look like callous indifference to you?"

He noted, however, that "when confronted by a tenacious lawyer" at trial, D'Angelo admitted that she "could have done it better." But that did not mean much, he argued. "We can always have done it better," he said, adding later, "Well, sure, she could have put on a hat and gloves and put splices in, too. We can always do something more." But not doing so certainly did not constitute "reckless" indifference, Levicoff held, using the same terminology needed for a jury to find punitive damages against his client. Avoiding a verdict against West Penn Power was Levicoff's goal, but he desperately wanted to at least dodge a jury finding for the generally more substantial punitive damages.

The linemen, Jeffrey Falo and Thomas Jones, also did not act recklessly, Levicoff asserted. Even if they failed to brush the wire (which he did not concede), they were just two typical workers doing their jobs the best they knew how. He asked: "Is it likely that those two guys are different than how many countless thousands of linemen all around the country who put these things up for our company or any other company? I mean, is it really likely they are just reckless and indifferent while others are not?"

"Don't you think that there would be evidence of some multiple number of these failures if, in fact, the failure occurs simply because a lineman some afternoon decides not to brush the conductor? It's an awfully thin reed on which to base certainly an award of punitive damages."

When the defense attorney finished, Judge Della Vecchia, who before the closing speech had mentioned that when younger, he had actually lived in Mr. Rogers' neighborhood (Fred Rogers was from Latrobe, about 40 miles southeast of Pittsburgh), now told them he had attended Catholic school. "The nuns had boxes of gold stars...I would give you [jurors] gold stars if I had them." Instead, he gave them something they undoubtedly preferred—the rest of the day off. As they filed from the courtroom and into the marble corridor, the jurors got another reminder of the trial's importance when they were met by a crew from KDKA-TV. Television cameras didn't show up for small potatoes.

Specter was glad that Levicoff had overshot his predicted one hour closing speech. He had taken two hours and 42 minutes, ending at 4 p.m., too late for the judge to allow Specter to respond. So not only would the plaintiffs' lawyer get the final word to the jury, but his closing speech would also come a day later, giving the jury more time to forget Levicoff's words. And Specter's words would be the last the jury would hear from either side before its deliberations.

But Specter doubted it would come to that. Soon, the agreement for the $50 million settlement would be finalized.

Chapter 137

After his summation, Avrum Levicoff did something unexpected. When the jury left, the defense attorney walked to the back of the courtroom and slid into the wooden pew where Mike Goretzka was seated. He placed a hand on Mike's back and said something to him very softly. The lawyer appeared to have tears in his eyes.

Levicoff explained that he had only done his job, which was to defend his client, though it had been emotionally difficult for him. He told Goretzka that he felt bad that his daughters had witnessed their mother's torment and that he admired his tenacity through such a long and difficult legal proceeding.

Mike didn't know how to respond, so he simply said thanks and nodded. After a few seconds, Levicoff patted him on the shoulder and walked away.

Chapter 138

Around this time, Maurice Nernberg, the local counsel in Pittsburgh who had originally referred the case to Shanin Specter's firm and who stood to reap a sizable sum of money from the settlement, emailed Specter that he had "informed everyone" at his firm of the great news of the $50 million settlement. He noted that he had run into another judge at the courthouse who had also heard about the deal, so "it is already out of the bag."

To which Specter responded: "There is no deal yet...please don't repeat the number and please don't confirm it to anyone who may ask." (He remembered the $1 million fine.)

Still, Nernberg found it hard to conceal his glee. He praised Specter's skill as a trial lawyer and negotiator. He also added a self-deprecating note: "I was very proud of myself not to let greed overcome the best interests of the client," referring to his decision to pass the case to Specter instead of attempting to try it himself. "Not only would I have gone outside of my comfort zone, but would never have achieved what you have here. As you know, many lawyers would like to have this case, but not many lawyers, if any, would achieve what you and your firm have."

Nernberg concluded in his email that he and his wife planned to go out to dinner that night and that "If you and your crew would like to join us and celebrate, you are quite welcome...We go out about 8."

Chapter 139

A half hour later, the red light flashed on Specter's Blackberry once again.

From: Avrum Levicoff
Sent: Wednesday, December 05, 2012 04:46 PM
To: Specter, Shanin

The insurers rejected. I am trying to determine if any leverage can be applied. I am also trying to find out where the blockage is. I will update you.

Levicoff told Specter that he had wanted a settlement of the case. Specter and his colleagues didn't doubt the intention of the defense attorney. They had heard him on one occasion shouting at an insurance company representative in a courtroom hallway. Levicoff told Specter that he was pushing his client, West Penn Power, to turn up the pressure on the insurance people to accept the settlement. Levicoff said he did not want to leave the matter to the jury. He did not want to gamble that it would not hand down a tremendous verdict. But apparently, at least one of the insurers was willing to roll the dice.

Time passed. Specter looked at his watch. It was 6 p.m.—drinks were now being served at the White House party. His name tag would be sitting on a table unclaimed. Finally, two hours after Levicoff's last correspondence, as Specter sat at the Fairmont Hotel bar sipping a Negroni (equal parts gin, sweet vermouth and Campari), his Blackberry flashed with an update.

From: Avrum Levicoff
Sent: Wednesday, December 05, 2012 06:48 PM
To: Specter, Shanin
Subject: Goretzka

My client clearly has no clue as to how to pressure insurers to settle. I will be working on this all evening. If anything can be done, I will do it. Please advise your client. I will update you immediately if anything breaks.

Specter showed the email to his colleagues. "What does it mean?" asked Baldwin. Specter smiled thinly and shrugged.

It sounded like there was a snafu. "If anything can be done...." That had a ring of hopelessness. Then again, Levicoff was on top of the situation, no doubt reading the riot act to the insurance people, maybe even threatening to sue if they didn't come up with the money and the whole thing went sour with a gigantic jury verdict. Or maybe Specter was being played. Perhaps it was a bit of gamesmanship. Perhaps the $50 million offer was never real, just a tease, a carrot offered to see if Specter would bite, which he had. Was $50 million an elaborate bait-and-switch? Were they trying to throw him off his game?

No matter, Specter wasn't going to let this latest development affect his performance in the courtroom. He would not be unprepared or disarmed by the dangling yet elusive $50 million offer. Whatever happened, tomorrow morning, he would be set to deliver his closing speech. In a quick staccato, he gave Baldwin and Guerrini their marching orders for the night, including a list of everything he would need for his closing. "And I need the blue company Bible for the speech," he concluded the list. "So you guys have a bunch of work to do, so I'll get going. We'll meet tomorrow morning and you can give it all to me. Eight a.m., OK?" They both nodded.

As Levicoff suggested, Specter did advise his client of the latest development. Mike Goretzka, who, like everyone else had believed the case was finally over, responded with incredulity.

"And it continues...unbelievable," he emailed Specter. "What is the strategy now?"

Specter wrote back a three-word response: "Show up tomorrow."

Chapter 140

The next morning, December 6, Specter took Mike Goretzka out of court and into the hallway. They walked down the corridor. Lawyer advised client. Specter had received word that the $50 million conditional offer had, in fact, been withdrawn. The other parts of the deal were done, including a full-fledged remediation program and an ironclad confidentiality agreement. But the monetary offer was gone and, without that, there was no deal at all.

"So what's the plan?" Goretzka asked.

"I don't know what they have," Specter replied, referring to a sum of money that might still salvage a settlement. He presumed the previous $40 million was still on the table. Maybe the defendants would up their offer. "But I don't want to be the first to ask. Let's do the closing speech and let the judge charge the jury and then we'll see."

Specter had seen cases settle while juries were deliberating, even moments before they returned to court with a verdict. It could easily happen here.

"You think maybe they'll go to 45?" asked Goretzka. He was clearly now willing to take $45 million if it was offered. He was tired of the courtroom, beaten down by the legal battle. It was exhausting him. If Specter was getting little sleep, Mike Goretzka was getting next to none. Ending this war was sounding better and better. He wanted a verdict, wanted to pronounce West Penn as the wrongdoer here and to the world, or at least the Pittsburgh news media. But $45 million was a lot of money, enough to punish the power company, even if the settlement would be confidential. It stuck in his craw but…

"I don't like the confidentiality agreement either," Specter admitted. "I can't agree to a $1 million fine. I have 110 employees. And what if your brother Chuck goes out one night and has a drink at a bar and mentions it?"

"I agree. But do you think they'll come back with 45?"

"There's no way to tell. I just don't know."

"Well, what do you think a verdict would be?"

"Mike, I think we have a 50/50 chance of it being more than $40 million. And there is value in a verdict, having it announced in court."

Mike nodded his head in agreement. The two men walked back into the courtroom, Specter taking his seat at the plaintiffs' table and Goretzka his spot in the first row directly behind the attorneys.

Judge Della Vecchia summoned both sides to his chambers, first a somber-looking power company executive, then Levicoff, then Specter. The courtroom was quiet in their absence.

When they came out, Specter walked directly back to his client. He had more news.

"They're back down to 25 million."

"What does that mean?" Goretzka asked.

"We give our closing speech."

Chapter 141

Judge Della Vecchia had never seen a plaintiff's attorney turn down a solid offer of $25 million, as Specter had, or anything close to that amount. But he didn't blame him. "He was reasonable in evaluating a case," Della Vecchia would say later, noting it was Specter's third case in his courtroom. He recalled that in the Blumer case, Ford had refused to accept Specter's demand of $3 million before a jury handed down its $8.75 million verdict.

The judge now blamed West Penn Power, which, he said, had indicated during the trial that it was willing to offer $35 million or $40 million to settle the case, but never made an official offer for those amounts. Della Vecchia commented: "They kept intimating. Frankly, you can wipe your ass with intimating. I wanted the money."

He never got it—until the offer of $50 million that both Specter and Levicoff signed. The judge, like Specter, thought the deal was done.

"But then they brought in this big bullshitter," Della Vecchia would recall about an attorney for First Energy Corporation, the Ohio-based holding company for West Penn Power and nine other regulated distribution companies, which boasted $50 billion in assets and $15 billion in annual revenues. The corporate attorney, he said, talked a lot but refused to commit to the deal.

"Finally I said, 'Are you going to pay the $50 million or not?' And he said, 'I'm not going to pay the $15 million,'" referring to the amount the company would have to advance beyond its $5 million deductible to make the deal work. "I have an insurance policy. Our insurance company has to pay."

The judge was fuming. "They made a deal and they broke it."

Guerrini, whom Della Vecchia had nicknamed "Little Dom" because of his boyish good looks, was the last to leave the judge's chambers. The judge told him that it was his job to keep Specter under control, to try to temper his boss during the settlement negotiations. He felt that Specter was close to exploding, and he didn't blame him. Then Della Vecchia, a first-generation Italian-American, pulled his "goombah" closer and, in words he would repeat in an interview nearly two years later, told him: "I'm so mad, I hope the jury gives you $100 million."

Chapter 142

As the hours and days mounted, so had the plaintiffs' cost for the Goretzka case. It would, in fact, become the most costly one that Kline & Specter had ever undertaken. The final tab would be $930,320.05.

Part of the reason for the high cost was that the trial was an "away game," requiring transportation for the 300 miles it took to traverse the length of Pennsylvania and hotel rooms for the whole team. And Specter didn't stay at Motel 6. Even after he negotiated a low rate at a very nice downtown Pittsburgh hotel, the Fairmont, the cost was still high. Rooms were needed for all the attorneys plus assistants and the well-stocked "war room" used for strategy sessions, readying expert witnesses, storing and making documents, eating and drinking.

On one trip to Pittsburgh, for instance, the group ran up a substantial hotel bill for absolutely nothing. It occurred during Hurricane Sandy when everyone had piled into various modes of transportation on Sunday, October 28, to beat the approaching storm and make it to trial. On Monday, however, after the trial team prepped over breakfast and then trudged the four uphill blocks to the county courthouse, the judge delayed the trial at West Penn's request. The reason: its employees, executives included, were needed at various other places to assist with the storm emergency. Specter, Baldwin, Guerrini, Grimmie and Mike Kutys walked back to the hotel and tried to pass the restive moments of the next three days. They couldn't get back to Philadelphia, where Sandy had now taken up residence. The Pennsylvania Turnpike was closed.

Being in Pittsburgh with nothing to do was like being out at sea in a sailboat with no wind. While eastern Pennsylvania faced a hurricane, the legal team was in the middle of the doldrums. They had been all keyed up for the trial and now, nothing. So they had spent the next three days cooped up in the Fairmont with little to do except eat and sleep and ruminate about the case. A bottle of water from the minibar cost $6. Diane Grimmie initially tried to keep the bill down by purchasing drinks and candy across the street at a CVS drugstore and by lecturing about the cost of the hotel treats, once even mildly castigating one member of the group for opening a box of mixed nuts priced at $12. But she eventually abandoned the effort. The cost of the hotel stay alone for those futile three days was $9,722.65. For the entire case, including all pretrial travel by Baldwin and Guerrini to take depositions and interview experts, the cost of lodging, travel and meals came to more than $200,000.

Printing costs were astronomical. At the trial alone, Grimmie would use well over 8,000 sheets of paper and burn through a dozen toner cartridges. Color and black-and-white copy charges reached nearly $110,000, while the cost of transcripts would hit almost $38,000. The largest expense of the case, however, was the experts. They didn't come cheaply. The cost amounted to more than $500,000 for experts used and not used—both good and not-so-good—at trial. Much of the money went to John Dagenhart and Campbell Laird.

None of this mattered if Specter won the case. The costs would come out of any settlement or verdict that resulted. But plaintiff firms generally got reimbursed only if they won. As the law firm's website put it:

> *Kline & Specter, P.C. works on a contingent fee basis—which means we only get paid if and when you are financially compensated. Kline & Specter is paid a percentage of the amount recovered. Any costs incurred by Kline & Specter will only be charged if the client is financially compensated.*

And if not, the costs would be paid by Kline & Specter.

Chapter 143

At the rising of the sun and going down, I recall her.
At the blowing of the wind and in the chill of winter, I recall her.
At the opening of the buds and in the rebirth of spring,
At the shining of the sun and in the warmth of the summer,
At the rustling of the leaves and in the beauty of autumn, I recall her.

With those words, adapted from the Jewish mourning poem by Sylvan Kramer and Rabbi Jack Riemer, Specter began his closing speech in *Goretzka v. West Penn Power*. He did not explain his own adaptation of the poem (and did not state its author), but its meaning was clear. It was about a man who would never see his wife again, about children whose mother was gone for all seasons, forever. Specter didn't know how such a reading would come across, but he was glad when Juror number 5, George Coulston, smiled at him at its conclusion. Then Specter quoted the 18th-century philosopher Edmund Burke: "This is an event that's happened upon which it is difficult to speak and impossible to be silent."

"It's difficult to speak, and I have difficulty speaking," Specter told the jury, "but it's impossible to be silent about this. And when we're finished with the speeches and Your Honor charges you and you go deliberate and come back and announce your verdict, you will break the silence."

Specter quickly switched gears, his voice at first soothing, now rising with indignation.

"There are so many outrages here. There are just so many, it's hard for me to catalog them all. Let's start with this: This case should have never been tried. Never been tried...How can they, with a straight face for three and a half weeks, come in here and contest their responsibility for the death of Carrie Goretzka? That is such a moral outrage.

"This woman was minding her own business, taking care of her children, thrust into an emergency not of her own making, killed in her yard, her yard, by a power line that fell on a clear, sunny day, through no fault of her own.

"They make us prove their responsibility, and they have the outrageous insult to blame her for her own death!"

Res ipsa loquitor. Latin for "the thing speaks for itself," Specter told the jury, "We learned it in the first two weeks of law school."

He explained: "As the lawyer for the family, I could have tried the case very differently. I could have simply proven that it was a clear, sunny day and the line fell. I could have relied upon that fact by itself. I don't have to prove anything."

The power line belonged to West Penn Power, and it was the utility's responsibility to ensure that it didn't fall and kill someone. Pure and simple. "Under the law," Specter pointed out, "when something occurs that would not ordinarily occur, unless there was negligence— negligence, lack of due care—then the mere happening of that incident is sufficient to prove that the defendant is responsible."

He told the jury about a law school case in which a barrel fell from a second-floor window and hit a pedestrian. Nobody knew how or why the barrel had rolled out the window, and it didn't matter. "It's unimportant. The person who owns the property has a responsibility to keep barrels from rolling out the window," Specter noted. "The mere fact that you were struck by a barrel while walking down the sidewalk is enough."

Res ipsa loquitor.

"Now, we, of course, went a step further to show you exactly why it happened," he told the jury, "but we didn't have to do that." By merely showing that the accident happened on a "clear, sunny day"—a phrase Specter would repeat six times in the first few minutes of his speech—presented enough, the plaintiffs have "met our burden of proof." If the jury felt that the falling of a charged electric line would not ordinarily happen unless there was negligence in the installation or maintenance of the line, then, Specter asserted, "We've proven our case on negligence, period. End of story." He had presented the plaintiffs' theory of what caused the accident— namely, the lack of brushing and proper installation and the lax efforts, the "reckless" behavior, up the company ladder that allowed that to happen.

The defense had relied on a "common sense" theory that the failed part of the line must have been brushed because the intact side of the splice showed some evidence—faint as it was and only visible under magnification—of brushing. It was logical that if the person who installed that splice, whether Thomas Jones or Jeffrey Falo, had brushed one side, they had most likely brushed the other. But Specter took that same logic further down the line, literally. Jones and Falo had installed the other two splices on the same stretch of power line along the Goretzka property. There was no evidence, not even the faintest, of brushing of the wire on either side of those splices. Specter urged the jury, as had Levicoff, to use common sense to answer this question: If the same workers had installed two splices without brushing the wire, was it probable that they had brushed the wire with the third splice? At six places the line was placed into splices, two for each device. Four had no evidence of brushing, one had possible—though faint and debatable—evidence of brushing. What were the odds the sixth piece of wire, the piece that had been destroyed and fell to the ground, had been adequately brushed and properly installed? The odds did not seem good.

"Now," he asked the jury, "did you notice with Mr. Levicoff's two-hour and 42-minute narration, there was not a moment, not even a moment of discussion, about the other two splices that were installed by Jones and/or Falo on that very same day?"

Specter suggested the plaintiffs' witnesses, his witnesses, were highly credible. Take Chris Havlik, for example, an official at the Hubbell company that supplied splices to West Penn Power, a company that relied on the utility as a major customer. Havlik had not found evidence of wire brushing on the power line at the splice point. If he had, Specter suggested, he would have been a witness—a "star witness" at that—for the defense. Havlik would have naturally preferred to have testified on the behalf of West Penn Power, a big customer of Hubbell products. But he couldn't honestly do so. "The law firm of Kline & Specter isn't buying any Hubbell splices. And we're not likely to in the future, are we?" Specter asked.

He went on to contend that the defense witnesses were not credible. Lineman Jeffrey Falo testified that he recognized the importance of wire brushing, that failure to do so could result in a line burning down and endangering lives, and that he always wire-brushed a line before installation. Yet the evidence showed that at least four splice points on that very line along the Goretzka property had not been wire-brushed. Worse, while understanding the potential consequences of not brushing a line before installation, Falo testified in the same breath that if he saw another lineman, like his partner, Thomas Jones, not using a wire brush, he wouldn't say anything to correct him. He would let a line go into a splice without being brushed.

It was also "distressing," Specter noted, that trainers—even after the tragedy and even after the lawsuit—continued to insist that it was OK not to use a brush, that pliers or the back of a knife would suffice. Two trainers had admitted as much. "They've been doing it wrong decade after decade, even after we filed this lawsuit," Specter emphasized. "And they know what happened here. They know it. And these men come in and they say, 'We still do it this way. I still think it's OK not to wire-brush.'"

Moreover, the executives of the company didn't know—or worse, didn't care—that this practice was par for the course. "You got to bring the men in. You got to tell them this is unacceptable. You got to suspend some people, maybe fire people," Specter asserted firmly.

Chapter 144

Shanin Specter was just revving up. At the start of his speech, he had removed his watch and placed it on the wooden rail of the jury box so he could keep track of the time. But he knew at this point that he was going to run long, probably more than two hours. (His father, the veteran senator, used to do the same thing, placing his watch on the lectern when he started a speech. Then Arlen Specter would look up at the audience members and, with his wry smile, tell them: "I'm doing this to give you a false sense of security that I'm paying attention to the time.")

Specter launched into a diatribe about Jill D'Angelo and her actions, or lack thereof. While Levicoff told the jury of her good intentions, his opponent put the West Penn Power manager in a far different light. Not only did D'Angelo take minimal steps to make sure lines were properly installed and maintained, but she had been less than truthful.

Specter was speaking specifically of Jill D'Angelo's claim, under oath, that she had sent a company-wide email stressing the importance of splice cleaning. But when asked on cross-examination to find the email—and given overnight to do so—not only was D'Angelo unable to produce the email, but she had also conceded: "I guess it was never sent."

"That's kind of dirty pool, respectfully," Specter told the jury, "for a witness to say, 'I'm sure I sent an email way back when telling people how important it was to have proper splice preparation,' because the lawyer might not say, 'Well, go look for the email.' Right? Not every lawyer is going to ask her that question. But I did. You might say I called her bluff: 'Put up.' And it's not there. Now that's bad. That's bad."

D'Angelo was no innocent in all of this—that was the clear implication. She had tried to put one over on the jury. But perhaps worse, Specter added, her testimony was acknowledgment that D'Angelo could have, and should have, acted by sending such an email. And she had not. "That's very bad, because she's admitting she could have sent out that word, and she didn't. And that's very bad." She and her boss, Haven Bearley, had been aware of other splice failures, and they knew that the majority had failed because of poor wire preparation.

"Here is Haven Bearley saying, 'We have a problem here,' Specter continued. "God knows how many of these things there had been. They're not even keeping a log of them." There was not even a gathering of evidence or an in-depth investigation—and certainly no conclusion —after the line had fallen on the Goretzka property five years before the fatal incident. "That's a disgrace all by itself!" Specter declared. Instead of setting off alarm bells and thoroughly investigating and tracking any and all such failures, the company managers largely ignored the problem. "No quality assurance. No discussion on retraining. No evidence-gathering. No analysis. No discipline of the men." And, if D'Angelo, as she had testified, had told other managers at West Penn Power that the "importance of wire brushing cannot be over-stressed," then, Specter wanted to know, "Why wasn't it stressed!" He was shouting the words out now. All this lack of action to safeguard customers constituted "reckless indifference," he told the jury. And that meant that punitive damages were warranted.

Specter offered a comparison. What if Levicoff was driving his car down Fifth Avenue, the main drag in Pittsburgh, and he looked down for a moment to fiddle with the radio dials and got into an accident in which someone was injured. That, Specter submitted, would be negligence but not recklessness. "But," he continued, "if Mr. Levicoff decides he's going to close his eyes driving down Fifth Avenue and he hits somebody, damages to compensate? Yeah. Damages to punish? Yeah." West Penn Power, he was telling the jury, had essentially closed its eyes. "That's what we have here. They're not doing anything to solve this problem. They know it's dangerous."

The company didn't act even after Mike Goretzka expressed concern for his family's safety after the line fell the previous time, Specter submitted, waving aloft the company email noting Goretzka's complaint to West Penn. But the company did nothing in response—a clear-cut case of "callous indifference." He asked the jury: "I mean, if this doesn't justify the imposition of punitive damages, what does?"

Next, he discussed Levicoff's main expert witness, Joe Turek, a man Specter called a "sacrificial lamb." The person who helped author the main report for the defense, Dr. William O'Donnell of O'Donnell Consulting Engineers—the "real guy," as Specter called him—hadn't appeared in court to support the defense position even though he worked only 12 miles away.

Why hadn't he testified instead of Joe Turek? Because, Specter contended, he would have been embarrassed to walk into the courtroom and say under oath that it was "Aeolian winds" that made the line come down. Specter called it "lawsuit abuse." He explained to the jury: "They have abused the system by bringing you a guy like that to make a preposterous claim like that." An even greater affront, he said, was the defense claim, supported by yet another expert, that Carrie had walked into the downed, energized power line. To advance such a theory was not only "the height of lunacy," it was malevolent, a "disgrace."

"The idea that Carrie Goretzka would walk out there and walk into a downed power line, it is a sacrilege to her memory. And she's not here to defend herself, but I am," Specter exclaimed, his face twisted in anger.

Specter's fury was real, not a rehearsed emotion meant for the jury. But his expression of any emotion, whether ire or sorrow, was always under control. He could count on one finger the number of times he had truly lost power over his feelings in a courtroom, and that single time, with an overly belligerent witness, he felt the jury did not disapprove. "The emotion comes from the heart, but it is tempered by the brain," he would say. Unless Specter felt the emotion was justified and would be shared and approved by members of a jury, he kept it in check.

"And this idea from Mr. Levicoff that 'I'm not blaming Carrie Goretzka' is bull. West Penn Power has accused her of contributory negligence. You have to answer that question on the [verdict] form because that is their affirmative defense. They didn't have to make that claim. They could have dropped that claim. That's their claim, and it is deeply, deeply offensive, and I represent the Goretzka family in saying that."

Chapter 145

Specter was not permitted to suggest dollar figures to the jury beyond economic losses, such as Carrie's potential income over her lifetime. But while barred from recommending a specific award of damages, he told the jury simply that its verdict should be very large. "It is a lot of money. It just plain is."

He briefly discussed the loss Mike Goretzka suffered, how he and Carrie had had a wonderful marriage, how they had been "soulmates," and what it would mean "for Mike to be without Carrie every second of every minute of every hour of every day or every week of every month." Goretzka sat erect in the front row of the courtroom as his lawyer spoke, his face red but resolute, his jaw clenched tightly as he swabbed his eyes with a clump of tissues. Finally, he let his head drop toward his lap. At one point, Specter removed his wire-rimmed glasses and wiped his eyes as well. But he went on, mentioning that in the years since Carrie's death, Mike Goretzka had been unable to get past his grief, had been unable to go out on even a single date. Specter described a depression so deep that Goretzka still found it difficult to sleep or to push away the thoughts of suicide that assailed him in his darkest moments.

Specter mentioned the loss endured by Chloe and Carlie, the irreplaceable loss of a mother. He reminded the jury of the testimony about two little girls who still slept in their father's bed, who could not go to sleepovers with friends, who had trouble developing relationships with other children. They were children who, having witnessed their mother's death, lived every day in fear. Now many of the Goretzka family members and friends who crowded the first two aisles were crying, filling the courtroom with sniffles and stifled sobs.

Specter briefly addressed Carrie's own suffering. First, he lambasted the defense for trying to minimize the severity of her experience, how Levicoff had questioned whether 7,200 volts had actually coursed through Carrie's body. "Remember that discussion?" he asked the jurors, "How incredibly offensive. 'How many volts did she really get?' I want you to know that I am not an electrical engineer, but I have figured out exactly how many volts of electricity Carrie Goretzka got for 20 minutes. I figured it out exactly. Enough. Enough! Enough to kill her."

Carrie had suffered third-, fourth- and fifth-degree burns over almost her entire body for those 20 minutes. It was another 25 minutes before she got enough pain medication to render her unconscious. "So," Specter added, "it's 45 minutes of the most gruesome pain and suffering any human being could possibly endure."

He mentioned the three pictures of Carrie following the incident that would be sent back to the jury room for deliberations. Specter said he had refused to force the jurors to look at the photos during the trial, but that they were "very important" and the jurors should be able to see them. The photos would be placed in an envelope, he explained, holding the piece of white and green-bordered stationery in his hand. Jurors who wished to see the photos could look inside the envelope. Those who did not want to look would not have to.

Finally, Specter addressed the subject of punitive damages. He noted the power company's net worth of $244 million, and asked for a large award, one that would "speak very loudly." While Specter was not allowed to suggest an amount for punitive damages, he used a comparison, likening West Penn Power to a person who had "only $10 to their name...and you are called upon to decide how much you're going to take from them in order to punish them for the reprehensible thing that they did and deter them and others from this kind of conduct."

So what are the options available to you? A fairly wide range. You could take a penny from this person who is worth $10. And you have to ask yourself, will that punish and deter him?

With that, Specter took a penny from his pocket and placed it on the wooden railing between him and the jury. It looked very small and indistinct.

What will the person say who is worth $10 from whom you've taken a penny? I suggest to you, respectfully, they would brush the award off their shoulder like lint. Let's say that you take a dime from them. They have $10, and you take a dime. What will they say? Well, it's more than lint off the shoulder, but not much more.

The dime on the railing looked more pronounced than the penny, but still very small.

Next, Specter placed a dollar bill next to the two coins. It was much larger, much more noticeable.

Let's say that you take a dollar from them. That probably hurts. Now, I'm not suggesting that you take ten percent from them, which is what a dollar would be. Or one percent, which is what a dime will be. Or one-tenth of one percent, which is what a penny would be. What I do suggest to you as the appropriate way of looking at this is to say what would it be if it were a guy with $10? How much would that be? To make him feel it. To make him not do it again. And then just go do the math on that $244 million. That seems to be the most reasonable way of approaching that issue.

Specter closed his speech as he had begun, with lines from a poem. It was titled "Dirge Without Music" by Edna St. Vincent Millay, and it suggested resolution and hope even in tragic times. With a quavering voice, Specter made a last request of the 12 peers of Carrie Goretzka.

I am not resigned to the shutting away of loving hearts in the hard ground. So it is, and so it will be, for so it has been, time out of mind. Into the darkness she goes, the wise and the lovely. Crowned with lilies and with laurel she goes. But I am not resigned.

"I ask you not to be resigned," Specter continued. "Be not resigned. I ask you to conduct your deliberations with honor for everyone in this case. Go through each question with exquisite care. To vindicate Carrie Goretzka...to vindicate the people of this community who need to hear from you about what you decide is the culpability of this company for its conduct in relation to its power lines. And to deliver a message to them through your verdict that will make them change, that will deter them from this kind of conduct in the future.

"I noticed that my opponent did not ask you for a verdict in favor of West Penn Power. Remarkable. I will not follow that lead. I ask you for a verdict for the Goretzka family on each of the questions that are asked. I ask you to find that Carrie was not negligent. I ask you to award very substantial damages in each element of these damages, and I ask you to award very substantial damages to punish. I thank you for your attention to me. God bless you."

Chapter 146

Judge Della Vecchia gave Specter a little poke at the end of his closing. With the courtroom crowded with people, many of them lawyers from the building who had come to witness his speech, the judge simply couldn't resist:

"I have to just make this observation because I see so many veteran lawyers in the crowd. Only a lawyer would stand up and offer an inferential criticism of another lawyer for speaking for two hours and 42 minutes and then speak for two hours and 34 minutes. We're the only people on earth who do that."

Specter smiled with the judge. He had gone on longer than he had expected, but there had been so much he wanted to say and needed to say. He did not feel the length of his speech had alienated the jury. Early in the trial, Specter had felt he had the jury on his side. Now he felt that more so.

The lawyers filed into the judge's chambers. Della Vecchia went over his instructions to the jury, his charge, for one last time. He would tell the panel about "evaluating the believability" of witnesses and about the scales of civil justice—how, if after all the evidence and speeches were concluded, the jury felt they tipped "ever so slightly" in the plaintiffs' favor, the jury must find for the plaintiffs, while if the scales tipped in favor of the defendants or were evenly balanced, the defendants would win the day. The judge would explain how "a person remains responsible for his or her conduct when that causes harm even if other causes contributed to the harm." He would tell the jury not to allow sympathy to influence its decision. And he would explain the meaning of a damages award that was fair to compensate the plaintiffs for their loss and also the meaning of punitive damages.

"If you find that the conduct of the defendant was outrageous, you may award punitive damages," he would say, explaining that "outrageous" meant conduct that is "malicious, wanton, willful or oppressive, or shows reckless indifference to the interest of others." Then he would instruct: "Again, on all damages, [just] because I'm instructing you on them doesn't mean you have to award them."

After there was agreement on the language Della Vecchia would use, the judge and the lawyers filed back into the courtroom. The room was sealed, with no one allowed in or out once the charge began. When it was completed, the judge sent the jury to its task with a few unscripted words.

"So, thank you. Now you're going to retire to the best-furnished jury room in western Pennsylvania. Judge McCarthy himself furnished it…He's quite the decorator," quipped Della Vecchia, his humor eliciting two rows of tired smiles. "You'll go up there. This is the time when you finally begin talking about this and work this out."

And talk they did. The jurors had barely closed the door when a cacophony filled the room, a burst dam of chatter. Multiple conversations broke out at once. George Coulston was immediately chosen as the jury foreman—the idea had been mentioned to him days earlier by several jurors—and his first act was to let his colleagues go, to let them talk out their excitement.

"There was a lot of discussion. It was not loud but not quiet either," he would recall. "People were talking over one another, there were a lot of conversations going on. I let that run throughout lunch, let them speak their minds. Then we started going through the questions."

Chapter 147

Specter never showed any signs of weakness. Throughout the trial and the initial settlement offers from West Penn, he had been unflinching, a rock. The utility and its insurance companies would make an offer, and he would remain pat in his refusal to bend. When his opponent would relent and up the offer, he would still refuse to give an inch.

But Specter was tiring. The burden of responsibility was starting to take a physical toll. His weight had dropped to its lowest since college. He wasn't sleeping well, having trouble dropping off some nights even in the puffy hotel bed, and when he did, waking at all hours of the morning—2:30 one morning, 4:15 the next—and finding it hard to fall back to sleep. He had special pillows brought to his room and a humidifier, but nothing seemed to help. Some nights he resorted to sleeping pills.

Specter's self-assuredness—he was unable to imagine a scenario in which he could lose the case—had begun to waver ever so slightly. The rock was showing tiny fissures. His resolve not to take anything but a colossal settlement, if he took one at all, began to dissipate. He had stood in the face of a powerful opponent and refused, with great exterior calm and without hesitation, several offers that would make Mike Goretzka a very wealthy man. But now Specter was feeling twinges of doubt. Had he been right to reject such large settlement offers and press on with the trial, moving inexorably to a jury verdict? Maybe a jury would feel that a modest verdict would be enough for Mike Goretzka, who had a nice home and made a good living. What if the jury awarded less, maybe far less, than West Penn and its insurers had put before him on a silver platter? The $40 million offer was gone. Specter, the courageous risk taker, was now questioning himself.

Having a cocktail one evening as the trial was nearing its conclusion, he confided in Kila Baldwin, exposing a trace of something she had never seen before in her boss—fear.

"I just don't want to wind up with egg on my face," he told her.

Chapter 148

If anyone knew how unpredictable juries could be, it was Specter. Such seeming jury capriciousness came in the biggest case of his career to date, a case that produced a $150.9 million punitive award against the Ford Motor Company for the parents of a three-year-old boy killed by an F-series truck with a faulty parking brake. But an appellate court had thrown out the *White v. Ford* verdict and directed that a second trial be held to decide a new monetary award. Ford's culpability had already been decided by a first jury and upheld. Only the amount necessary to "punish" Ford needed to be decided. The presiding judge instructed the new jury accordingly.

After weeks of testimony, the second jury went off to decide an award. Three of its eight members told their colleagues they had arrived at a sum for punitive damages that seemed astounding. That sum was zero. Absolutely nothing. They were completely ignoring the first jury's verdict and the judge's instructions in determining that Ford should not pay a penny. A fourth juror, an older woman, said in those early deliberations that she wanted to award $1 million, an amount that was little more than nothing to such a large company. So half the jury wanted to "punish" Ford by making it pay little or nothing at all. Had one or two more jurors agreed with them, making a majority, Ford might have walked away with a hand slap. However, three other jurors, who had heard the identical case, came to contrary decisions. Two said right from the start that they felt Ford should pay $100 million in a punitive award, while a third called for $116 million in damages. The last juror suggested $10 million.

How could a group of people who listened to the same words from the same witnesses and experts and lawyers arrive at such polar opposite conclusions about the case? Specter didn't know the answer. But he knew that such a thing was a fact of human nature, and not a rarity at that. Different people saw things differently. It happened. Only one thing was certain: juries were impossible to predict. (In the Ford case, that eight-member jury eventually reached a compromise and awarded $52 million.)

Another troubling aspect of the Ford case for Specter was that it contradicted his theory that it was good to have at least one juror who was a technical thinker, someone who would understand how the parts worked and could explain it to the rest of the jury, and maybe even take the lead in deliberations. In the Ford case, he had gotten such a pick with car mechanic Allen Humphreys. Indeed, before the jury returned with its verdict, Specter had told David Caputo, his associate in the case: "I don't know if we're going to win or not, but I'm glad we kept that mechanic on the jury." As it turned out, Humphreys had been the most adamant of the three jurors who had initially wanted to award nothing in punitive damages.

In the Goretzka trial, Specter's technical juror was another middle-aged man whom he believed would understand and appreciate the case's complexities. He felt that Juror number 5, George Coulston, would take the plaintiffs' side and that he would lead the jury. Specter could only hope that his perceptions about Coulston were better than his hunch about Allen Humphreys.

Chapter 149

Was it really happening? Was the case actually before the jury? Had the settlement talks broken off for good? Were the jurors really in a back room discussing a verdict? Or was Specter imagining it, his sleep-deprived mind playing tricks on him?

His video technician, Mike Kutys, had disassembled the 12 × 12-foot video screen in the courtroom and taken down the TV screens that had been set up for the jury to view exhibits. Two young men had loaded up the wall of 60 document boxes that had been piled up in the back of the cramped courtroom, hoisting them onto a cart and rolling them off to a truck destined for a storage facility. The spectators had departed from the courtroom, leaving behind candy wrappers and empty water bottles on the blue fleur-de-lis patterned carpeting.

Maybe it was just a dream. But Specter didn't know the ending yet—whether it would be a good dream or a nightmare.

Chapter 150

Guerrini and Baldwin were sitting in the courtroom while the jury deliberated. They were supposed to have platooned for lunch, with one remaining at the plaintiffs' table while the other refueled at the small food court across the street from the county courthouse. But they were too nervous to leave for very long.

After just 30 minutes, the bare lightbulb on the wall in a front corner of the courtroom flashed on—a signal from the jury. The judge's tipstaff, an affable older gentleman named Ray Bender, who'd been around for years (and referred to himself in the third person), hurried to the jury room. He came back saying the jury wanted to see the photos of Carrie's injuries. The three photos in the sealed white envelope were sent back with Bender.

Dominic Guerrini emailed the news to his boss. It was good news, he thought. The jurors were not afraid to confront the gruesome reality of Carrie's end. Perhaps they were considering how much money to award the victim. Another hour went by and the jury light went on again. Bender went back once again to the private room.

"I wonder what they want now," Guerrini said to Baldwin. They had all the evidence and pertinent documents close by. Liz Deemer, Avrum Levicoff's co-counsel who had been posted in the courtroom, also stood at the ready.

Bender emerged in the courtroom once again. He shot Kila Baldwin a quizzical look, shrugging slightly.

"They have a verdict."

Chapter 151

Specter was at his noon haunt, Au Bon Pain, with Mike and Chuck Goretzka. They were having soup and sandwiches. Specter ate nothing. He was still full from his "big breakfast" of granola with berries and two percent milk. Besides, he was too engaged in the case, too wound up, to think about eating. He had also been skipping dinner some nights, and when he did sit for a meal, he often wolfed down just a piece of fish with a cocktail. Since the start of the trial, the six-foot-two Specter had gone from thin to skinny, his weight falling from 168 when he gave his opening speech to 159 for his closing.

The work was nerve-racking but also physically taxing, requiring long hours and constant thought. Only rarely did Specter let his mind diverge from the task at hand. Even during dinners with Baldwin and Guerrini, he would often interrupt his own stories about the Phillies to return to the trial, often quizzing his associates about a minuscule detail or barking out orders to be completed ASAP.

The small courtroom was hot, jammed with the Goretzka family on one side and the bevy of lawyers and insurance men on the other. In the later days, spectators had also shown up as word filtered through the courthouse about the "big trial" going on in Courtroom 710. By late in the afternoons, Specter could feel his crisp white shirt turning moist against his skin, literally sticking to his ribs.

The already palpable stress hiked when Specter's and the Goretzka brothers' cell phones sounded simultaneously. Specter hit the email from Guerrini that appeared on his Blackberry. The jury was back with a verdict.

Specter looked at his watch. A little more than an hour and a half had passed since the jury was charged. He felt something twist in the pit of his stomach. It was not a good feeling. Specter had had short deliberations in winning cases before—once a jury argued for just 40 minutes before awarding his client a large verdict—but it was atypical.

Chapter 152

It was a bad sign for the plaintiffs. The jury had taken just 90 minutes to render a verdict in such a complicated case, one that had a verdict slip comprising 11 questions and that included the calculation of a series of monetary awards—damages for Mike Goretzka for the loss of his wife, Carrie's pain and suffering, the economic loss, damages for JoAnn, damages for the kids, and, perhaps the largest consideration of all, punitive damages.

Did it mean that the jury had found that West Penn Power was not negligent, that it was not liable for Carrie's death? Such a finding would certainly have curtailed deliberations, eliminating the need to determine the various monetary awards. Or had it settled those claims but then found that punitive damages were not warranted? That would have shortened the deliberations as well.

Guerrini phoned the boss. He hadn't answered his earlier email. Specter arrived in a few minutes. So did the Goretzka family and friends. Levicoff, who had returned to his office some six blocks away, had still not appeared. So everyone waited. Would Levicoff show up with a final settlement offer? Would a $50 million deal finally be made formal?

Specter fidgeted noticeably in his seat, one hand picking at the nails on the other. He couldn't sit still, so he didn't. He walked out into the hallway, where Dominic Guerrini was already pacing. Specter sat in one of the wooden chairs lined up against the wall, his head down almost between his knees. Guerrini approached hesitantly, as one would walk up on a wounded lion. When Specter looked up, his mere expression—his face drained of any bravado—betrayed his self-doubt. Guerrini didn't know what to say, so he said nothing. And, for a while, neither did Specter. But then he did.

"I don't like this at all," he said.

His younger colleague disagreed. He reminded Specter that he had told the jury in his closing speech that they shouldn't spend any time deciding negligence because the issue was so clear-cut. Maybe they had taken his advice. "They probably went right to damages," he assured his boss. "That's what you told them to do."

Specter was not placated. He looked at his associate. "I'm worried about this," he said. For the first time in the trial, for the first time since he had started work at the law firm, Guerrini saw uncertainty in Specter's eyes.

Then Levicoff came walking down the hallway. Specter looked at his adversary, who looked back at him and merely shrugged. No settlement offer was forthcoming. The jury would announce its decision.

"Maybe you won," Specter said to Levicoff, meaning it.

"No way," the defense attorney responded, not expounding.

The exchange was exceptional. Two generally confident attorneys admitting to one another, face to face, that they felt they may have lost the case. And it was not, at least on Specter's part, a mere exchange of pleasantries. With the jury's relatively fast deliberation on such a long and complex verdict slip, he was truly worried about the outcome. The possibility that the years of work and arduous weeks at trial could produce a verdict in favor of the defense roiled in his gut like food poisoning.

The lawyers followed one another into the courtroom. They would know who was right soon enough.

Chapter 153

The combatants—the lawyers, the insurance people, the family members—waited to hear the verdict. It had been three and a half years and one day since Carrie Goretzka died. Mike Goretzka sat still, a stern look on his face. Specter left his seat at the plaintiffs' table and walked back to sit beside his client. His sister Carol nervously joked that her gold, satiny blouse had become stained with perspiration. She was shaking.

The jurors entered the courtroom in single file and took their seats for the last time. "Do we have a verdict?" asked the judge.

The jurors, eyes intent on the judge, indicated that they had. Juror number 5, George Coulston, handed the verdict sheet to the tipstaff, who handed it to the judge.

Della Vecchia read the first question on the ballot. He would also read the answers.

"All right. The verdict in this matter: "Was the Defendant West Penn Power Company negligent?"

"The jury answers, 'Yes.'"

But that was only part of the decision. For the plaintiffs to win, the jury also had to decide that that negligence had caused Carrie's death.

"Do you find that the Defendant West Penn Power's negligence was a factual cause in the injury and death to Carrie Goretzka?"

"The jury answers, 'Yes.'"

Now it was a question of how much the jury would award. Would it reach the last settlement offer that Specter had turned down—$25 million? Would it be less than the $50 million tentative offer that West Penn Power and its insurers had pulled from the table in the last hours of the trial?

"Question number 3: State the amount of Wrongful Death Act damages you award."

"Ten million dollars."

"Question number 4: State the amount of Survival Act damages you award."

"Twenty-nine million dollars."

"So that's a total of $39 million."

Hearing the verdict and these large awards, Mike Goretzka put his hands to his eyes. His shoulders bobbed violently, but for the first time in years, with a sense of relief. His legal war was over. There was more to the verdict, but victory was palpable. It was real.

"Question number 5: State the amount of damages you award to JoAnn Goretzka."

"One million dollars."

The judge did a quick tally. "That brings the cumulative total to $40 million."

"Question number 6: State the amount of damages you award for Chloe Goretzka."

"Four million dollars."

"That's $44 million."

"Question number 7: State the amount of damages you award for Carlie Goretzka."

"Four million dollars."

"That brings the total to $48 million."

Many of the family members now were crying. Several of the jurors looked over at them, smiles on some of their faces, sympathy in their eyes.

But there was more to come from the jury. For one, was it convinced at all by the defendant's argument that Carrie was partly to blame for her own demise? If it found her any percentage liable, that would reduce the verdict. It would also, no doubt, stab Mike Goretzka in the heart.

"Question number 8: Was the Plaintiff, Carrie Goretzka, herself negligent in causing the injuries complained of?"

"The answer is, 'No.'"

Mike Goretzka's face unclenched in relief. Slight smiles formed where his family and friends huddled together. But the total award was still less than the $50 million settlement offer that West Penn Power had dangled but pulled away at the last moment. Some insurance company stood to save $2 million if the verdict stayed this way.

The big question that remained was whether the jury had found punitive damages in the case, whether it saw fit to go beyond compensating the Goretzkas to punishing West Penn Power.

"Question number 11: Do you find the Defendant West Penn Power Company's conduct was outrageous?"

"The jury answers, 'Yes.'"

"The award of punitive [damages]: $61 million."

"For a total of $109 million award."

Seated next to Mike Goretzka for the verdict, Shanin Specter slapped his open hand so hard on the wooden seat that it made a sound like a shot from a pistol. Now he was crying, too. The normally stoic attorney held a fist to his mouth and bawled. After several seconds, he composed himself, placing one hand on Mike Goretzka's bouncing shoulders and using a handkerchief to dab his eyes with the other.

"OK. Ladies and gentlemen," cautioned the judge, "please contain yourselves for a couple minutes." He proceeded to poll the jurors one by one.

"Ladies and gentlemen of the jury…Juror number 1, is this your verdict?"

"Yes."

The next 11 gave the same answer, "Yes." The verdict had been unanimous.

Before excusing the jury, Judge Della Vecchia added one more note, mentioning that the verdict was, as far as he knew, the largest in Allegheny County history.

Chapter 154

It had been a perfect storm of sorts. Virtually every move Specter had made—right down to his reading of a poem at the end of his closing speech—turned out to be the right move.

George Coulston had indeed led the jury deliberations, and he proved sympathetic to the Goretzkas' plight. All the evidence and debate about brushing the wires, which consumed probably half of the trial, was virtually meaningless to the jury. And its members would be inflamed by all they had seen and heard.

Asked after the verdict if there had been any difference of opinion among the jurors on whether West Penn Power had been negligent, one juror, Maureen Noyes, replied, "We decided negligence almost immediately, the first question. There was no discussion. We all just said yes."

"That line came down on a clear, sunny day," said George Coulston, echoing Specter's catchphrase, "The whole question of brushing, at the end of the day, becomes almost irrelevant because for us it was that the line shouldn't have come down. The fact that it came down was a problem, and it was not some act of nature. If West Penn did brush the line and followed all the proper procedures and it still came down, it's still incumbent upon them that the lines don't come down."

The jury, however, had not completely discounted the notion that proper installation with wire brushing should be followed. Even if failing to do so caused only one in a million lines to fail and drop to the ground, West Penn Power probably had a million lines in the air, reasoned Coulston, and that meant that one was bound to fall if the utility didn't make a better effort.

The jurors also were convinced that West Penn Power did not follow proper procedures, from the linemen right up the corporate ladder. Coulston noted that Jill D'Angelo had sent a cautionary email, "but she couldn't even answer who was on the list to get word….Where's the documentation that the right people got the message? Where's the field audits that there was any follow-up? Not that Jill D'Angelo is a bad person, but there was a culture that came through loud and clear at West Penn Power that no one was really taking things to a level that would go above and beyond what their narrow job scope is....If they were really serious, they would have asked after the prior line failures not only why it fell but 'What do we have to do to ensure that it never falls again?'" (Coulston suggested the line could simply have been placed underground.) That lack of effort, he said, constituted "callous indifference, to use the Specter term."

"Their basic culture is not adequate for the line of business they're in and that's a leadership problem that goes all the way to the top of the company," added Coulston. He felt strongly about it, going so far as to say that he believed West Penn's entire executive group should be replaced.

Deciding that West Penn Power was liable—and that Carrie was in no way responsible for her own death—took the jury seconds. Deciding how much to award each victim took longer—but minutes, not hours.

A few of the jurors threw out numbers to compensate Mike Goretzka under the Wrongful Death portion of the verdict slip. The initial thought was $2 million, based on the calculation that such a sum invested at 5 percent would earn an annual $100,000 for the widower for the rest of his life. George Coulston had come up with the idea. But then, he added, "It just didn't feel right." It somehow didn't feel like enough. So the jury agreed to set the number at $5 million, enough to earn annual interest of $250,000.

Jurors had some disagreement on what to award to Chloe and Carlie under the same category for the loss of their mother's guidance and tutelage. Some felt the children deserved more than their father, some thought less. They toyed with the idea of giving them equal amounts of $5 million each, but several jurors protested that $15 million for all three survivors seemed high. They decided finally on $2.5 million each. "So the total's $10 million," under the Wrongful Death statute, said Coulston, "Let's move on."

Deciding damages for Carrie was tougher. "To what extent do we compensate Carrie Goretzka for pain and disfigurement being that she died and did not have to live with that? So how do you award for that?" Coulston asked. "But we tried to follow the judge's instruction that the power company should not benefit from the fact that Carrie died."

So the decision was based on an entirely different matrix: "She had these horrific injuries. If she had lived, what should the compensation be?"

The jurors considered the surgeries she would need, the medications, the "excruciating pain for the rest of her life." When nobody spoke up with a monetary amount to equal such a dismal existence, George Coulston picked an arbitrary number: $20 million. This produced a soft groan from some of the jurors, not because they felt it was too much, but because it was not enough. (As they tried to decide, the envelope Specter had given the jury with photos of Carrie's injuries sat on one end of the table. None of the jurors had opened it. Not until after the final verdict was reached would a few of the jurors, and only a few, take a quick look.) After a minute or two, Coulston upped the number to $25 million and there was unanimous agreement. Then $4 million—rounded up from the estimate of Specter's financial expert—was added for economic loss and the total for the Survival Act award was set at $29 million.

For the injuries, physical and psychological, suffered by JoAnn, Chloe and Carlie, the jury set damages at $1 million and $4 million for each child. The jury figured that JoAnn was older and she would have to live with her awful memories far fewer years than her grandchildren.

This brought total compensatory damages to $48 million.

Punitive damages were often a tougher issue. But the Goretzka jury decided the issue, said Coulston, with "no hesitation."

Maureen Noyes, a retired computer programmer and IT manager, cited Mike Goretzka's call to the power company expressing fear for the safety of his family and West Penn Power's failure to act: "If there's a bug somewhere, you've got to figure out where that is because the problem's only going to get bigger over time. That's been drilled into me over the years. Them not figuring out why these wires were falling down is just amazing, especially for a company that big" and one dealing with people's lives. "I found it hard to believe they didn't have that level of care."

The jurors voted unanimously that West Penn Power had acted recklessly and outrageously. So how much to award in punitive damages? While one juror expressed concern that a large punitive award could force the utility to cut jobs or, worse, to go out of business, the sentiment in the room was not one of concern for West Penn Power. George Coulston reminded his colleagues of the judge's words: "We're not to worry about whether the company can pay and how it would do so." Frankly, said Coulston afterward, his own point of view was: "If they go out of business as a result, then so be it."

"What Specter said in his closing speech was very helpful," Coulston noted. "A person on the street might have $10 in their pocket, and if they do something wrong and you want to change their behavior, how much of that $10 bill are you going to take from them?" Specter had also noted that West Penn Power's retained earnings were not $10, but $244 million.

Coulston posed the question to his peers. Three spoke up immediately: "Take half." Or $122 million. But a few others recommended only 10 percent, or $24.4 million. So the jury foreman asked: "Would 10 percent change their behavior?" Most of the jurors shook their heads. "Would 20 percent?" Now several of the same heads nodded yes.

"Then somebody in the room said 25 percent," Coulston reported. And there was more agreement.

"We felt that would hurt them enough," said Amy Siniawski, a homemaker and former human resources manager.

With 25 percent, or $61 million, on the table, Coulston added, "We all said OK."

And that was that.

"The fact that that was the [second time] that happened, to me that was an alarm," said Tina Wojton, an account manager, about the line falling on the Goretzkas' property. "We tried to be fair on punitive damages, but we wanted to make a statement that that shouldn't have happened....I hope they [West Penn Power] will now take the precaution that's warranted."

"I think $61 million is enough to get West Penn Power's attention and the attention of every electric utility company across the country," George Coulston asserted. "They all should be looking at this verdict and taking note."

The jurors left the courtroom after the verdict to find Mike Goretzka standing out in the hallway waiting to greet them and say thank you. They all shook his hand and most hugged the man who had sat silently just a few feet away from them in the courtroom for all those days. They had seen his anguish, and some had felt it.

"I feel really bad about what the family went through and what they're going to go through in the future, but I'm glad I was part of that experience and that I could help them in some way," said Noyes, a computer programmer.

Many of the jurors also spoke with Shanin Specter, and he would travel to Pittsburgh months later to take a large group of them to lunch and talk about the case. They had appreciated his no-nonsense, take-no-prisoners style.

"He beat up on some witnesses, but no more so than they should have expected. We never felt he was abusive. He made a point of being polite to Jill D'Angelo—I kind of rolled my eyes a little at that," said Coulston, noting that Specter's manner may have been polite, but his questions were anything but. "At the end of the day, it's about trying the facts of the case, getting to the facts. If you hurt somebody's feelings in the process, then too bad."

Several jurors felt that Specter had been "a little theatric at times" during the trial, but, Coulston added, "Not over the top, never to the point of being annoying." Even Specter's reading of a poem at the end of his closing speech and also a lyrical speech by Bobby Kennedy was fine with the men and women of the jury. Kennedy, at a 1968 election rally in Kansas, had told his audience, essentially, that not everything is about money.

> ...The gross national product does not allow for the health of our children, the quality of their education or the joy of their play. It does not include the beauty of our poetry or the strength of our marriages, the intelligence of our public debate or the integrity of our public officials. It measures neither our wit nor our courage, neither our wisdom nor our learning, neither our compassion nor our devotion to our country, it measures everything in short, except that which makes life worthwhile.

"It helped me very much," Coulston noted. "I'm very analytical about numbers, and it was helpful to his cause to remind me before going into deliberations about an award amount that the value that we as individuals bring to society is so much more than the directly calculable economic value we bring. It's so much more."

Mike Goretzka stood in the hallway with his family after the jurors went home. His mother and brother Chuck, his sisters and family friends continued to hug and kiss and cry. The tears were joyful.

"I feel great," he observed. "Today there was justice for Carrie. For three and a half years we never gave up. It took courage. I couldn't be more proud of my family. Today was Carrie's day. The closing and the verdict—that was her voice."

Chapter 155

Despite all of Thomas Edison's macabre efforts to discredit AC power, George Westinghouse eventually won the "War of Currents." AC was simply a superior product, its power able to be transported long distances with relatively minimal loss over lengthy power lines used to service a sprawling population. But one Edison-inspired invention, the electric chair, remained in use for decades, though only in America (and for a time in the Philippines after American occupation). The electric chair has largely been done away with, though it remains a seldom-used option in a handful of states.

By 2014, the 32 states that still had the death penalty had enacted lethal injection as a more humane manner of carrying out the ultimate punishment, according to the Death Penalty Information Center. Six states—Alabama, Florida, Kentucky, South Carolina, Tennessee and Virginia—still allowed all or certain prisoners (depending on date sentenced) to choose between lethal injection and electrocution. In some cases, outlawing death by electrocution came after botched or unusually gruesome executions in which convicts suffered profuse bleeding or their heads caught on fire. Today, the use of the electric chair is rare, with some states banning electrocution as "cruel and unusual" punishment, even for the most heinous of murderers.

As of 2015, the electric chair was last used in Virginia to put to death Robert Gleason, a convicted murderer who strangled two fellow inmates in prison and vowed to keep killing until he was put to death. He chose the chair over lethal injection.

His final words, delivered in Irish Gaelic, were: "Pog mo thoin."

Translation: "Kiss my ass."

Chapter 156

In the late afternoon of January 31, not quite two months after the trial, a tall, distinguished gentleman in his sixties stepped from the elevator at Kline & Specter and made his way to Specter's office. He knew the way. Mark Aronchick, a well-known Philadelphia lawyer, a former city solicitor and past chancellor of the Philadelphia Bar Association, had known Shanin Specter for more than 20 years. They would occasionally chat at court appearances or political functions. The two shared a mutual respect and genuinely liked each other. They had a kinship. Which made Aronchick the right man for the job, the job of trying to reach a settlement of the Goretzka case on behalf of West Penn Power.

Mark Aronchick was, in Specter's words, "not a bullshitter." When he agreed to meet, he knew Aronchick would not try to throw him any curves. He complimented Specter on his handling of the trial, especially his meticulous avoidance of "hot-button issues," those that might have left the verdict vulnerable to appeal. And Specter had indeed been careful. He had, for instance, intentionally not asked the judge to preclude the contributory negligence claim against Carrie from the verdict slip because he knew that doing so, even if the judge agreed, could jeopardize any verdict in the appellate courts. He had also been careful to avoid using inflammatory language in his closing speech in seeking punitive damages.

West Penn Power filed post-trial motions within the required 10 days after the verdict. Such motions were typical for a defendant seeking action by the presiding judge, generally claiming errors by the judge during trial and asking that a verdict be thrown out or reduced. What was not typical was the response fired back in the Goretzka case by Kline & Specter's chief appellate attorney, Charles "Chip" Becker. Becker, educated at Yale Law and son of the highly respected federal appeals chief judge Edward R. Becker, anticipated the post-trial motions and he was ready. When Levicoff followed the motions with a 39-page brief, Becker fired back with a response that was 94 pages and which was, he felt, airtight. The response gave West Penn Power a glimpse of how Specter's firm would defend against an appeal. It could not have liked what it saw.

Not only was Becker's brief likely to convince Judge Della Vecchia to keep the verdict intact, but it would also help give him fodder to write an opinion to the appellate courts refuting West Penn Power's motions. And now, since Pennsylvania law mandated 6 percent interest to accrue annually after a verdict, it was costing West Penn Power, if it eventually lost the post-trial motions and a later appeal, roughly another $550,000 every month.

And it seemed destined to lose. On January 20, a Sunday afternoon, the loquacious Becker sent Specter a three-page, single-spaced email detailing the strategy and prospects of battling a possible appeal. He summed it up: "Generally, I think the chances of a new trial are not very good."

Mark Aronchick's visit to Specter came just a few days after West Penn Power got Becker's written motions response. It had apparently touched some nerves at the power company.

"I'm here to make you rich," Aronchick told Specter, then added with a smile, "Excuse me, richer."

He conceded that he did not give his client much of a chance of overturning the $48 million in compensatory damages awarded by the jury, but he told Specter that he could envision a higher court voiding or reducing the $61 million punitive verdict.

"You're not going to get that either," said Specter, "but even if you did, then what would happen after a new trial was granted?"

"We'd settle," Aronchick replied.

"Right, so why should I settle now when I may never have to?" Specter also knew that Aronchick was aware of the mounting interest. Appeals could take years and, if it eventually lost, West Penn Power's bill would be mounting by nearly $7 million a year.

Shanin Specter was normally a vision of calm. But here, in his office, with Mark Aronchick seated on a leather couch and squinting to keep the afternoon sun out of his eyes, Specter held all the good cards, and he seemed even more self-assured than usual.

There was a brief silence. Aronchick broke it. "Listen," he said, "I'm not going to dick around with you. I'll tell you what I have. I have $95 million."

It was a solid offer. Specter knew that with interest that started accruing on compensatory damages one year after suit was served, the verdict now amounted to roughly $115 million. So $95 million was a good offer indeed. He didn't know if Aronchick "had $95 million"— meaning it was all his client was willing to pay—or the sum was his starting gambit. Specter did not say "rejected," his usual answer to initial offers. Although he didn't say yes either.

"It's a good-faith offer. It's a good first step," he granted.

It was even better than that. Aronchick also told Specter that West Penn Power had settled the complaint against it with the PUC by agreeing to remediation, to inspect and fix its power lines.

Specter got the clear impression that someone high up at the power company's parent company, First Energy, perhaps its chief executive officer or its board of directors, wanted the Goretzka case to go away—badly. He also felt that Aronchick spoke directly for whomever or whatever entity that was. All good.

Specter didn't get a sense of how strongly West Penn Power might have felt about keeping the terms of any settlement confidential. He knew the company didn't want such a large number as $95 million (or larger) to get out. "By paying something like $100 million, the company is admitting its conduct was outrageous, that it was not a runaway jury, that the plaintiffs' lawyer didn't simply pull the wool over the jury's eyes," Specter maintained. He knew the utility would push to keep a settlement under wraps. But he also doubted that it could. A judicial ruling to seal the agreement, he felt, would probably not hold up against a news media challenge since the matter was in the public interest.

Specter sent an email about the meeting to Baldwin and Guerrini:

On Feb. 1, 2013, at 10:16 AM—FYI, on behalf of West Penn Power, Mark Aronchick offered 95mm yesterday. I told him this was a good start. He said West Penn Power has settled with the PUC. Apparently, West Penn Power will retrain the linemen, put into place an infrared program and retain a third-party expert to assist in implementing the program under the PUC's continuing oversight. He had no info on confidentiality. I told him to get me the details of the PUC settlement with the PUC and West Penn Power's position on confidentiality. He is to get back to me. I spoke with Mike Goretzka this morning and received blanket authority...

Overall, Specter felt good about his sitdown with Aronchick. "Settlement negotiations are comparable to a dance," he said shortly afterward, "and if this is a dance, we're at the point where we've moved from rock to the slow music."

Chapter 157

The rest of the dance would take place over the telephone and through emails. Specter said he would accept $110 million. Aronchick countered with $100 million. Specter said no.

"There was no reason to take $100 million because I knew they'd pay more," Specter said later, "because when the exposure is $115 million and they've already offered $100 million, the CEO has told his insurers that it must be settled *now*. If they had wanted to try to appeal or get a real discount, they would have offered $48 million for the compensatory damages, or $48 million plus a little for punitive."

It might have been worthwhile for West Penn Power to fight the $61 million in punitive damages, Specter surmised, noting that appellate courts found punitive awards generally unfavorable, often chopping them down or sending them back for new trials. Specter had won punitive damages in three cases during his career: one for $15,000, which was thrown out, and two in *White v. Ford*, both remanded for new trials. But he felt the Goretzka verdict was on sound footing. If the power company wanted an appellate fight, he was ready to give them one. Aronchick said he would get back to Specter.

Later that Friday, on February 15, Aronchick emailed Specter a draft proposal outlining the deal. Specter sent an answer at 5:36 p.m., after most people had left the office for the weekend. In his email, he accepted all the proposals (with some wording changes) except for one: "With respect to dollar amount, pursuant to specific client authorization, your offer of $100 million is respectfully declined. My clients feel that the verdict should be paid, or something very close to the verdict. I am confident they would accept my advice to take $105 million if this is offered."

Specter's phone rang.

"Will you be available over the weekend?" Aronchick asked.

"I'm not sure," Specter replied, "because I'm in the middle of negotiating seven other cases with $100 million offers."

Both lawyers laughed.

"If I can get 105, will you take it?" asked Aronchick.

"Well, are you sure you can get it?" Specter questioned him.

"I'm confident that I can."

"Then I'm sure I can take it."

The deal was finalized on Monday. The case of *Goretzka v. West Penn Power* was over.

Chapter 158

The settlement negotiated with Mark Aronchick was all about the money, with nothing concerning the remedial steps West Penn Power would have to take. That was now in the hands of the Public Utility Commission. Throughout the Goretzka case, Specter had stayed in contact with the PUC, communicating with its staff even during the trial. He was aware of the steps being considered by the Pennsylvania agency. Aronchick told Specter that West Penn Power had settled with the PUC, too. Now Specter would put his nose into that business.

Only days before the $105 million settlement was reached, the PUC's Bureau for Investigation and Enforcement filed a petition seeking to settle its proceedings against West Penn Power. It outlined remedial steps that would have to be taken in light of the Goretzka case and Specter's original complaint against the company. Specter felt the steps were not strong enough. On February 26, he filed a "Petition to Intervene" with the PUC, stating that although the settlement proposed with West Penn Power was "good and constructive," the remedial measures were insufficient. For one thing, he felt it was not stringent enough for all linemen to be retrained on proper installation within one year and then again at unspecified "regular intervals." He also felt the agreement that West Penn use infrared technology and inspect all splice connections within three years did not provide any protection beyond that initial three years. "This is not enough," he wrote in the petition. "If it is important enough to require West Penn to check all splices once, it is important enough to require such inspections at regular, specified intervals going forward." And there was one other thing. Specter sought to require splice inspection not only for West Penn Power, but also for all electric utilities across Pennsylvania. "If it is important enough for WPP to perform these inspections," he reasoned, "it is important for all other power companies to follow suit."

It took almost another year for the PUC to take formal action. When it did, at a public meeting on January 9, 2014, it addressed all three points and one in addition.

West Penn Power would retrain all linemen within one year on the proper installation of splices—including the importance of wire brushing—and would conduct refresher training one year later (not at "regular intervals"). The company was also required to invite the PUC to observe the training and to hold quarterly meetings for the first 18 months with the agency on the program's progress.

The power company would inspect all splices within three years using infrared technology, with any at-risk splices removed and replaced and reported to the PUC. West Penn Power would also have to follow up with spot checks of 5 percent (or 100 splices, whichever was greater) of all its splices in an annual reliability report.

All electric distribution companies in the state would be required to conduct visual "ground patrol" splice inspections every one to two years. While infrared inspections were not required, the PUC noted that West Penn Power was using the technology and that it would enable companies "to find overheating and resistance issues with splices"—a suggestion that infrared was a smart thing for power companies that didn't already use the technology. The commission further mandated that West Penn Power hire a third-party independent contractor approved by the PUC's technical staff to perform within one year a review of its inspection and maintenance procedures. West Penn Power estimated that all the steps would cost the company $2.5 million. That was in addition to the PUC's relatively small fine of $86,000 for the company's failure to answer queries.

The government agency took one additional action as an outgrowth of the Goretzka case. It created a new Electric Safety Division and staffed it with engineers to initiate investigations of electrical injuries throughout the state. No longer would the PUC rely solely on reports by utility companies. It would be active rather than passive when it came to electrical injuries.

Chapter 159

Dr. Allen Ault was for many years the corrections commissioner for the state of Georgia, a job in which he supervised the carrying out of the death penalty in the electric chair. In a 2014 interview with the BBC, he spoke of the horrors he had witnessed, recalling about one inmate's execution: "I could see the jolt of electricity running through his body. It snapped his head back and then there was just total silence...and I knew I had killed another human being." Ault later regretted his role even though he knew the prisoners put to death had committed heinous crimes. "I still have nightmares," he said.

Epilogue

Nearly two years after the trial and more than five years after Carrie's death, things had gotten better for the Goretzka family. Not perfect, but better. Mike Goretzka had finished building the family's new house, a large and beautiful brick structure on more than two acres in a new neighborhood not far from the old West Hempfield address. Goretzka proudly noted that he had not used a penny from the settlement to build the house, which was started two months before the trial. In fact, he had not spent any of the money at all—"I feel like I don't deserve it," he said—putting the lion's share in trust funds for his daughters. (He did get rid of the old Dodge Dakota that didn't have any heat and bought a new Ford F-150 pickup.) He continued to work at his old job, needing to keep busy and feeling a commitment to stay at the place where he had begun with his father 26 years earlier. He also didn't want to let down his boss, Norm Rish, who had been like a father to him. Mike Goretzka's sister Carol lived with him and Chloe and Carlie during the week, taking the kids to their private Catholic school and staying the day as a volunteer. Truth be told, Carol had always carried a speck of guilt in her heart over Carrie's death because it was she who had informed her brother about the "Gay Days" celebration in Orlando back in 2009, causing him to change the date of his family's trip to Disney World: "If I hadn't told him that, the whole thing with Carrie might have never happened." Carol knew it was silly to feel that way, and the sentiment was waning, but she wanted to do everything she could for Carrie's daughters in her absence.

The new house was only partially furnished and finished. Bare lightbulbs hung from the ceilings in the foyer and master bedroom. Mike Goretzka had not yet gotten around to purchasing and installing ceiling fixtures. At the urging of others, he had hired an interior decorator, then fired her. Her taste was simply not that of the man who was still more comfortable wearing sweatshirts and dining at Applebee's and Chick-Fil-A. For now, he used the living room furniture from the old house in the new master bedroom. Carrie's father, John, whom the girls called "Pap-Pap," visited them every Friday and Sunday. John, remarried and living in nearby Luxor, planted a tree outside his mobile home and kept a red candle burning near the tree as a vigil for Carrie. "I look at it every night and I just get a good feeling," he said. "It just gives me a good feeling, like she's there or something."

There were no beds in the girls' rooms. Although Chloe and Carlie were doing well in school, getting good grades and making friends and no longer seeing a psychologist, they still slept in their father's bedroom. In his bed, in fact. They didn't want to spend the night apart from him. Mike Goretzka slept on the carpeted floor. "I'm used to it," he said. "It's not so bad, as long as I don't sleep on my side. Then I wake up sore."

There were other signs, often subtle and less frequent, that the children, particularly the older one, still felt pain over the death of their mother after more than five years. Chloe exhibited anxiety and longing in a poem she wrote for school. It was accompanied by three photos. One was of their dog, one was a tornado and the third was a picture of Jesus Christ in heaven.

"I Am" Poem
by Chloe Goretzka

I am a good friend and a good person.
I hear water falls that relax me.
I see my mom in heaven.
I want to have kids someday.
I wonder what my kids will look like.
I am a good friend a good person.
I pretend I am a mom when we play baby.
I feel bad when my friend hurts my feelings.
I touch my dog and feel the warmness.
I worry if my house is going to get hit by a tornado.
I cry when people die.
I am a good friend and person.
I understand that my family loves me.
I say I love my friends and family.
I dream about the future.
I try to do my best in school.
I hope I will see my mom one day.
I am a good friend and a good person.

Besides getting a new house and the dog, a mini Golden Doodle they named Jackson, Mike Goretzka noted, "Nothing's changed." Time had not healed his wounds, at least not yet. He still felt off-kilter in his everyday life. His blue eyes held a dull sadness, though he still refused to see a psychologist. He kept things inside, though he willingly talked about Carrie and how much he still missed her. He went to the gym every day at lunchtime, feeling that the physical exercise helped steady him and helped him sleep at night. He did go on one date but it didn't go well. He had felt clumsy, and guilty. Friends tried to fix him up with women, but he politely declined.

"I find it hard to balance everything, to work a job and to be with the girls. I need a better balance," he said. Mike Goretzka was thinking about maybe working part-time, maybe undertaking a new endeavor, maybe going on some trips or to a Super Bowl, maybe finishing the interior of the house. But the motivation wasn't always there. And he didn't know when it would be.

"I do believe the girls are adjusting well and will continue to grow. As for me, my life will never be what I wanted. I already had everything I ever dreamed of. I had my career and the kids, and I had Carrie."

After the Goretzka case, Kila Baldwin and Dominic Guerrini, along with a group of other attorneys, were made partner at Kline & Specter. They kept up with Mike Goretzka long after the trial. Guerrini chatted with him over the phone, and he and Specter played golf with their former client in the Pittsburgh area. Baldwin continued to talk to Mike from time to time. She placed the framed photo he sent her of Chloe and Carlie, both smiling in lovely blue dresses, on a shelf in her office with pictures of her own two children. "It reminds me sometimes, when I am tired and don't feel like working, why I do it." Next to the photo was a snow globe with an angel holding a heart on her knees, also a gift from Mike with a note saying that Kila was his family's angel.

Shanin Specter talked a great deal about the Goretzka case in the months and years after the trial. There were lessons to be learned, wisdom to impart. He discussed the case with his students at the University of Pennsylvania Law School, where he taught two classes, including "The Civil Justice System as an Agent of Change," a class motivated by his successful efforts to achieve remediation through his cases. He lectured on the case to fellow lawyers at Continuing Legal Education classes. Pennsylvania law required lawyers to take 12 hours of CLE classes every year and most did so grudgingly, often showing up to sparsely attended sessions armed with coffee and Danish, newspapers and crossword puzzles. But Specter's lectures on the Goretzka case played to packed houses of attentive attorneys eager to learn how to beat a powerful corporation. One Specter CLE was so jammed that there was not a seat left for the guest lecturer, so he stood for the three-hour session. He welcomed his guests and then launched into the now-famous case he had tried in Pittsburgh. Specter began by flashing a photo of a pretty woman on a TV monitor.

"This," he said, "is Carrie Goretzka...."

Acknowledgments

To the participants of the case who graciously agreed to do interviews with me, especially jurors, witnesses in the case and Judge Michael Della Vecchia. (Avrum Levicoff declined to speak on the record regarding this matter.) To the Goretzka family, who endured my endless questions and were always friendly and generous, even in the heat of battle. To those who helped with innumerable details, especially Barbara Carberry. To my early reader and friendly critic, Tracy Leonardis; to Nelson Imhof, who helped fact-check parts of the book, and to Dawn Kudgis, who was of real help with the photos. And finally to my chief editor and constant source of encouragement, Avery Rome.